D0808025

The Many Facets of
Diamonds Are Forever

The Many Facets of
Diamonds Are Forever

James Bond on Page and Screen

Edited by Oliver Buckton

LEXINGTON BOOKS
Lanham • Boulder • New York • London

Published by Lexington Books
An imprint of The Rowman & Littlefield Publishing Group, Inc.
4501 Forbes Boulevard, Suite 200, Lanham, Maryland 20706
www.rowman.com

6 Tinworth Street, London SE11 5AL

Copyright © 2019 by The Rowman & Littlefield Publishing Group, Inc.

All rights reserved. No part of this book may be reproduced in any form or by any
electronic or mechanical means, including information storage and retrieval systems,
without written permission from the publisher, except by a reviewer who may quote
passages in a review.

British Library Cataloguing in Publication Information Available

Library of Congress Cataloging-in-Publication Data

Names: Buckton, Oliver S., editor.
Title: The many facets of Diamonds are forever : James Bond on page and screen / edited by Oliver
    Buckton.
Description: Lanham : Lexington Books, [2019] | Includes bibliographical references and index.
Identifiers: LCCN 2018060489 (print) | LCCN 2019006217 (ebook) | ISBN 9781498567589 (Elec-
    tronic) | ISBN 9781498567572 (cloth) | ISBN 9781498567596 (pbk) Subjects: LCSH: Fleming,
Ian, 1908-1964--Characters--James Bond. | Bond, James (Fictitious char-
    acter) | Fleming, Ian, 1908-1964. Diamonds are forever. | Diamonds are forever (Motion picture)
Classification: LCC PR6056.L4 (ebook) | LCC PR6056.L4 M365 2019 (print) | DDC 823/.914--dc23
LC record available at https://lccn.loc.gov/2018060489

Contents

Acknowledgments   vii

Foreword   ix
    Tom Cull

Introduction: The Many Facets of *Diamonds Are Forever*   1
    Oliver Buckton

1: Sound, Affect, Adaptation, and Intertextuality in *Diamonds Are Forever*

1   The Scorpion as Emblem of Affect in *Diamonds Are Forever*   15
    Elyn Achtymichuk-Hardy

2   The Sounds of *Diamonds Are Forever*   39
    Jesc Bunyard

3   Transforming Bond: *Diamonds Are Forever* in Its Contexts   55
    James Chapman

4   James Bond, Meet John Blaize: Identity Theft and
    Intertextuality in Ian Fleming's *Diamonds Are Forever* and
    The Diamond Smugglers   73
    Oliver Buckton

2: Gender and Sexuality in *Diamonds Are Forever*

5   My Adversary, Myself: An Examination of James Bond and
    How Wint and Kidd Reflect His Own Psyche in *Diamonds
    Are Forever*   91
    Grant C. Hester

6   The Devolution of Tiffany Case   105
    Jennifer L. Martinsen

7   The Eyes of Tiffany Case—And What They Tell about Ian
    Fleming's First Successful Female Character   121
    Ihsan Amanatullah

3: Culture, Consumption, and America in *Diamonds Are Forever*

8   Attitudes Are Forever: America Disdained   141
    Matthew B. Sherman

9 The Desert of the Real: *Diamonds Are Forever* as a
       Hollywood Novel   157
       Mark David Kaufman

10 A Happy Selection: The Representation of Food and Drink
        in the Book and Film of *Diamonds Are Forever*   177
        Edward Biddulph

Index   199
About the Editor   205
About the Contributors   207

Acknowledgments

First of all, my thanks go to the contributors to this volume for producing such exciting and original work on Ian Fleming's *Diamonds Are Forever* and Guy Hamilton's film adaptation. It has been a pleasure working with such a dedicated and talented group of scholars and critics. I would also like to thank the South Atlantic Modern Language Association, especially Dan Abitz, for its support of the original panels on *Diamonds Are Forever* held at the 2016 conference in Jacksonville, Florida. My thanks to Tom Cull, who publicized the conference panels and the call for papers for this volume on his superb "Artistic Licence Renewed" website. Tom also generously agreed to write the foreword to this volume. I would like to express my thanks to the Lilly Library at Indiana University, Bloomington, for providing a visiting fellowship that allowed me to consult archival material on Ian Fleming and *Diamonds Are Forever*. The director and staff at the library have been unfailingly welcoming and helpful in assisting me with my researches on Fleming. My thanks to Lexington Books, especially my editor Jessica Thwaite, for encouragement and support of this project. Thanks go also to the anonymous reader for the Press who made valuable suggestions for improvement. I am grateful to my students at FAU who have taken my courses on James Bond over the years and offered stimulating discussions of the fascinating world of James Bond and Ian Fleming. Finally, I am grateful to my wife, Laurice, for her continuing love and support and for sitting through more James Bond films than either she or I can remember.

Foreword

Tom Cull

Ask many Fleming readers, which is their favorite James Bond novel and you will often hear *Casino Royale* or *Moonraker* or *From Russia with Love*, and for very good reason. These are classics in all of spy fiction, let alone within the Fleming canon. For *Diamonds Are Forever* to be sandwiched between *Moonraker* and *From Russia with Love* makes it even more difficult to fight for attention, making it one of the most overlooked novels in Fleming's writing career. As such, it perhaps has become an easy target among aficionados to pick holes in it, but this would be unfair, and I for one am pleased that in this edition of marvelously varied essays it is finally getting the attention it deserves.

It holds a special place for me also, as an Englishman who has lived in the Northeast of America and visited many of the places that this novel is set, such as Saratoga Springs (often shortened to Saratoga), and even the place where much of the novel was inspired and written, on the Vermont/New York State border where Ian's best friend Ivar Bryce had a house that Fleming would visit in the summers. Given the more claustrophobic nature of *Moonraker* and *From Russia with Love*, reading *Diamonds Are Forever* often feels like you're breathing the fresh air of Vermont. It is worth noting that any real Bond fan should make the trek to Saratoga, probably the most unchanged public Bond site in America, where you can follow in Fleming's footsteps much the same as he did.

Diamonds Are Forever is also one of the most fun Bond adventures with some of the most sparkling and funny dialogue, and introduces one of the best Bond women to the entire series in Tiffany Case, who manages to steal Bond's hardened heart, at least for a time, back to the King's Road. Case is the heart of the book and quite rightly the subject of two essays in this collection, which shows how much stronger Fleming's characterization of his female protagonists had become and how this was arguably lost in the 1971 film of the novel.

At the time the novel was published, it received great praise from some of the people whose approval Fleming craved the most—his peers. Raymond Chandler for one, as Oliver Buckton discusses in his introduction, who marveled at Fleming's realistic portrait of America. Fleming's love/hate relationship with the United States has always been a source of fascination for me, especially from the American perspective, given the legions of American readers of James Bond. Fleming mercifully did not do enough to damage the "special relationship," which has in my experience, brought many Anglo-American Bond fans together.

While Fleming had always wrestled with the idea of a diminishing British Empire and used Bond as a buttress against this, he was equally excited by what the rest of the world had to offer and found that in America. His enduring friendships with Ivar Bryce, Ernest Cuneo, and William Woodward Jr. (to whom the book is dedicated in part) were hugely important to his inspiration for writing, and probably not least to his mental health. His road trips with Cuneo and Bryce helped inspire some of the best scenes in *Diamonds Are Forever,* including scenes at the racetrack in Saratoga, which are some of the best descriptive passages Fleming ever produced. Ernest Cuneo would of course have a cameo in the novel as Ernie Cureo the cab driver. Really, without these friendships, one wonders if Fleming would ever have written so extensively about America in his stories. It was in 1954, that Fleming and Cuneo went on a transcontinental rail trip via Chicago, Los Angeles, and Las Vegas. These trips helped Fleming, with his trusty notebook at hand, to absorb even the finest of details as Cuneo remarked in an interview in the 1980s: "He said that at the end of each day, he had compiled notes. These he amplified and typed out, no matter what the hour, at the rate of about 800 words a day."[1]

Fleming often said that Cuneo provided much of his material for *Diamonds Are Forever* and there is an underlying theme of friendship in the novel, manifested by the relationship between Bond and Felix Leiter. Their journey in the Studillac to Saratoga Springs mirrors that of Fleming and Cuneo, taking in all sorts of Americana, and the food of course, which Edward Biddulph describes in his essay contained in this volume. But this novel is by no means a glorified travelogue.

As Tiffany Case is the heart of the novel, Felix Leiter provides the American soul. In his previous outings, he'd had a hell of time, particularly in *Live and Let Die.* This time, Fleming goes easy on him and provides him with some of the best lines in the novel. "'It'll be one-twenty in the shade out there. Only there isn't any shade.'"[2]

By this novel, Leiter was no longer working for the CIA and Fleming had taken a break from the Soviets as the central threat. This provided new villainous terrain to be explored for Fleming and he introduced American gangsters in the form of the Spang Brothers, pitted against Bond and Leiter. Critics of the novel have often pointed to this aspect as one of the major weaknesses, for they lacked the real menace of Le Chiffre, Mr. Big, or Hugo Drax. It's arguable that this diluted the impact, compared to the previously larger-than-life main villains. The Spang Brothers, with their homosexual hitmen Wint and Kidd joining the fray, did not quite hit the mark with readers. With no connection to the Cold

War, Fleming was not able to conjure up the same amount of foreboding he could with SMERSH or SPECTRE. Despite Fleming writing without an obvious villain, Wint and Kidd are better drawn characters than the Spangs, proving, even in a small measure, that he could successfully write against his own formula. That physically unimposing people can also be feared is a real world touch overlooked. It's perhaps fitting then, that one of the most memorable aspects of the film version was Wint and Kidd, who managed to create the right amount of menace—one of the few elements that improved on the novel.

This most American of British thrillers was overshadowed by *From Russia with Love*, the next in the series, which caught the attention of President John F. Kennedy and was simply a *better* novel by many literary benchmarks, but *Diamonds Are Forever* arguably has more heart and is more fun to read. Even the *New York Times'* Anthony Boucher—described by the first Fleming biographer, John Pearson as "throughout an avid anti-Bond and an anti-Fleming man"[3]—noted that "Mr. Fleming's handling of America and Americans is well above the British average."[4]

This collection of essays is a worthy and overdue reevaluation of a novel that Fleming threw everything at, and I'm sure, he would be thrilled that we're still talking about it.

NOTES

1. Fergus Fleming, ed., *The Man with the Golden Typewriter: Ian Fleming's James Bond Letters* (New York and London: Bloomsbury, 2015), 83.
2. Ian Fleming, *Diamonds Are Forever* (Las Vegas: Thomas and Mercer, 2012), 128.
3. John Pearson, *The Life of Ian Fleming* (London: Jonathan Cape, 1967), 99.
4. Anthony Boucher, "Report on Criminals at Large," *The New York Times*, 28 October 1956.

Introduction

The Many Facets of Diamonds Are Forever

Oliver Buckton

This collection of essays emerged from two panels on *Diamonds Are Forever* (*Diamonds*) organized for the 88th South Atlantic Modern Language Association (SAMLA) convention in 2016, to mark the sixtieth and forty-fifth anniversaries of the novel and film, respectively. The panels attracted papers from international critics and scholars on a range of topics about both Fleming's novel and Guy Hamilton's 1971 film adaptation. These essays, revised and expanded for publication, have been augmented by several other pieces written specifically for this collection, which provide essential insights into aspects of the novel and film not covered in the original conference. Giving roughly equal attention to both novel and film, the essays in this collection place both works in the contexts of Ian Fleming's career, the history of spy fiction, gender and sexuality in popular culture, Fleming's attitudes toward America, and the development of the James Bond film franchise. This is the first full-length collection of essays on Fleming's important and influential novel and the 1971 film adaptation of the same name directed by Guy Hamilton—the last official Bond film to feature Sean Connery in the starring role.

Published in 1956, *Diamonds Are Forever* was the fourth James Bond novel by Ian Fleming and is distinctive in a number of ways. It was, as Fleming himself noted, a departure from the previous 007 adventures— for example, while set largely in the United States it was, as Fleming wrote to Raymond Chandler, "an America of much more fantasy than I allowed myself in *Live and Let Die.*"[1] In his 1965 essay "Narrative Structures in Fleming," Umberto Eco noted further discrepancies between *Diamonds* and the Bond canon: "Only the evil characters in *Diamonds Are Forever* have no connection with Russia. In a certain sense the international gangsterism of the Spangs appears to be an earlier version of Spectre."[2] Thus while the previous three Bond novels—*Casino Royale, Live and Let Die,* and *Moonraker*—each featured a villain working for the Soviet spy agency, SMERSH, *Diamonds* anticipates the later fiction of Fleming, beginning with *Thunderball* (1961), in which the international terrorist organization SPECTRE is the chief adversary.

Diamonds may be considered an anomaly in the Bond canon in other respects: for example Bond's American counterpart Felix Leiter is no longer working for the CIA but—having sustained serious injuries as a result of a shark attack in *Live and Let Die*—is now a private detective working for Pinkerton's agency. Considering Fleming's well-known love of cards and gambling, it is surprising that *Diamonds* is the only Bond novel to be set in the American gaming capital of Las Vegas. The novel gives perhaps the most critical view of American society of any Bond novel, overall, while also attempting to move the Bond series into new territory of American gangsterism that would feature in later works such as *Goldfinger* (1959) and *The Spy Who Loved Me* (1962). These departures from the conventions of the Bond canon make *Diamonds* a fascinating subject for an extended close study, being open to a variety of critical, theoretical, and textual perspectives as demonstrated by the varied essays in this collection.

Following the entirely English setting of its predecessor *Moonraker*—which had provoked some raised eyebrows from critics and readers—Fleming returned Bond to the international scene in *Diamonds*. Yet to some extent the novel's unusual plot and villains reflect Fleming's growing dissatisfaction with the Bond formula that he had launched with *Casino Royale*. In a letter to Chandler, Fleming described his Bond novels as: "straight pillow fantasies of the bang-bang, kiss-kiss variety."[3] Fleming's self-deprecating comments about his character respond to Chandler's suggestion that he should write to a higher level, to which Fleming objected: "My talents are extended to their absolute limits in writing books like *Diamonds Are Forever*. I am not short-weighting anybody and I have absolutely nothing more up my sleeve."[4] Fleming was already looking about for other outlets for his literary interests beyond James Bond, as is demonstrated by his book published in the following year, *The Diamond Smugglers*. This nonfictional account of the actual operation to prevent diamond smuggling in Africa—on which *Diamonds* was also based—features another protagonist, John Blaize, who was considered by Fleming as a replacement for James Bond. The publication of *From Russia with Love*—also in 1957—further emphasized Fleming's disillusionment with his spy protagonist. Bond does not even appear until the second part of the novel, and the story ends with him having apparently met his end from the poisoned shoe-blade of SMERSH's Colonel Rosa Klebb. Even by the time *Diamonds* was published, then, Bond faces replacement or elimination by his own creator.

Yet while this may imply that *Diamonds* is representative of Fleming's creative exhaustion, it would be a serious mistake to read the novel as a case of artistic decline. For in several respects, *Diamonds* is one of Fleming's most significant and innovative efforts in spy fiction which changed the course of the series. Significantly, this was the first of Fleming's Bond novels to be serialized in the *Daily Express* newspaper in Britain and thus, as Fleming's bibliographer Jon Gilbert notes, "proved to be the template for future Bond novels and short stories in the UK."[5] The lack of SMERSH villains means that the author has to be more creative in developing adversaries for his hero, drawing on the gangster story and hard-boiled detective novel (such as those penned by Chandler) for inspiration. Anticipating the displacement of SMERSH that would be confirmed by the films' preference for SPECTRE as the chief enemy organization—beginning with *Dr. No* in 1962—*Diamonds* offers Fleming's most detailed and, in some respects, satirical portrayals of crime in America. If, as Christopher Moran has argued, Fleming was generally enthusiastic about promoting the "special relationship" between Britain and its World War II ally—and especially in highlighting the collaboration of SIS and the CIA—then *Diamonds* offers a counterargument against this claim.[6] Leiter has been cast off by the CIA, leaving him to pursue race-fixing in Saratoga as a Pinkerton's detective, rather than address matters of national security. America is portrayed as a largely corrupt, materialistic, and culturally anemic society, in which everything from the cuisine to the obsessive gambling of Las Vegas is subject to scathing critique. Yet the heroine, Tiffany Case, is one of the few American women in Fleming's novels with whom Bond becomes sexually and romantically involved. With her hard-nosed attitude toward diamond smuggling, gambling, and men, she emerges as one of the novel's great strengths, carrying the plot for much of the novel while serving as Bond's counterpart: an emotionally damaged, ruthless professional who is not prone to sentimental liaisons. Indeed, the significance of Tiffany Case in particular—and gender roles in general—in both novel and film are the focus of several of the essays in this collection.

Precisely because the novel was written at a point of crisis in Fleming's career, *Diamonds* is significant as a work of transition, notable for its challenges to conventional gender and sexual identities. If Tiffany Case represents one interesting aspect of the novel's gender politics—her fierce independence and sexual desire challenging the stereotype of the passive "Bond girl"—another is apparent in the Spangs' gay hitmen, Mr. Wint and Mr. Kidd. Identified by Leiter as "homos," some of whom make the "worst killers," Wint and Kidd bring a new dimension to the sexual menace embodied in the Bond villain.[7] If the genital beating administered to Bond by Le Chiffre in *Casino Royale* evoked a bizarre eroticism—implicating Bond in an intimate queer scenario from which heroine Vesper Lynd can scarcely rescue him—then Wint and Kidd suggest a lethal violence that defies the 1950s stereotype of the effeminate homosexual. Wint's obsessive sucking of the wart on his thumb may suggest an infantile oral fixation (also evoked by Drax's splayed teeth in *Moonraker*) but there is nothing childish about the violence inflicted by him on the jockey Tingaling Bell at the Acme Mud and Sulphur Baths. *Diamonds* is also significant in that it is based on experiences Fleming shared with his Eton schoolfriend Ivar Bryce, who had (through his wife, Jo Hartford) a home in Vermont called Black Hole Hollow Farm, where Fleming stayed while researching and revising the novel, and from which he visited the horse-racing town of Saratoga in upstate New York.[8] With Bryce's lawyer-friend Ernest Cuneo, Fleming made an ill-fated expedition to a Sulphur bath that resulted in the famous episode from chapter 13 of the novel. While *Diamonds* contains some of the disturbing racial stereotypes that also appeared in *Live and Let Die*, the novel makes an intriguing contrast between British and American racial attitudes. In describing his aversion to being handled by the black attendant at the mud baths, Bond comments "how lucky England was compared with America where you had to live with the colour problem from your schooldays up."[9] *Diamonds* is thus intriguing in its expression of some of the cultural, racial, and sexual anxieties that haunted Fleming's imagination while also reflecting the values and assumptions of the time period in which he wrote.

If the novel is an important anomaly in the Bond novel canon, the same may be said of Guy Hamilton's 1971 film in its relationship to the film franchise. The film of *Diamonds* was the seventh in the Broccoli-Salzman series, and the second of four Bond films directed by Paris-born British director Hamilton. The first of Hamilton's efforts, *Goldfinger*, is viewed by many as the archetypal Bond film, in which the 007 screen formula was definitively established. *Diamonds* in some ways replicates the plot and settings of *Goldfinger*, with its story of smuggling precious commodities, its American setting, and its focus on gangsterism. But whereas in the earlier film, Sean Connery was at the peak of his powers (and his popularity) as 007, *Diamonds* was his final appearance in the role. Moreover, Connery was lured back by the offer of a huge paycheck following the abrupt departure of Australian actor George Lazenby after only one film, the critically admired but commercially disappointing *On Her Majesty's Secret Service* (OHMSS, 1969). Thus Connery's performance was a stopgap measure, until a permanent replacement could be found, and Hamilton's third and fourth Bond films would feature the new cinematic incarnation of 007, Roger Moore. Notably, Hamilton's film—based on a screenplay by Richard Maibaum and Tom Mankiewicz—would significantly reduce the role of the gangster villains of Fleming's novel, while reintroducing Bond's nemesis Ernst Stavro Blofeld, at the helm of SPECTRE. Played by British actor Charles Gray—who had previously appeared as a Bond ally in 1967's *You Only Live Twice*—Blofeld exhibits a camp style that links him more closely with Wint and Kidd. Yet Fleming's gay hitmen—who are lethal and sinister—are treated as a comic sideshow of effeminate stereotypes in the film version, signaled by Wint's obsessive spraying of himself with cologne. In this and other respects, the film suggests the shift in Bond films toward a caricature of the spy genre, rather than the more realistic portrayal of espionage (and closer representation of Fleming's work) in films such as OHMSS.

The essay collection is divided into three sections of related chapters: the first section, "Sound, Affect, Adaptation, and Intertextuality in *Diamonds Are Forever*," includes critical discussions of the soundtrack of the film, the production and historical contexts of the film, and the connection between Fleming's novel and his nonfiction book, *The Diamond Smugglers*, published the following year. The first chapter, "The Scorpion as Emblematic of Affect in *Diamonds Are Forever*," by Elyn Achtymichuck-Hardy, features a detailed discussion of the scorpion that opens the novel and explores a key example of affect in Fleming's novel. While the author notes that the scorpion evokes fear and danger in the novel's African opening, this danger is "beautiful, even sexualized." The scorpion emerges as a sublime object, conveying both awe and terror. The essay argues that the scorpion functions in certain key ways as a metaphor for Bond himself. For example, the scorpion is portrayed as a deadly predator—demonstrated by its ravenous consumption of the beetle—but also a vulnerable creature, who will encounter and be destroyed by a more powerful enemy. Ultimately, however, Achtymichuck-Hardy is more interested in using affect theory to explore the scorpion's power to shape emotion in the reader, that is its "affect." Like Bond, that is, the scorpion embodies what the author terms the sublime "beauty of violence." The emotions of fear, danger, and excitement evoked by the scorpion are essential to the reader's engagement with the novel and foreshadow the dangers that Bond himself will face. Using both Aristotle's theory of "catharsis" and the affect theory of Sarah Ahmed, this chapter makes a compelling argument about the disturbing treatment of themes of race, violence, and sexuality in Fleming's novel.

In the second chapter, "The Sounds of *Diamonds Are Forever*," Jesc Bunyard explores the moments of "sonic interest" in Guy Hamilton's film adaptation, starting with the obviously Scottish accent of Sean Connery as James Bond, which highlights the "British" (rather than English) nationality of the spy. Given the Welsh singer Shirley Bassey's singing of the title song (as she did for *Goldfinger*, Hamilton's previous Bond film), Bunyard argues that the soundtrack may be considered a classic example of British film music. Bunyard also addresses the "acousmatic" nature of Bond's (Connery's) voice in the film's opening scenes, as Bond's face and mouth cannot be seen. The acousmatic voice as Bunyard—following Mladen Dolar—defines it, is the voice whose origin and source cannot be seen or identified. Paradoxically, the revelation of Bond's identity in the opening sequence results in a loss of power as the origin of the voice is exposed. The chapter goes on to explore other intriguing sonic aspects, such as the "leitmotif" of James Bond, as well as that of Mr. Wint and Mr. Kidd—the gay assassins—which ends with a "sting," evoking the deadly scorpion at the film's opening. Bunyard explores the intriguing vocal exchanges between Blofeld and Willard Whyte, whose voice Blofeld appropriates for his plot of global domination. This results in an "already visualized acousmêtre" — in which a voice that has previously been seen with its appropriate body but is then acoustematized: thus Whyte's voice becomes acousmatic when Blofeld uses it to talk to his accomplices on the phone. The essay demonstrates the sonic complexity of Hamilton's film as well as arguing that the film demonstrates the malign adaptability of capitalism, in the form of Blofeld's appropriation of Whyte's empire.

The third chapter, "Transforming Bond: *Diamonds Are Forever* in Its Contexts" by James Chapman, places the 1971 film in the specific context of its predecessor, *On Her Majesty's Secret Service*, and its successors featuring Roger Moore's first appearances in the role of Bond. Chapman's essay discusses how the disappointing critical and commercial reception of OHMSS—the only film to star Australian model George Lazenby as 007—was partly responsible for a significant change in style with *Diamonds Are Forever*. The author notes that the box-office failure of OHMSS represented a change in film culture, in which blockbuster entertainments were supplanted by a new kind of Hollywood product such as Mike Nichols's *The Graduate*. Hence *Diamonds* would define itself as "the very antithesis of OHMSS" representing one of the most dramatic stylistic shifts in the history of Bond on film. While incorporating some of the visual excess of *You Only Live Twice*, *Diamonds* also introduced a camp sensibility and shrewd political commentary that set it apart. In particular, the film of *Diamonds* is more blatant in its depiction of Britain as a third-rate world power, unlike earlier Bond films which perpetuated the myth of Britain's superpower status. Chapman offers illuminating commentary on the significance of Sean Connery's return to the role of 007 after a four-year hiatus, and examines ways in which his performance in this film established the tone for Moore's films, beginning with *Live and Let Die* (1973)—also helmed by *Diamonds* director Guy Hamilton. Noting that the film of *Diamonds* begins a process of the films distancing themselves more emphatically from Fleming's novels, Chapman examines a film sensibility in sharp contrast to the serious and somber mood of its predecessor, *On Her Majesty's Secret Service*—a film that, unlike *Diamonds*, closely follows Fleming's novel.

In chapter 4 "James Bond, Meet John Blaize: Identity Theft and Intertextuality in Ian Fleming's *Diamonds Are Forever* and *The Diamond Smugglers*," Oliver Buckton offers a different slant on the theme of "adaptation" of Fleming's work. Presenting a comparative reading of *Diamonds Are Forever* and the nonfiction book Fleming published the following year, *The Diamond Smugglers*, this chapter examines several key examples of intertextuality and influence between the works. The discussion is framed by considering Fleming's growing disillusionment with James Bond by the mid 1950s, and his attempts to develop alternative protagonists and even to kill off James Bond at the end of *From Russia with Love*. Noting that both books were based on the same real-life operation to shut down diamond smuggling from the African diamond mines—headed by the retired former head of MI5, Sir Percy Sillitoe—this chapter illustrates how a knowingness about the blurring between fact and fiction permeates both narratives. Fleming introduced a substitute for Bond in *The Diamond Smugglers* in the character of "John Blaize" (having the same initials as Bond), a pseudonym for the real-life head agent of Sillitoe's operation, John Collard. Buckton goes on to note that *The Diamond Smugglers*, while lacking the kinds of erotic fantasy and "Bond girls" typical of a Bond novel, restores, in the enigmatic figure of Monsieur Diamant, the more traditional Soviet-backed villain that is lacking in *Diamonds Are Forever*. In the portrayal of this hugely successful diamond smuggler, Buckton argues, Fleming depicts an arch-villain who in some ways anticipates future Bond baddies such as Dr. Julius No, Auric Goldfinger, or indeed Bond's nemesis Ernst Stavro Blofeld.

The second section of the book, "Gender and Sexuality in *Diamonds Are Forever*" features discussions of the complex and shifting gender roles and relations in the novel and film. This includes a study of the queer dimensions of the novel and the film, specifically the notorious gay hitmen Wint and Kidd, as well as in-depth discussions of women in the novel and film, especially Tiffany Case. The essays in this section explore the fascinating representations of gender and sexual politics in both Fleming's novel and Hamilton's film, linking both to other seminal works in the Bond canon. While several of the essays address the main female characters and gender roles, the opening essay of this section takes as its starting point the presence of homosexual villains in Fleming's novel.

In the fifth chapter, "My Adversary, Myself: An Examination of James Bond and How Wint and Kidd Reflect His Own Psyche in *Diamonds Are Forever*," Grant C. Hester develops a challenge to the superficially heteronormative world in which James Bond acts. Through close analysis of Fleming's coded language, this chapter opens up other interpretations that suggest a repressed homosexuality in Bond. Noting that the homophobic period in which Fleming wrote (his death in 1964 occurred three years before homosexuality was decriminalized in Britain) meant that only "coded" language could be used to invoke same-sex desire, the author considers Mr. Wint and Mr. Kidd as among the most overt references to queer desire in the Bond canon. Hester demonstrates the context of queer characters elsewhere in Fleming's novels, before proceeding to a detailed discussion of how Wint and Kidd's "sexual identity provides a unique parallel and vantage point for an examination of Bond's own sexuality." Deploying theoretical insights by Judith Butler, Laura Mulvey, and Susan Sontag, Hester suggestively argues that Bond's masculinity is "performative," functioning to mask an inner queer desire that abruptly surfaces at moments in the text. Noting that Bond's emotional entanglements with women are always temporary and often superficial, Hester makes a compelling case that Bond himself becomes the object of the desiring gaze, adopting the position typically assigned (in Laura Mulvey's now-classic argument) to the woman: "To-be-looked-at-ness." Bond, in this perspective, becomes a mirror image of his own adversaries, especially the queer hitmen Wint and Kidd. As an example of this mirroring, the chapter notes that Bond's meeting with the gay hitmen takes place in the Acme Mud and Sulphur Baths, a significant location in that the gay bathhouse was a vital part of queer culture even during the homophobic 1950s.

The sixth chapter, Jennifer L. Martinsen's "The Devolution of Tiffany Case," focuses on the leading female character in novel and film, contrasting Fleming's strong independent heroine with the "floozy" the character is transformed into in Guy Hamilton's film version. Martinsen provides a strong counterargument to the dismissal of Fleming's novels as misogynistic, pointing out "there are enough examples throughout Fleming's texts to indicate that the 'Bond Girl' is not simply there to look pretty and warm Bond's bed. Instead, she often helps Bond and serves as an asset to his mission and to the story." Martinsen argues that Fleming's Case, while initially an object of sexual desire for Bond, demonstrates control of her own body and sexuality, while also possessing an agency and level of control that makes her Bond's counterpart in the diamond smuggling mission. In Fleming's plot, Case—whose traumatic girlhood experience of being gang-raped provokes sympathy in Bond—emerges as "a true asset," for example by helping Bond escape from Spectreville—Seraffimo Spang's fantasy version of a Western town—after being beaten up by Wint and Kidd. At first, in Guy Hamilton's film version, Case seems to possess a similar sexual confidence and agency, as she makes it clear that her scantily-clad appearance is for her own rather than Bond's (and the viewer's) pleasure. However, in subsequent scenes, such as her appearance in Bond's hotel bedroom, Case is portrayed merely as a means to an end for Bond and as a sexual object or "bimbo" on display for Bond's (and the male viewer's) consumption. Using Laura Mulvey's theory of the masculine gaze, Martinsen shows Case's "to-be-looked-at-ness" as a degradation of her character, especially with the camera's obsessive fixation on her buttocks in the scenes on Blofeld's oil rig. The chapter intriguingly links this "devolution" of Case from novel to film version to a backlash against the feminist movement in the early 1970s, as the film attempts to reassert a patriarchal version of female identity that had been challenged by feminist discourse. Martinsen concludes by arguing that the debasement of Case also weakens the character of Bond in the film, as he is at his best when challenged by a female counterpart with agency and intelligence.

Chapter 7, "The Eyes of Tiffany Case: And What They Tell about Ian Fleming's First Successful Female Character," by Ihsan Amanatullah considers how Case's sexual trauma as a girl instilled a determination to be independent of men, even though she is in the power of the patriarchal gangsters of the Spangled Mob. The chapter offers a dazzling examination of Fleming's (and Bond's) close attention to Case's eyes, registering the hero's uncharacteristic sensitivity to a woman's emotions in this novel. This analysis includes some striking parallels between Case's eyes and the diamonds that become the first object of desire in the novel. While Amanatullah also considers the character of Case as the most complex female figure Fleming had yet created, and the most compatible with Bond's character, his chapter concludes by noting that in the next novel, *From Russia with Love*, Case's future is separated from Bond's.

The third and final section of the book, "Culture, Consumption, and America in *Diamonds Are Forever*" takes a close look at issues of consumption—including food, drink, clothing, sex, and other commodities—in Fleming's novel and the film adaptation. In chapter 8, "Attitudes Are Forever: America Disdained," Matthew B. Sherman argues that *Diamonds* is notable for its extensive use of an American setting that is hardly flattering to Britain's chief postwar ally. *Diamonds*, according to Sherman, offers a frequently satirical take on American manners, gambling, materialism, cuisine, and consumption. The chapter offers a thought-provoking reading of "America disdained" in Fleming's novel, noting the folktale qualities of Bond's quest in which "it is often an inept United States and not just women in peril who need rescue." Sherman demonstrates that *Diamonds* contains negative commentaries on many aspects of American society from drug trafficking to inferior food and obsessive (and unglamorous) gambling in Las Vegas. He also notes the negative imagery often used by Fleming in describing American towns and landscapes, especially in Las Vegas. In contrast to the elegant gambling surroundings of *Casino Royale*, *Diamonds* also features the inferior (in Fleming's view) food of America, offering what Sherman terms "a dystopian view of greed and consumerism." The chapter extends the analysis to include the 1971 film of *Diamonds Are Forever*, demonstrating that the disdainful portrayal of America is, if anything, intensified as compared to the novel. In particular, Sherman notes, the portrayals of American characters as incompetent or foolish is a surprising feature of a film designed, presumably, to reach an American audience.

Chapter 9, Mark David Kaufman's "The Desert of the Real: *Diamonds Are Forever* as a Hollywood Novel," focuses on the America of Fleming's *Diamonds Are Forever* as "a land of simulacra," a site of illusions of which Hollywood is the ultimate producer. By comparing Fleming's novel to "Hollywood novels" such as Nathanael West's *The Day of the Locust* and Evelyn Waugh's *The Loved One*, Kaufman situates Fleming in a group of writers who both satirize the illusions and corruptions of Hollywood, and use the setting to undermine the distinction between reality and simulation in mainstream American society. While Fleming's novel is not primarily set in Hollywood, Kaufman defines the "Hollywood novel," following Chip Rhodes's argument, more broadly as a genre that exposes America as a "land of simulacra." Moreover, Kaufman demonstrates that the film industry plays a significant part in Fleming's novel, such as Felix Leiter now sounding like a private investigator from film noir rather than a spy. The highlight of the Hollywood-esque spectacle and illusion, Kaufman argues, is Seraffimo Spang's faux-Western town, "Spectreville," described as being like a film set, in which Bond and his adversaries are all "actors" playing out scripted roles. Fleming's novel, then, tests the boundaries between reality and illusion/performance in America, ultimately finding little to separate them.

In chapter 10, "A Happy Selection: The Representation of Food and Drink in the Book and Film of *Diamonds Are Forever*," Edward Biddulph explores one of the most enduring and intriguing topics in Fleming's fiction: the consumption of meals. Biddulph carefully analyzes the numerous references to food and drink in *Diamonds Are Forever*, noting the details of Bond's consumption of all comestibles and beverages in both the novel and film. Biddulph's chapter also offers remarkable insight into the wide range of references to food and drink throughout Fleming's novel, noting the recurrence of dishes such as Brizzola and (especially) scrambled eggs in Bond's cuisine. Indeed, the recurrence of scrambled eggs has been linked by critic Elizabeth Hale to Bond's "power," a symbol of his role as man and killer. Though the author questions this assumption, he recognizes the important symbolism food often has in Fleming's fiction. For example, Biddulph notes that the abundance of food and drink in America would have been enticing to British readers still enduring postwar austerity, but argues that Bond is far from flawless in his food and drink choices. Despite his apparent expertise, Bond appears as a "food tourist" in the novel and film. The proven ability of Tiffany Case to make sauce Béarnaise is an indicator that she is the kind of woman Bond might marry.

Yet, for Biddulph, uncouth or unsophisticated dining practices are still a sign of the villain, such as the American gangsters' gluttony in *Diamonds*. By charting Bond's consumption of food and drink in meticulous detail throughout the novel, Biddulph investigates how changing food practices and tastes have shaped readers' responses to the novel and film of *Diamonds* over the years. Paying particularly close attention to how the Bond of the film is "altogether a different beast" than Fleming's creation, Biddulph shows how food and drink are used by Hamilton's film as a means to establish Bond's expertise rather than as a source of pleasure. Moreover, lack of knowledge about wine is a sign of the villains in the film of *Diamonds*, as it had been in *From Russia with Love*. Biddulph's chapter provides intriguing insight into how dishes and ingredients (such as avocados) that would have been an "exotic novelty" in 1956 have since come to seem quite ordinary. Clearly, in the realm of food and drink, Fleming was ahead of his time. And yet, Bond tends to play it safe in his culinary choices, sticking to dishes he knows and enjoys. As Biddulph's chapter demonstrates, Bond is a less adventurous "food tourist" than we might imagine.

With its diversity of characters, its blend of suspense and humor, its nontraditional villains, its unique female lead character, and its ambivalent portrayal of America, *Diamonds Are Forever* is surely in need of much closer critical scrutiny. The aim of this collection of essays is to open up the "many facets of *Diamonds Are Forever*" — both the novel and the film — for further critical discussion. The editor and contributors are hopeful that this volume will lead to similar case studies of other single novel/film pairings in the Bond canon. As unique landmarks of the James Bond series, both novel and film of *Diamonds* offer intriguing challenges for readers and critics in the twenty-first century.

NOTES

1. Fergus Fleming, ed., *The Man with the Golden Typewriter: Ian Fleming's James Bond Letters* (New York: Bloomsbury, 2015), 225.

2. Umberto Eco, "Narrative Structures in Fleming," *The Role of the Reader: Explorations in the Semiotics of Texts* (Bloomington: Indiana University Press, 1979), 153.

3. Fleming, ed., *The Man with the Golden Typewriter*, 228. Chandler had criticized the novel, in part because he felt it had too much "padding" and didn't stick to the action (Ibid., 100).

4. Fleming, ed., *The Man with the Golden Typewriter*, 232.

5. Jon Gilbert, *Ian Fleming: The Bibliography* (London: Queen Anne Press, 2017), 128.

6. See Christopher Moran, "Ian Fleming and the Public Profile of the CIA," *Journal of Cold War Studies*, Volume 15, Number 1, Winter 2013, pp. 119–46.

7. Ian Fleming, *Diamonds Are Forever* (Las Vegas: Thomas and Mercer, 2012), 119.

8. Black Hole Hollow Farm is today located in New York state, just west of the Vermont state line.

9. Fleming, *Diamonds Are Forever*, 110.

BIBLIOGRAPHY

Eco, Umberto. "Narrative Structures in Fleming." *The Role of the Reader: Explorations in the Semiotics of Texts*. Bloomington: Indiana University Press, 1979. 144–72.

Fleming, Fergus, ed. *The Man with the Golden Typewriter: Ian Fleming's James Bond Letters*. New York: Bloomsbury, 2015.

Fleming, Ian. *Diamonds Are Forever*. Las Vegas: Thomas and Mercer, 2012.

Gilbert, Jon. *Ian Fleming: The Bibliography*. London: Queen Anne Press, 2017.

Moran, Christopher. "Ian Fleming and the Public Profile of the CIA." *Journal of Cold War Studies*, Volume 15, Number 1 (Winter 2013): 119–46.

1

Sound, Affect, Adaptation, and Intertextuality in *Diamonds Are Forever*

ONE

The Scorpion as Emblem of Affect in *Diamonds Are Forever*

Elyn Achtymichuk-Hardy

Rock scorpion, n. A scorpion that frequents rocky places: (a) any of several large black scorpions of the Old World, esp. Pandinus imperator of Africa; (b) (more fully flat rock scorpion) any of several flattened scorpions of the genus Hadogenes, of southern Africa.[1]

The Black, or Rock Scorpion, is nearly as venomous as any of the serpent tribe.
—W. Paterson[2]

The great Rock-scorpion of Africa is much dreaded by the natives.
—J.G. Wood[3]

Typically, a scorpion is neither a symbol of pleasure, nor of beauty. Rather, the image of the scorpion is striking in its capacity for insectoid violence and danger. However, the scorpion featured in the opening chapter of Ian Fleming's *Diamonds Are Forever* is sensuous, exotic, and brimming with powerful emotional impact, conveyed by paradoxical symbolism that succinctly captures the essence of the text that follows. *Diamonds Are Forever* begins and ends in the same place, forming a symmetrical narrative depicting two scenes in the desert region near the intersection of three West African countries: Sierra Leone, Liberia, and—in 1956—French Guinea.[4] Of particular relevance is the opening part of the narrative frame, which describes a magnificent scorpion.[5] Unlike a typical scorpion, the arachnid featured in Fleming's novel symbolizes pleasure and fear in tandem. Paradoxically, the scorpion expresses violence in addition to an aesthetic of fear: danger in this passage is beautiful, even sexualized. The image of the scorpion transgresses a number of taboos that would otherwise suggest that sex and violence remain separate, and

15

that there is neither beauty in danger, nor sensuality in death. As the scorpion hunts and kills the beetle, it is easy to see the violent nature of the scene, but its evocation of pleasure is equally important, although more difficult to parse out. The scorpion therefore also introduces these paradoxical themes within the person of James Bond. Finally, the scorpion takes on racialized characteristics by the end of its existence: that is, certain stereotypical identities are ascribed to its blackness, and thus the image becomes more than just a physical trait, but rather also a symbol of racial prejudice and the exploitation of Africans: their bodies, their labor, and their country. One could argue that the scorpion is a metaphor for Bond himself without much controversy; like the scorpion, he is violent, dangerous, sexy, and undeniably influenced by the colonialist and imperialist practices of the time.

However, applying the concept of metaphor to this phenomenon is too simple: if one claims that the scorpion is a metaphor, one must also determine why that matters. Therefore, it is more thought-provoking to consider the scorpion as an affective symbol. In simple terms, affect is the shaping power of emotion.[6] Affect is not, then, the transfer of emotion, or the mobility of emotions across bodies, but the real capability of emotion to shape bodies, ideas, and objects. In Sara Ahmed's model of the sociality of emotions, she writes:

> Emotions create the very effect of the surfaces and boundaries that allow us to distinguish an inside and an outside [of an object] in the first place. Emotions are not simply something "I" or "we" have. Rather, it is through emotions, or how we respond to objects and others, that surfaces or boundaries are made: the "I" and the "we" are shaped by, and even take the shape of, contact with others.[7]

The scorpion is capable of affect because it makes us powerfully aware of the danger and, to a lesser extent, the sexuality of the text: it produces an emotive response that does not simply move across bodies, but creates an internal emotive response. In reading, I react emotionally to the text, feeling both fear and desire for the characters and their lifestyles. Ahmed objects to the notion that emotions are like a contagion—the emotion is given and taken like a possession—because of the way emotions are changed and reinterpreted when they are received.[8] Thus, she speaks of emotions as passing through objects. The emotions that we receive from the scorpion shape our feelings on the scorpion, but they also shape how we feel about Bond: once we interpret the myriad of emotions that the scorpion is meant to elicit, we are afforded a more complete interpretation of Bond if we recognize that those emotions reoccur when we encounter Bond in similar situations of fear, violence, disgust, beauty, and sexuality.

Primarily, the scorpion embodies fear, and yet it also embodies the appeal of Bond: his violence, yes, but also his beauty and his almost insatiable need for pleasure, even at the expense of his personal safety. As a result, the scorpion *creates* our impression of Bond, and it *produces* our assumptions about Bond's abilities. Ahmed puts this in economic terms: she writes that "the movement between signs or objects converts into affect . . . affect does not reside in an object or sign, but is an effect of the circulation between objects and signs."[9] It is the circulation of the signs through the reader which produces the affective response, and thus the relationship between emotions as they pass through the scorpion, through the reader, and back to Bond. If we read the scorpion as a simple metaphor, the scorpion exists to make us see Bond as the scorpion. But in my reading of this passage, we *feel* that Bond is the scorpion. We are therefore also more attuned to the disgust suggested by the mixing of fear and sex that the images of the scorpion suggest: affect makes us more perceptive to the rape metaphor of the scorpion's meal, its black and polished shell shining elegantly; combined within the violent creature, we are discomfited by the relationship between fear and sex that the scorpion elicits. The perception of danger, violence, and beauty is pressed upon and through us, and we feel these concepts emotionally rather than intellectually. In *Diamonds Are Forever*, Fleming's scorpion foreshadows the danger that Bond is in, and it also instantly transfers those emotions of fear to the reader; disquietingly, the reader perceives the beauty of the scorpion, despite its ravaging of the beetle. Therefore, an additional emotion transferred to the reader is that of desire, as the reader is captivated by the scorpion's fastidiousness, efficiency, and elegance, even in spite of its violence. In short, we desire its success, rejoicing in its pleasures, while fearing for its failures. Therefore, the scorpion is not just a symbol for danger, violence, and beauty, but an affective symbol which evokes an emotive response which is paradoxical, conflicting, and emblematic of the entire text.

One could dismiss the scorpion as phenomenology, or an element of kitsch, which is a stylistic quirk that appears frequently in Fleming's writing. The garishness of "kitsch"—apparent in gaudy and sensationalized details—is a source of Fleming's appeal, but one wonders whether such style is meant ironically, suggesting literary prowess, or otherwise. Umberto Eco writes at length regarding the "minute and leisurely concentration with which [Fleming] pursues for page after page descriptions . . . apparently inessential to the course of the story."[10] Without reading the scorpion as affective, the scorpion in this case is obviously inessential; one could read the rest of the text without giving the scorpion a second thought. Amongst other similar examples from other Fleming texts, Eco offers this very scorpion: "It is . . . 'purposeless' to introduce the diamond smuggling in South Africa[11] [sic] in *Diamonds Are Forever* by opening with the description of a scorpion, as though seen through a magnifying glass . . . as the protagonist in a story of life and death at animal level . . . Then the action of the book begins."[12] Arguably, the novel is not about the scorpion, and its message of the frailty of life is hardly necessary to the telling of the larger narrative. Thus, Eco wonders if such an inclusion is "purposeless." In Eco's conclusion on the reason for including details like the scorpion, he determines that such imagery provides relatability. Eco writes,

> Fleming takes times to convey the familiar with photographic accuracy because it is with the familiar that he can solicit our capacity for information . . . Our credulity is solicited, blandished, directed to the region of possible and desirable things. Here the narration is realistic, the attention to detail intense, thus creating a world which the reader can identify with by including everyday objects. [13]

It is this flourish of expressive prose that Eco uses to suggest the merits of Fleming's literary abilities, but his primary argument is that the minute details are more likely to make the more fantastical details—car chases and epic fight scenes, disarming an atomic bomb or traveling in space—seem more realistic simply by association. Michael Denning quotes Kingsley Amis, who calls this the "Fleming effect": it is Fleming's attention to detail in the ordinary world which creates the illusion of plausibility in the extraordinary. [14] However, Eco's claim of relatability, and of identifying with the rest of the text, fails to capture what occurs when one reads the scorpion as a symbol of affect: if I feel disgust or fear at the presence of the scorpion, I am not meant to simply acknowledge the existence of such a creature in reality. Rather, I am meant to feel its visceral presence, and I internalize the emotions it gives me and then feel them again when I witness Bond in a similar predicament. By association, because the scorpion appears to be aesthetically pleasing, and the language used to describe it is of sexual arousal, the connections between the scorpion and Bond are strengthened. Because the emotions change when they are transferred through me as the reader, my feelings will inevitably change when I see fear and disgust embodied by Bond. Perhaps because his beauty and sexuality are more convincing than that of the scorpion, the sensual relationship between the two is less apparent. However, because the scorpion expresses violence, beauty, sensuality, and danger in tandem, the mechanism by which affect works is meant to explain how I can view Bond in latter scenes of violence or of sexuality, and recognize my fears on his behalf as *the same ones* that were first introduced by the scorpion. In short, the scorpion shapes my feelings on what can be sexual and violent in the novel, and what objects can induce those paradoxical feelings of disgust and desire.

The scorpion is decidedly Bond-like as it casts around for signs of oncoming danger, considering whether it needs to retreat. [15] Bond is usually this careful: Fleming's first novel, *Casino Royale*, contains plenty of examples of his caution. The first few pages establish his attention to detail and precision: he searches his room for a misplaced hair, checks for disturbed talcum powder on a drawer handle, and verifies the correct water level in the toilet's tank to determine if there were intruders in his absence.[16] *Diamonds Are Forever* is particularly interesting by comparison, because the scene with the scorpion foreshadows Bond's potential for distractions: while the scorpion is deadly and cautious, it still dies at the mercy of a more powerful enemy, which may also turn out to be the case for Bond. For Bond's part, he completely underestimates the American gangsters. He says disparagingly that there's nothing that concerns him regarding American gangsters,[17] and refers to them as "teenage pillow-fantasies," or in other words: the infantilized desires of inexperienced adolescents.[18] In addition to dismissing their legitimacy as criminals, he is easily distracted by Case, which compounds his problems. One might argue that in previous novels, Bond has slipped up more than once, trusting women because he underestimates them, or missing details that he only notices much later. However, the sheer number of these cases is overwhelming in *Diamonds Are Forever*, which will be outlined below. Bond ignores or disparages a variety of warnings from at least three prominent sources, which further compounds the problem of his tendency to be diverted by beautiful females. One such example of his lack of precaution is that he is unaware that he and Case are followed onto the ship departing for England at the end of the novel.[19] Since Bond's initial departure from England, the reader is aware that Wint and Kidd have been following Bond; his failure to recognize Wint during the auction onboard the ship contributes to Bond and Case being cornered at the climax of the novel.[20] He seems to be slipping, and the scorpion is the first indication that this might happen. Like Bond, the scorpion's violence is precise and cautious, but not enough: the scorpion still gets killed.

The very first lines of the text suggest the inherent violence of the arthropod in question. The novel begins with the *pandinus* scorpion emerging from its hole, with "claws held forward": it is alert, and sensitive to danger.[21] The narrative goes on to describe the scorpion's hunt of a beetle: mere inches away, the beetle is unaware of its peril. Meanwhile, the scorpion attacks without warning: the beetle's legs "[wave] in protest" as the scorpion's claws snap its body in two, its sting simultaneously lancing the helpless beetle, killing it violently and instantly.[22] The scorpion eats the beetle meticulously, and Fleming takes care to note that the meal lasts for an hour, as if the beetle were some particular delicacy. The scorpion's hunt suggests what the reader already knows about Bond: he is ruthless, violent, and swift. Bond is also painstaking and excessively cautious. Perhaps he is just as fastidious as the scorpion, particularly when it comes to his cuisine. He eats smoked salmon and Brizzola with Leiter,[23] caviar and champagne with Case,[24] and speaks disgustedly of the fish—mislabeled as fresh—which had, undoubtedly, spent months far away in a freezer. In the same breath, he disparages the American waitresses who are unconcerned and disinterested, suggesting Bond's further shaming of the American service industry, as well as its lack of attention to etiquette.[25] For his part, Bond is as particular about his food as the scorpion. However, just as the scorpion meets his untimely end soon after his lunch is over, Bond's arrogance, ignorance, and distractions all make him vulnerable. In a typical Bond novel, the scorpion's kill could be a metaphor for Bond's purposeful hunt for the American gangsters and their relationship to the diamond smuggling ring, and that would be the end of it. But in this novel, the scorpion dies due to its ignorance and vulnerability. This leaves one to think that the same might occur for Bond.

In fact, one of the major themes of *Diamonds Are Forever* is that Bond fails to take the American gangsters seriously, and thus gets caught off-guard multiple times, despite warnings from other characters. M is the first to warn Bond that this will be a difficult task, first checking to make sure that Bond is physically ready for it. M warns Bond that there are "tricky people" whom Bond has not made contact with yet: a polite way of saying that Bond can hardly be omniscient about criminal elements in the world.[26] Bond is naturally irritated at this inference, but the scene is critical because it is the first one that foreshadows several points: first, if Bond is physically unfit, he may not be successful; second, that Bond is continuously warned, and each of those warnings goes unheeded; third, that Bond is not fully prepared for, or aware of, his potential global opponents. Finally, while Bond is typically distracted by women in the franchise—a kind of hallmark for the way that he treats women—he is particularly distracted by Tiffany Case, which serves to exacerbate his lack of appreciation for his opponents' strengths.

Further comparison between the scorpion and Bond is therefore illuminating: the scorpion briefly senses something is amiss, but its ignorance is a fatal flaw. Before hunting the beetle, the scorpion had been warned of a potential threat by two sets of movements, the first of which were identifiable as belonging to the beetle. The second set, however, was beyond the scorpion's scope of experience: these sounds turn out to belong to the smuggler when he arrives. However, the scorpion, who has neither the experience nor the intelligence to infer such things, can only be said to find these vibrations as "incomprehensible."[27] The reader can identify the rhythmic trembling in the ground as a vehicle, and has the capacity of memory to not let those sounds become normalized. Not so for the scorpion, who begins to forget the urgency attached to those vibrations as they become background noise.[28] This point is of particular relevance when one considers that Bond's life is constantly at risk, so he becomes desensitized to the rhythmic hum of incessant danger, thus making him less prepared for the gangsters. The scorpion's final act is to ignore these warning signs and pursue the beetle: in its greed to collect its prey, the beetle forgets about the sounds that suggest danger, and leaves its place of safety.[29] Critically, Bond is lured away from his instincts as a result of his greed for Tiffany Case, thus linking his actions to those of the scorpion.

One assumes that the scorpion is the predator—at least until the moment it is killed. The scorpion therefore suggests a pair of dualities present in the narrative: it is both killer and victim, predator and prey. This is not unlike Bond himself. One can extrapolate from the scorpion's scenes that Bond is the predator of this novel, but that he will often be distracted from danger by his prey: both Bond and the scorpion are practiced killers, predators in their own right. Yet, both will become prey by novel's end. The scene therefore introduces a further theme which the novel engages: there is a difference for both arachnid and man between what is known and what is unknown, based on what each is capable of understanding. That is to say, the scorpion cannot know what it is incapable of comprehending: the scorpion is inherently limited by its own inexperience. Similarly, Bond's experience of international conflict has resulted in his dismissal of the American threat, which is influenced by his classist and colonial perceptions. He perceives that America is inferior because of its history as a former colony. His understanding of America is limited by what Benedict Anderson would call the "imagined political community," which in Bond's case is his perception of Britain's global superiority, both past and present.[30] Despite having worked in the United States previously (in *Live and Let Die*),[31] Bond's loyalty to the British nation inadequately informs him of the nature of the nation-state, and he is therefore limited by his feelings about Britain. He fails to see the cultural understanding of the nation—any nation—as a secular, unifying force that provides purpose and meaning for *all* of its citizens. Bond dismisses the notion of the nation-state existing in America, which causes him to underestimate the capabilities of its people; regardless of how one might feel about the morality of the gangsters, they undeniably identify as Americans. Shady Tree is angry when Bond seems to dismiss the credibility of his crew. Calling Bond a "Limey" (and therefore implying that he is correspondingly clueless), Tree is offended that Bond seems to think their criminal organization is composed of amateurs.[32] Tree's pride in his gang is unmistakable, and his insult of Bond is particularly indicative of how Tree sees their main difference as one of nationality; Tree refers to America as a place where progress has occurred, thus an Englishman could not be expected to be aware of this, nor of how prideful he is of their operation. This interaction suggests that Bond's feelings of nationalism have given him a profound flaw: the inability to recognize the legitimacy of people with loyalty to other states. Thus, Bond can no longer distinguish between what he knows and what he cannot know in order to predict and then eliminate the threat. The scorpion eats the beetle carefully, feeding delicately on each "morsel of . . . beetleflesh,"[33] relishing its catch in the same way that Bond might relish his vacation from real espionage, or his latest conquest of the female persuasion. As one might

lick their fingers over a particularly luxurious meal, the scorpion precisely and meticulously devours its kill. When the scorpion and Bond have
made their conquests, neither has enough information or experience to
know that they are still in danger: they are still the prey.

In addition to the warning from M, Bond also receives warnings from
the Chief of Staff, who becomes impatient with Bond's incredulousness.
Bond wonders why M is so concerned: what might be worrisome about
opponents who are not acting in the name of communism, or some other
known entity?[34] This suggests that he sees the Soviets alone as a serious
threat, and the reader is predisposed to agree, thus falling for the misdirection. Jeremy Black confirms that this was one of Fleming's goals, as it
rang true for the majority of his contemporary audience: "the belief that
Communists were encouraging agitation both in the trade unions and the
empire was widespread. Fleming both contributed to such attitudes and
derived benefit from their popularity."[35] In this case, Fleming uses the
audience's Cold War paranoia to complete the tension: Bond's larger
nemeses comprise the communist forces, so the American gangs are auto-
matically of less concern.

If the reader had previously dismissed the parallels between the scor-
pion and Bond, they might accept this misdirection, and believe in
Bond's confidence that the American gangsters are not a threat. When the
Chief of Staff continues to insist that M has a healthy respect for the
American gangs, Bond replies, belittlingly, that American gangsters are
inferior criminals. He also claims that they are not Americans, but rather
Italian immigrants, concluding with some rather demeaning—if colorful—insults.[36] But the point of these is not the insults themselves, but
rather that Bond's dismissal of these warnings relies heavily on a stereotype of Italian immigrants, as well as America as a former colony: he
rejects the notion of an *American criminal* because that would suggest that
the nation of America has both a distinct identity, as well as the capability
of turning out formidable criminals. Much of Bond's erroneous impression is tied up in racist and colonial perceptions of America, which are
evidently mistaken. This colonial perception leads him to think of America as an inferior country, and its people as weak reflections of their former heritage, rather than their new, wholly American, culture. The Chief
of Staff continues to warn Bond, serving as the second time a character
warns Bond that he should not be disdainful of the American criminals.
However, Bond fails to heed the advice of the Chief of Staff, dismissing
the warning.[37] Bond's overconfidence suggests that he takes neither
man's advice very seriously.

The third explicit warning is once again from M, in the form of a
memorandum from his personal communications. The communication
suggests that the American government recognizes the Spangled Mob as
a powerful gang and a significant threat; the mob has ties to the police, as
well as protection from politicians at multiple levels of government.[38]

This clear warning from both M and the United States government only serves to provoke Bond's pride. Bond's devotion to England makes him hesitant to rely on the Secret Service, and in some ways, he believes himself to be protecting M's pride, also: M would have to speak with the Secret Service if Bond were to fail, making them all appear cowardly.[39] His feelings of personal and national pride are now at stake, and so he decides to prioritize his personal discretion in determining how dangerous the Spangled Mob might be. His feelings of nationalism are not isolated to this one instance: as Jeremy Black writes,

> [Bond is a] British agent and Fleming's [novel is] very much an account of Britain. That it [is idealized does] not detract from his presentation of Britain at a particular moment. This [is] late-imperial Britain, as the decades of defense took their cumulative toll, and the tide of empire ebbed under the pressure of the hostile world.[40]

Fleming has Bond consider the political and national implications of his personal failures because Bond represents not only himself, but—quite melodramatically—also the success of an entire empire. Black goes on to say that, in the first few novels (those concerned with Soviet enemies, as opposed to the international terrorist organization SPECTRE), Bond defines and reflects an entire worldview:

> [Bond is a] central figure in the paranoid culture of the Cold War. The novels . . . charted a period when Britain was making adjustments to her world status in uneasy alliance with the United States against Communism, and, increasingly, offering skill, brains, and professionalism, instead of mere might.[41]

In accepting the American criminals as legitimate, it would be harder for Bond and MI6 to convince themselves of the inferiority of the CIA and FBI, because it would mean that the CIA and the FBI are as equally capable as MI6 with regards to dealing with enemies of the state. Because MI6 has never been called to help the CIA and FBI with the gangster problem, it suggests that the latter are confident that they can deal with them. Bond's racist and stereotypical preconceived notions about the American criminals reflects, in part, Fleming's attitudes. Black writes: "Fleming's notion of the appropriate equivalence of territory and ethnicity, of a proper spacing, of what, to him, were clearly distinguished racial groups, was questioned by the success of the deracinated United States."[42] Bond still views immigrant populations as identifying with their homelands, rather than America: in the case of the Spangs, they are Italian rather than American, grounding his criticism in racial and geographical prejudice toward both nations. Thus, America's perceived lack of identity causes Bond to see the criminals as less of a legitimate threat: his racist and classist perceptions cloud his judgement.

Bond's final explicit warning against the Spangled Mob comes from his old counterpart in the CIA, former agent Felix Leiter. Leiter's warning is particularly interesting, because Bond greatly respects his old companion, and takes him seriously as a skilled partner. Leiter tells Bond that he would be acting unwisely if he were to take on the Spangled Mob alone.[43] He warns Bond a second time in the same conversation, acknowledging that Bond dismisses the gangs in comparison with SMERSH and Bond's other enemies. However, Leiter tells him that the Spangled Mob is likely one of the most serious threats in all of America.[44] Bond's response to Leiter is curiously absent, but he does take Leiter's offer of companionship, as they work together to undermine the horse race which the Spangled Mob had put together. These many examples of explicit warnings seem intentionally obvious when taken together, and indeed, Fleming can be heavy-handed with his clues: references to A B C—the anonymous contact for the operatives in the diamond smuggling operation—are often proximate to references to one or more of the Spangled Mob or its associates. Tiffany Case refers to the two brothers, and in the next sentence, she refers to a *third person* called A B C, which is, in fact, an alias for Jack Spang.[45] Shortly afterwards, Bond has someone follow Rufus B. Saye, in addition to warning London of *an additional person* named A B C, completing the misdirection: both characters help to set up the illusion that A B C is a separate person from either of the Spangs.[46] After escaping Seraffimo in Spectreville, Bond realizes that Jack Spang and A B C were the actual people behind the smuggling ring, but he still fails to realize that Jack Spang, Rufus B. Saye, and A B C are aliases for the same person.[47] Fleming is persistent in his repetition of these details, all in an attempt to make the outcome clear by the end of the text. The warnings given to Bond exacerbate the reader's perception of tension, particularly when Fleming gives information to the reader that Bond is not given, and it further suggests that Bond ignores details that seem particularly obvious in retrospect.

For a brief moment, Bond betrays a sense of vulnerability, which he immediately disregards—or forgets—as soon as he begins his assignment. This might be the one place in the text where his instinct could save him from his continual disregard for the warnings that he receives, but it is not to be. On leaving London to smuggle the diamonds, he realizes that he will be away from the safety of MI6, as he would be out of their reach if he ever needed them. Paradoxically, he also recognizes that, even if he does need them, he would not be able to make such a call: it would undermine his pride to do such a thing.[48] He briefly acknowledges that there may be some danger; however, it is a moment which is countered by his pride, because he knows he would never willingly ask for help, even if he were in danger. He immediately forgets this brief moment of introspection and susceptibility upon leaving his hotel room, and he once again dismisses an important survival instinct. Taken with the others, this passage clearly demonstrates that Fleming is purposefully laying clues that Bond is ignoring signs of danger—both explicit and implicit—as a result of his personal pride; his inexperience with American gangs; and his nationalist tendencies. These circumstances deepen the comparison between himself and the scorpion, which is distracted by its inexperience and limited animal instincts.

The scorpion and Bond are likewise similar as a result of their capacity for violence. Fleming constructs an aesthetic of violence through the murderous and violent description of the scorpion. The scorpion is fast, precise, and ruthless. There is something greatly appealing about that precision and skill. Joel Black argues that "(if) any human act evokes the aesthetic experience of the sublime, certainly it is the act of murder." [49] If the awe-inspired beauty of the sublime is demonstrated in the *human* act of murder, then certainly there is also beauty in the scorpion's *anthropomorphized* murder of the beetle. The aesthetic of violence introduced by the scorpion aids us in our appraisal of Bond's appeal to the reader. During the Las Vegas car chase, Bond shoots at the vehicle that is chasing him without hesitation and with undeniable skill: he times the shots perfectly, and completes them with impeccable accuracy. [50] The scene is revealed through Bond's narration, reducing the act of the shot to a series of onomatopoeic sounds—"cracks"—which emphasize the precision and accuracy of his targets: he can not only perfectly estimate the distance to the target, but also hit it with a minimal number of shots. The car that was pursuing him goes over the curb and bursts into flames. The aesthetic of violence is therefore achieved in a number of ways in this scene: there is beauty in the logic and precision of the violence, as well as in the perceived satisfaction of justice, and the satisfaction of the hero's goals. The element of grotesque beauty is present in the flames enveloping the vehicle, and the splatter of blood. Bond's actions are ruthless, but they are also precise and skilled. For those of us without a license to kill, the act of ruthless, yet logical and skillful killing is sublime: it is the beauty of violence.

The affect of violence is apparent in the passage. The sublime that Black refers to above—the murder of another human being—fills us with awe, fear, and, depending on the context, delight: particularly if the person murdered is an enemy of Bond or of the state. It is this complex combination of emotions which transcends the text, affecting the reader. As previously mentioned, Ahmed writes that differences between bodies—between the "I" and the "We" which give us both similarities and differences—comes as a result of our emotions, and "how we respond to objects and others"; it is through the process of responding to emotions that "surfaces or boundaries are made." [51] The distinction between "I" and "We" here takes on a significant meaning when the "I" is confronted with the "other"—yet another object which changes the surfaces and boundaries of self-identity. The people Bond kills are the "other," and this "other" shapes our fears by their existence. It is also the destruction of the "other" which inevitably removes those fears. The appeal of a Bond novel is in fact this complex combination of emotions: Bond as a phenomenon takes shape from its contact with the audience, and our understanding of Bond comes from our contact with awe, fear, and delight. In addition, because of the way that affect works, Bond may fulfill the audience's pre-existing fantasies of success or seduction, which thenceforth become associated with his embodiment of the character. Further, we take pleasure in the process of "othering" objects which are separate from "us"; we take further pleasure in the other's destruction. Our boundaries of what can be fearful or delightful are tested. This complex set of emotions is of particular importance to our perception of Bond in *Diamonds Are Forever*, because while Bond is still violent, his skills are potentially becoming less astute.

The primary emotion at play with regards to the scorpion is fear: the scorpion's decisive movements, its ruthless ability to kill, and its possession of deadly poison are all sites of fear. Our feelings on scorpions are shaped by this kind of narrative. We come to associate fear and danger with the scorpion, and we adjust our perceptions of fear as a result. The scorpion becomes an affective symbol for danger. Ahmed writes that "fear does not simply come from within and then move outwards,"[52] and that we should not think of emotions such as fear as possessions which we "have" or "do not have."[53] We do not possess the fear that drives our feelings toward the text (even though that is how we would refer to it linguistically). Instead, our reaction of fear to Bond's situation (coupled with pleasure and desire) is inherently exciting, which we register unconsciously on physical, intellectual, and emotional levels. Thus, fear has shaping power when it is evoked by either the scorpion or Bond, because we are both afraid for, and afraid of, man and arachnid. One comes to expect certain qualities from Bond which will ease those fears, but there is no denying that his skill and coldness are terrifying: whether or not we imagine he is on our "side," one should not be desensitized to his capacity and taste for violence. The presentation of fear within the opening section of the text prepares us to be afraid, and if the reader is paying attention, it should—at least in this novel—have them feel afraid *for* Bond. According to affect theory, one's perception of Bond as a character is shaped by the relationship one has with this emotional input.

The experience of fear and anxiety is critical to the text as a whole, and thus affect becomes a critical part of understanding Bond. Here, Aristotle's "tragic catharsis" can be modified into a more current theoretical framework: the *catharsis of anxiety*, in conjunction with Ahmed's affect theory. I borrow from the Aristotelian notion that entertainment performs a social good: he claims that tragedy evokes fear and pity in its audience, providing them with *catharsis*, or a "purgation" of the emotions of "fear and pity."[54] Before Bond's audience can act on their negative thoughts, their feelings can be purged by experiencing anxiety through their entertainment. This catharsis allows the audience to vicariously experience temptation to do that which is forbidden; one views temptation and purges oneself of those feelings, without having engaged in the danger of temptation. The audience feels that catharsis both because they no longer desire the dangerous activity, but also because Bond defeats real-life dangers that pose a significant threat, such as nuclear annihilation or resource extraction. In either case, affect explains how the audience experiences fear as a result of the novel, but then also how the fear is removed from them, reifying their emotions toward Bond, but also becoming shaped by the relief that Bond's success affords. The catharsis of anxiety is the affective transfer of emotion between bodies and objects. The texts elicit an emotive response of fear, and the presumed audience responds, transferring that fear onto the text. However, that transfer through affect works in the opposite direction, also, because the films and texts emphasize, exaggerate, and even parody minor cultural concerns, presuming that the audience will respond with fear. Both audience and text are shaped by the movement of fear between them. The appeal of Bond is that one can expect him to resolve all of these cultural anxieties: thus, we live vicariously through his actions to the point where we can feel the threat of danger, but the danger is removed before we are harmed by it (whatever the threat might be). The catharsis of anxiety and the audience's associated affective responses turn danger, violence, and fear into a pleasurable experience.

The scorpion provides a microcosm of this catharsis of anxiety. As the reader imagines the black and polished scorpion hunt its prey and then feast upon it, one is meant to feel disgust at the event; one is meant to understand the violence of the situation. The readers project their own fears onto the scorpion. Incidentally, the scorpion is also meant to shape the reader: they are to understand that this is a dangerous place to be. But their fears are immediately assuaged when the scorpion meets its end without a sound, despite its staring upwards in vain: it is ultimately ineffectual against the superior enemy.[55] Of course, the scene cannot be a perfect catharsis, but only a tantalizingly close one: the scorpion's death suggests that, although skilled, Bond is actually in danger in this novel. Affect allows the reader to understand that Bond is both predator and prey, and thus, may meet his match. So while the reader may feel momentarily delighted that the object of their fear is removed, its very removal requires consideration of Bond's abilities: will he be capable of defeating the enemy this time? Thus, the affect of this catharsis—in this passage—is limited, but there is a new object for fear which drives the narrative onward.

In addition to fear, there is also beauty in the description of the scorpion. In the opening passage, the light of the moon throws "sapphire highlights" off of the "hard black polish"[56] of the arachnid's body. The scorpion here is not just dangerous, but also visually appealing. The primary emotions of fear and desire—which are usually anathema to one another—are produced by the scorpion, thereby "shaping" the reader. According to Ahmed, "emotions . . . move between bodies."[57] The color black is particularly sexualized in *Diamonds Are Forever*, as Tiffany Case is first seen dressed—at least partially—in the color: the "black" of her brassiere, or the similarly black "lace pants"[58] that are on prominent display, create a striking first impression. When Bond meets Case to eat in New York, he admires her dress, saying that he loves "black velvet."[59] Fleming equates the color black with sexuality through the person of Case, but echoes of the shining black scorpion remain, suggesting that we should view the color as a purposeful aesthetic choice: the color denotes elegance, beauty, and visual appeal. In thinking of the scorpion and the reader as two separate bodies between which emotions are transferred, one can see how affect theory is useful in considering how fear and attraction are irrevocably coupled within the text. In Bond, the shaping-power of fear is appealing, even desirable.

The beauty of diamonds is also reflected in the description of the scorpion. Just as diamonds are polished and shiny, so is the scorpion; and just as Bond and the scorpion inspire lust and danger, so do the diamonds. Interestingly, Fleming uses the vocabulary of diamonds, gemstones, and rocks throughout the text, referring to all manner of objects, including diamonds, the scorpion, and people as well. Of Case, Bond notices a "chatoyance" within her eyes. Hobart M. King writes that "Chatoyance is an optical phenomenon in which a band of reflected light . . . moves just beneath the surface of a cabochon-cut gemstone,"[60] and Bond notices the light moving in Case's eyes, observing that the color changes with respect to the light.[61] In keeping with the theme, Fleming describes Rufus B. Saye as a piece of "quartz": hardened and rough.[62] Notably, the description of Saye lacks appeal, as he is compared to a stone of very little worth, while Case is described as having a gem-like quality. Shady Tree's eyes, by contrast, are said to be made of "china,"[63] and as such, are blank and lifeless, as glass eyes would be. Fleming takes care to construct both Saye and Tree as being like worthless objects: quartz and glass. This is the kind of attention to detail that Amis refers to regarding the Fleming-effect. Fleming uses descriptive language to refer to the luster of certain people—with some variance on how positive those comparisons are—but he begins the theme of these word choices by referring to the scorpion in similar terms to how one might refer to rare stones, specifically using the word "sapphire," an association which suggests both beauty and elegance, as well as a quality of blue color within the black shell.

In addition to its visual appeal, the scorpion is undeniably sexual. The "moist white sting"[64] is both dangerous and phallic, especially when the scorpion lowers its guard: the sting slowly returns to its sheath, and the poison sac below the sting slackens.[65] The phallic sting relaxes, and the poison sac—not unlike testicles—also releases some tension, evoking the sexualized imagery of male genitalia following coitus. In that sense, the helpless beetle's legs waving and protesting suggest rape. It feels controversial to discuss violence and sex in the same image, but there is no doubt that Bond himself embodies both of these ideas at once, as both the perpetrator of violence and the seducer. Case offers a similar dual imagery, as both object of desire and victim of rape, which both explains and comes as the result of her tragic history. Leiter tells Bond about Case's past, telling him that, at sixteen, her mother upset the gangs by failing to pay their protection dues. As a result, multiple members of the gang raped Case as punishment.[66] She is thus capable of embodying the result of sexual violence as well as sexual desire. The scorpion's beauty is sexually appealing, and the language used to describe its poison sac is sensual, although disturbingly so. Affect is palpable here in our discomfort: we resist thinking of sexuality and danger in the same context, so for the scorpion to so obviously represent sexual imagery fills the reader with discomfort. The reader is shaped by that discomfort, and their perception of Bond is shaped similarly: are his sexual conquests so innocent, or should readers question his powers of persuasion and manipulation, particularly in the context of Case's potential vulnerability due to past traumas? In terms of the duality of the scorpion and Bond, is it possible that Bond is a predator? One can see this as a recurring theme throughout the franchise.

Of slightly less prominence than the sexualization and violence of the scorpion, is the fact that when the scorpion dies, its body becomes racialized. As soon as the scorpion loses its power and becomes prey, it becomes a hated and exoticized object, identified as "black" and thus associated with indigenous Africans. This allusion is illustrated when the human who kills the scorpion brings a heavy stone down on the scorpion, declaring, "Black bastard," and then watches the scorpion writhing on the ground as it dies, evidently enjoying its suffering.[67] The man yawns, bored of the death that he has inflicted, but in this act has exposed much of the zeitgeist and underlying racial politics of Africa at the time. The word *black*—within the text and outside of it—carries all kinds of racial codes. It holds within it multiple negative and demeaning associations which are particularly relevant to Africa. The scene is set in West Africa, and the narrative makes a number of unflattering references to the local African people stealing diamonds from the mines, inferring that they are both desperate and exploited by the smuggling ring: the dentist controls the price of the diamonds, and without him the indigenous Africans have no means of participating in the market on their own.[68] This helps to provide context that indicates that the racism of the system is so deeply ingrained that, for Africans, social mobility is impossible, and they are prohibited from reaping the benefits owed to them by virtue of the resources existing on their land. Further, this passage also indicates that they are reliant on the whims and designs of the white colonizers who literally exploit them for their black bodies: for their labor in mining the diamonds; for their mouths and teeth to hide the diamonds. When the diamond smuggler kills the scorpion and calls it *black*, he is transferring the coding of the word to the scorpion. The word black as the diamond smuggler says it is not the same way that Fleming uses it, to describe the aesthetic of the arachnid, but rather to denote the unpleasantness of the scorpion; that it is undesirable; and that the creature is worthy only of being destroyed. The political nature of affect is apparent here: because the word black is racially coded, and the reader knows this chapter to be located in Africa, the association between race—and every feeling the reader has about race, or racialized bodies in particular—at once becomes associated with the scorpion. As a twenty-first-century reader, I feel disgust at the treatment of black Africans, and I come to feel that the death of the scorpion was racially motivated, as a reflection of the despicable desire to exterminate beings which are perceived to be worthless or inferior. As aforementioned, because of the shaping power of emotions, the reader's knowledge of race becomes transferred onto the scorpion simply by the use of that one coded word: black.

In addition to the scorpion's physical description, the context of the novel is critical to how we glimpse race and colonization in this short frame. The smuggling ring is based on the exploitation of black Africans. The diamond smuggler, who is a white Afrikaner, despises the woman who gives him his alibi as he passes off the smuggled diamonds. He refers to her home as a "hut" to distance himself from the act that he must perform there which he finds so revolting. In exchange for her alibi, he must have sex with her, and according to his crude recollection, she would accept no other payment: she allegedly wants his "white body." [69] This is a frankly racist and stereotypical characterization of an insatiable, exoticized African woman whose purpose is purely sexual. He is disparaging of her home and her poverty, taking advantage of her desperation—she apparently lives in a hut, after all—by buying her silence. His revulsion comes from a flipping of the script, where instead of his paying her for sex, he is paying her for her silence with his body. And yet, there is some sense in which she is being exploited for and reduced to her body, as well. He perceives her as *wanting* his *white* body, and will not be satisfied with his company nor his money, suggesting both the perceived superiority of his body, as well as the inferiority of her racialized one. In using the coded word *black* to refer to the scorpion, this racist and unpleasant man refers to an arachnid which is considered, at worst, dangerous, and at best, a nuisance, but thereby also associates it with the hated and oppressed "Other" of West Africa: the Africans themselves. *Black bastard* is a loaded phrase which expresses both the inherent racism of the time and place, as well as the racialized body of the scorpion.

The diamond smuggler's unjustified anger at the scorpion—now rendered helpless—and the smuggler's need to extinguish the life of the scorpion are deeply symbolic of how he feels about black Africans: his unnecessary anger reflects the illogical and troubled disposition of racist people; his actions suggest an instinctive desire to do the same to other Africans, particularly the ones he codes as black. The scorpion's body is thought of with disgust and beauty, reflecting the aesthetic of the grotesque, which unfortunately coincides with the kind of perception given to black female bodies at the time. At the end of the novel, we return to the framing device that casts the diamond smuggler in the middle of the three West African countries. The scorpion is now replaced by a column of ants: first, he throws dirt on them, but they dig their way out. Next, he slaps his shoe against them. They overcome this, also, and the ants continue on their path.[70] This is when we discover that the ants are black, too. Once again calling them black bastards, he stamps all over their line of soldiers. At this point, the connection that the diamond smuggler draws between the colour black and racial hatred is made absolutely, undeniably certain: as the helicopter approaches, the diamond smuggler then forgets "the hatred he [has] *for all black things*" [emphasis mine].[71] At this point, there can be no more doubt that the diamond smuggler associates his racial hatred with the ants as well as the scorpion. In both cases, he acts out his racist frustrations by killing the offending creatures, and in the case of the ants, becoming more and more enraged at their continued existence. In the context of this text, one is affected by the relationship between the word black and our associations of racial discrimination.

The scorpion therefore reflects a perceived racial threat which is not only felt locally, but globally as well. Africa's resources are of importance to British interests: it is not the American gangs that bring Bond to the United States, but rather Britain's leak in the diamond pipeline. The exploitation of Africans is not at all the issue, but rather, who is exploiting them: the British would continue to mine the diamonds in West Africa, colonizing and exploiting the continent's riches, until they are interrupted by the American gangs intercepting a large percentage of the diamonds extracted. Bond is not above racism himself, as he says he had a "natural affection" for those of African descent, but he also claims that England is "lucky" because he perceives this his country has avoided the racial problems that America has. Bond euphemizes the racial tensions, unable to confront the possibility that black and African bodies are continuously discriminated against and endangered: he is more concerned with *what it might be like to be white* in that situation, thereby locating white bodies in the position of discomfort, even as victim.[72] It is clear that Bond feels removed—physically and morally—from the problems of racism and discrimination, as well as from the exploitation of Africa's wealth to benefit his own country. He can therefore act on behalf of MI6 and feel *lucky* to be able to ignore the problems of colonization which he is participating within. On a micro-level, the scorpion is an immediate threat to the diamond smuggler, and so must be exterminated, controlled, or removed. Similarly, one can have a supposed affinity for Africans and African Americans—as long as they stay in Africa and America; for Bond, his affection comes from being distant from the issues of race relations. The novel implicitly suggests that removing the diamonds from Africa is also a legitimate act, but only if you own the mines. Black people—whether African or American—are purposefully excluded or exploited throughout the text, and the scorpion—again, coded black, and associated with the lack of worth that the diamond smuggler ascribes to that word—represents, at least for a twenty-first-century reader, the visceral disgust that such exploitation engenders.

The connection between sexuality, danger, and violence is further deepened by Bond's relationship to Case. When he first meets her, she is sitting provocatively and mostly undressed: her position excites him, "whipping"[73] at his senses, and threatening to distract Bond from his purpose. He knows that he must use this relationship for the purpose of breaking the smuggling ring, but he expresses conflicting feelings: he both likes her and knows he must betray her to do his job.[74] While he recognizes his duty, he is further distracted by his desire to talk to her and be with her.[75] Bond and Case become closer during the trip on the *Queen Elizabeth*, in many ways fulfilling the readers' expectations of the relationship between Bond and his love interest. All thoughts of danger are put aside as they consummate their relationship on the ship, and the sweetness of their newfound understanding belies the true tension of the moment: Bond and Case are in danger, pursued by Wint and Kidd. As Fleming has correctly pointed out, Bond is once again putting Case before his duty, and before his responsibility to protect his mission—not to mention themselves. At the point where Bond and Case are finally agreed as to the nature of their relationship, Wint and Kidd are on the *Queen Elizabeth* with them, planning Bond and Case's demise.

Claire Hinds points out that "women in the 007 films . . . are integral to the formula and success of the series,"[76] and that includes finding a time and place to consummate the relationship *du jour*, as occurs on the ship back to England in *Diamonds Are Forever*. Hinds identifies Honey Rider as being "at once beautiful and resourceful, sexually available, and independent," but these characteristics can be seen in the female characters of many of the novels as well: in addition to Tiffany Case, characters like Vesper Lynd (*Casino Royale*) or Pussy Galore (*Goldfinger*) come to mind as women who demonstrate capability in addition to their sexuality. The scorpion does not represent these women so much as the apparent contradictions that these women—and Bond—contain; the paradox is that a woman can be both independent and enjoy sex, and Bond can be an enigmatic lover as well as violently dangerous. In some cases, becoming James Bond's lover can be fatal, too, as being associated with him often makes the female characters into targets. In experiencing the affective nature of the sexual and dangerous scorpion in the first chapter, the reader is able to feel at a visceral level the complex nature of Bond's character.

Bond is so distracted from his purpose that he is unable to correctly identify the threat posed by Wint and Kidd throughout the entirety of the narrative. While he is on the plane to America, Bond considers Wint briefly, as someone who has a great deal of anxiety about flying. However, his thoughts are interrupted when Case appears in front of him.[77] Wint and Kidd continue to follow Bond, even boarding the *Queen Elizabeth* as Case and Bond cross over to England. Bond fails to recognize Wint immediately, which is directly contradictory to both Bond's experience in previous missions, and to his professional instincts. Although he hears a voice and looks around, his incomplete thought mirrors his interrupted assessment of Wint on the plane.[78] He is unable to place the two men because his thoughts about them had been previously distracted by Case. If he had realized that they were on the plane with him from England—a strong clue being Wint's demonstrating clear signs of panic about travel, an important identifying characteristic—he would immediately have recognized the suspicious nature of their being on the same boat headed back from America. However, because of his desire for Case, he has incomplete and ignored data. Fleming foreshadows that, if Case had not entered his thoughts at that particular moment, Bond might have remembered that important detail.[79] Once again distracted from his purpose, Bond is unable to prevent their predicament on the boat. Similarly, Felix Leiter explicitly warns Bond about Wint and Kidd before they are even present on the boat, sharing obvious details that Bond should connect back to the plane trip, and then later to the auction—but for some reason fails to do so. Leiter tells him that Wint is afraid of traveling,[80] which Bond should have connected back to the man on the plane, whom he had previously noted.[81] Bond's slipping instincts become a theme throughout the novel, which is particularly foreshadowed by the scorpion. However, the other theme indicated by the scorpion is that of misdirection: if we are at first meant to believe that the scorpion has the upper hand before it is killed, then the number of times that Fleming misdirects our gaze away from actual dangers reflects the first chapter's scene in that way, also. Fleming directs us away (and yet toward!) A B C as Rufus B. Saye; he makes Bond think that the Soviets are more powerful enemies; and he sends Bond after Case repeatedly. All the while—from the moment Bond first leaves England, in fact—he is being followed by Wint and Kidd, who were on the same plane from England; who were referred to by Leiter at the races; and who were in Spectreville working for Seraffimo Spang.[82] When we fail to see the rock above the scorpion's head, we are just like Bond, failing to see the wart on Wint's hand, connecting the dots of these mysterious men intending to kill him.

It is somewhat surprising, given the many warnings that Bond dismisses or ignores, that he is ultimately successful. Through a series of misdirections, Fleming creates tension for the audience in giving Bond critical flaws which seem to make his dire situation plausible. Finally, it is the tail in London that discovers that Rufus B. Saye and A B C are the same person, and suddenly the information forms a clear picture, and Bond experiences a revelation.[83] From this point on, Bond is no longer at a disadvantage, and his ruthless ability and instincts return to him. He kills Wint and Kidd and dispatches the bodies, covering the evidence at the scene and making it possible for himself and Case to get away. It is in this scene that Bond breaks away from the set-up of the scorpion, and becomes the predator that the reader expects him to be.

Affect offers us a theoretical framework for thinking about violence, beauty, and even race in James Bond, in this novel and throughout the rest of the series. The scorpion in *Diamonds Are Forever* offers a useful microcosm which enables us to engage with themes of Bond's capability, as well as his capacity for distraction. The image of the scorpion is one which Umberto Eco saw as similar to a highly detailed scene in a film; however, I see it as more than just a cleverly designed opening, but rather an exploration of the themes of the text which make us feel the most. The ending of the frame narrative provides a kind of symmetry, but also a sense of satisfaction as everything ends where it began. Bond reflects that he has had to kill many of the Spangled Mob, but he did not like it. He also admits that he was assisted by luck and his companions.[84] The immediate contrast between Bond and the diamond smuggler of the previous pages is that Bond kills without emotion, and purely out of duty. Bond's sense of duty, his capabilities as a spy, and his—somewhat variable—ability to remain emotionally distant are the skills he needs in order to overcome the distractions and misdirection that became common themes throughout the novel. The scorpion dies because it cannot know or process the danger it is in; once Bond has learned a healthy enough respect for the American gangs, he is no longer in danger of letting his preconceived notions of Americans get the better of him; once Case is safe in his apartment, she is no longer an immediate distraction for him; finally, because he has killed so many of his enemies, the threat they previously posed is now removed.

In part because of the nature of a Bond novel, and also because of the way that the catharsis of anxiety works, Bond must now prevail. It is his success which provides the greatest emotional release, as we feel the pleasure of his putting the pieces together, killing Jack Spang, and attempting to secure amnesty for Case, suggesting that he will get the girl in the epilogue. For Bond, it was all just "another adventure."[85] In sum, the thing that gave Bond the excitement of adventure was about death and beauty, fear and pleasure in tandem. To conclude on this note, above all, provides a satisfying ending for the reader. All at once, we are given a taste of the complexity of emotions available to us throughout the text: we feel fear for Bond, disgust at the number of grisly murders, discomfort at the racial prejudices, pleasure at the success of the protagonists, and desire for the aesthetically pleasing bodies, food, and locales. And it is affect theory which enables us to consider this conflicting swirl of emotions as the central appeal of James Bond.

NOTES

1. "Pandinus Scorpion," *Oxford English Dictionary Online*, last modified June 2017, http://www.oed.com.cyber.usask.ca/view/Entry/275109?rskey=sclkNQ&result=1.

2. "Pandinus Scorpion," *Oxford English Dictionary Online*.

3. "Pandinus Scorpion," *Oxford English Dictionary Online*.

4. The colony of French Guinea would become the independent state of Guinea in 1958, two years after the publication of *Diamonds Are Forever*.

5. Ian Fleming, *Diamonds Are Forever* (Las Vegas: Thomas & Mercer, 2012), 2.

6. Sara Ahmed, *The Cultural Politics of Emotion* (New York: Routledge, 2015), 7.

7. Ahmed, *The Cultural Politics of Emotion*, 10.

8. Ahmed writes, "The model of emotional contagion, which is often influenced by Silvan S. Tomkins' work, is useful in its emphasis on how emotions are not simply located in the individual, but move between bodies. . . . In suggesting that emotions pass in this way, the model of 'emotional contagion' risks transforming emotion into a property, as something that one has, and can then pass on, *as if what passes on is the same thing*" (emphasis mine) (Ahmed, *The Cultural Politics of Emotion*, 10).

9. Ahmed, *The Cultural Politics of Emotion*, 45.

10. Umberto Eco, "Narrative Structures in Fleming," in *The James Bond Phenomenon: A Critical Reader*, Second edition, ed. Christoph Lindner (New York: Manchester University Press, 2011), 49.

11. Eco likely means to refer to West Africa here.

12. Eco, "Narrative Structures in Fleming," 51.

13. Eco, "Narrative Structures in Fleming," 52.

14. Michael Denning, "Licensed to Look: James Bond and the Heroism of Consumption," in *The James Bond Phenomenon: A Critical Reader*, ed. Christoph Lindner, (New York: Manchester University Press, 2011), 57.

15. Fleming, *Diamonds Are Forever*, 1.

16. Ian Fleming, *Casino Royale* (Las Vegas: Thomas & Mercer, 2012), 10.

17. Fleming, *Diamonds Are Forever*, 19.

18. Fleming, *Diamonds Are Forever*, 99.

19. Fleming, *Diamonds Are Forever*, 215.

20. Fleming, *Diamonds Are Forever*, 210.

21. Fleming, *Diamonds Are Forever*, 1.

22. Fleming, *Diamonds Are Forever*, 2.

23. Fleming, *Diamonds Are Forever*, 65.

24. Fleming, *Diamonds Are Forever*, 73.

25. Fleming, *Diamonds Are Forever*, 82.

26. Fleming, *Diamonds Are Forever*, 14.

27. Fleming, *Diamonds Are Forever*, 3.

28. Fleming, *Diamonds Are Forever*, 3.

29. Fleming, *Diamonds Are Forever*, 3.

30. Benedict Anderson, *Imagined Communities* (New York: Verso, 2006), 6.

31. Ian Fleming, *Live and Let Die* (Las Vegas: Thomas & Mercer, 2012).

32. Fleming, *Diamonds Are Forever*, 61.

33. Fleming, *Diamonds Are Forever*, 3.

34. Fleming, *Diamonds Are Forever*, 18.
35. Jeremy Black, *The Politics of James Bond: From Fleming's Novels to the Big Screen* (Lincoln: University of Nebraska Press, 2005), 6.
36. Fleming, *Diamonds Are Forever*, 19.
37. Fleming, *Diamonds Are Forever*, 20.
38. Fleming, *Diamonds Are Forever*, 44.
39. Fleming, *Diamonds Are Forever*, 45.
40. Black, *The Politics of James Bond*, 1.
41. Black, *The Politics of James Bond*, 4.
42. Black, *The Politics of James Bond*, 26.
43. Fleming, *Diamonds Are Forever*, 66.
44. Fleming, *Diamonds Are Forever*, 70.
45. Fleming, *Diamonds Are Forever*, 75.
46. Fleming, *Diamonds Are Forever*, 79.
47. Fleming, *Diamonds Are Forever*, 190.
48. Fleming, *Diamonds Are Forever*, 46.
49. Joel Black, *The Aesthetics of Murder: A Study of Romantic Literature and Contemporary Culture* (Baltimore: John Hopkins University Press, 1991).
50. Fleming, *Diamonds Are Forever*, 157.
51. Ahmed, *The Cultural Politics of Emotion*, 10.
52. Ahmed, *The Cultural Politics of Emotion*, 62.
53. Ahmed, *The Cultural Politics of Emotion*, 9.
54. Aristotle, *Poetics*, n.d.
55. Fleming, *Diamonds Are Forever*, 3.
56. Fleming, *Diamonds Are Forever*, 1.
57. Ahmed, *The Cultural Politics of Emotion*, 10.
58. Fleming, *Diamonds Are Forever*, 33.
59. Fleming, *Diamonds Are Forever*, 73.
60. Hobart M. King, "Chatoyant Gems - The Cat's-Eye Phenomenon," *Geology.com*, October 20, 2018, https://geology.com/gemstones/chatoyancy/.
61. Fleming, *Diamonds Are Forever*, 35.
62. Fleming, *Diamonds Are Forever*, 30.
63. Fleming, *Diamonds Are Forever*, 57.
64. Fleming, *Diamonds Are Forever*, 1.
65. Fleming, *Diamonds Are Forever*, 1.
66. Fleming, *Diamonds Are Forever*, 69.
67. Fleming, *Diamonds Are Forever*, 4.
68. Fleming, *Diamonds Are Forever*, 8.
69. Fleming, *Diamonds Are Forever*, 8.
70. Fleming, *Diamonds Are Forever*, 226.
71. Fleming, *Diamonds Are Forever*, 226.
72. Fleming, *Diamonds Are Forever*, 110.
73. Fleming, *Diamonds Are Forever*, 33.
74. Fleming, *Diamonds Are Forever*, 38.
75. Fleming, *Diamonds Are Forever*, 39.
76. Claire Hinds, "'Entertainment for Men': Uncovering the Playboy Bond," in *The James Bond Phenomenon: A Critical Reader*, ed. Christoph Lindner (New York: Manchester, 2011), 100.
77. Fleming, *Diamonds Are Forever*, 50.
78. Fleming, *Diamonds Are Forever*, 208.
79. Fleming, *Diamonds Are Forever*, 210.
80. Fleming, *Diamonds Are Forever*, 119.
81. Fleming, *Diamonds Are Forever*, 50.
82. Fleming, *Diamonds Are Forever*, 170.
83. Fleming, *Diamonds Are Forever*, 215.
84. Fleming, *Diamonds Are Forever*, 228.

85. Fleming, *Diamonds Are Forever*, 235.

BIBLIOGRAPHY

Ahmed, Sara. *The Cultural Politics of Emotion*. New York: Routledge, 2015.

Anderson, Benedict. *Imagined Communities*. New York: Verso, 2006.

Aristotle: Poetics. *Internet Encyclopedia of Philosophy*. October 1, 2016. http://www.iep.utm.edu/aris-poe/, n.d.

Black, Jeremy. *The Politics of James Bond: From Fleming's Novels to the Big Screen*. Lincoln: University of Nebraska Press, 2005.

Black, Joel. *The Aesthetics of Murder: A Study of Romantic Literature and Contemporary Culture*. Baltimore: John Hopkins University Press, 1991.

Denning, Michael. "Licensed to Look: James Bond and the Heroism of Consumption." In *The James Bond Phenomenon: A Critical Reader*, edited by Christoph Lindner, 56–75. New York: Manchester University Press, 2011.

Eco, Umberto. "Narrative Structures in Fleming." In *The James Bond Phenomenon: A Critical Reader*, edited by Christoph Lindner, 34–55. New York: Manchester University Press, 2011.

Fleming, Ian. *Casino Royale*. Las Vegas: Thomas & Mercer, 2012.

Fleming, Ian. *Diamonds Are Forever*. Las Vegas: Thomas and Mercer, 2012.

Fleming, Ian. *Goldfinger*. Las Vegas: Thomas & Mercer, 2012.

Fleming, Ian. *Live and Let Die*. Las Vegas: Thomas and Mercer, 2012.

Hinds, Claire. "Entertainment for Men: Uncovering the Playboy Bond." In *The James Bond Phenomenon: A Critical Reader*, edited by Christoph Lindner, 89–105. New York: Manchester University Press, 2011.

Oxford English Dictionary Online. "Pandinus Scorpion." Last modified June 2017. http://www.oed.com.cyber.usask.ca/view/Entry/275109?rskey=sclkNQ&result=1.

TWO

The Sounds of *Diamonds Are Forever*

Jesc Bunyard

Dedicated to the memory of Mark Fisher

When devoting time to discussing any film it is important not to diminish the role that sound plays. A film, excluding those made in the silent era, is an audiovisual medium. Therefore, in order to properly dissect a filmic work, the sound must also be analyzed. Sound within cinema is an all-encompassing, broad, and slightly generic term. Cinematic sound tends to include such diverse areas as sound effects, film score, and dialogue. Sound in the Bond films plays an incredibly important role in the theme music, sound effects, and dialogue and often plays a driving role. This is most prevalent in *Diamonds Are Forever*, where the voice takes on a force within the film and almost becomes a character on its own. Sean Connery's return to the role of James Bond in *Diamonds Are Forever* offers the most sonically interesting film of his tenure as 007. Each Bond film, regardless of lead actor, takes a filmic snapshot of the time. For an average of 126.25 minutes, the audience get a glimpse into the contemporary tastes at the time: the fashion, music, and cars. This is particularly noticeable throughout Sean Connery's reign where there is a period of dramatic aesthetic change from *Dr. No* in 1962 through to *Diamonds Are Forever* in 1971 (then later in *Never Say Never Again* in 1983) Indeed, during Connery's main era from the 1960s to the early 1970s there is a decade of substantial transformation and this is reflected not just in the visual aesthetics but in the character development and script. Bond in Ian Fleming's novels and Bond in the early films (*Dr. No*, *From Russia with Love*, and *Goldfinger*) is harsh, dark, clinical, and efficient. Bond in the later Connery films plays to the cinema audience with a joke and an accompanying wink and a raised eyebrow. Each of these later films comes with a layer of kitsch comedy.

In *Diamonds Are Forever* we get a snapshot of heightened life in America in the 1970s. The beginnings of Bond's overt covertness and knowing humor, that is continued in the Roger Moore era, is taken and thrown into extravagant Las Vegas in 1971. It is easy to get swept up in the visual opulence and fast pace of a Bond film but to ignore the role that sound plays in an ocularcentric approach to an audiovisual medium. Ocularcentrism is an approach that has dominated western philosophy. It is a method of thought that is ruled purely by the eyes, that the visual is above all other senses. To take an ocularcentric approach to any analysis of film is negligent as it dismisses the audiovisual nature of cinema. Within the Bond films there are numerous examples of how sound is an important part of film and not just a supplement. However, the focus here will be the 1971 film *Diamonds Are Forever*, which was directed by Guy Hamilton.

Within the Connery era in particular, we get a fusion of sonic regions that mean that the Bond films are less British and even further from any sonic sense of England. According to K.J. Donnelly in *The Spectre of Sound: Music in Film and Television*, Bond films are more "mid-Atlantic" than British:

> Although they are British productions, their background and assumptions are less English or even British, but more "mid-Atlantic." Arguably, the music has precisely the same (mid-Atlantic) tone as the other elements. Despite the use of some British singers for the title songs, there is nothing to mark this film music out as a particularly English or British. "British" as distinct from "English" rarely registers in films and probably never registers in film music.[1]

The only thing to mark the Connery films out as having something which is distinct within the liminal area of "mid-Atlantic" is the lead actor's Scottish accent. The title songs of *Diamonds Are Forever*, *Goldfinger*, and *Thunderball* don't stand out as being sung by Welsh singers, Shirley Bassey and Tom Jones respectively, and there's nothing about *From Russia with Love* (sung by Matt Monro) or *You Only Live Twice* (by Nancy Sinatra) that stands them out as being English or American songs. This blend of accents and music means that the Bond films are less English and, as Donnelly indicates, occupy a space within Western filmmaking that is more British/Atlantic. These Bond films have a makeup of British and American filmmaking influences and cultural links that mean they're more generically Western than anything distinct. However, this has changed over time and the Bond films and their music hold an important place within the canon of British filmmaking that they now feel inherently British, although their feel at the time was more "mid-Atlantic." The contemporary Bond films, with title songs sung by British singers (Adele and Sam Smith) and a lead actor (Daniel Craig) with a classic, sharp

English accent sell a concept or ideal of England or Britain and its talent through the films.

Although the prime focus of this chapter is *Diamonds Are Forever* it is important to recognize the lineage that exists through the Connery Bonds, in particular sonically. There are sonic threads which can be traced throughout the Connery era, including the use of sound effects within the fight scenes, weaving the opening title music in the rest of the film score and hiding the source of a voice for dramatic effect. The hidden voice was used in *Thunderball* but it dominates within *Diamonds Are Forever*. Both *From Russia with Love* and *Goldfinger* use music and in particular sound effects in ways that do more than just supplement the visuals. In particular, the fight scenes in these two films are led, almost choreographed, by their sound effects, there is rarely composed music used. This is most memorable in the fight on board the Orient Express train in *From Russia with Love* between Bond and Grant (played by Robert Shaw). The use of sound is also important in the scene inside Fort Knox in *Goldfinger*, where the fight between Bond and Oddjob (played by Harold Sakata) is amplified by the clanging of metal, footsteps pounding the floor, and grunts as punches are thrown.

One thing that unites all the Bond films, irrespective of which actor is in the lead role, is the theme music. The instantly recognizable theme music for Bond—composed by Monty Norman and originally arranged by John Barry for *Dr. No*—is not just the music for the Bond film series but it is the music for the character of Bond. It belongs to him, it signifies not only that there is a Bond film, but when heard within the film it heralds the appearance of James Bond on screen. The Bond theme music is a leitmotif, a piece of music that is personally assigned to a character. In *Music and Mythmaking in Film: Genre and the Role of the Composer*, Timothy E. Scheurer describes how the term "leitmotif" came from the composer Richard Wagner: "Film music composers it is generally held, borrowed the concept from Wagner but did not implement it in strict Wagnerian fashion. The reason is quite obvious: film is not an opera, and to even think that a composer could fully develop the potential of the leitmotif in a filmic context is not logical."[2] The leitmotif has been adapted from opera to film and is now a commonly used filmic trope. Another film example of leitmotifs besides Bond would be *Star Wars*. The *Star Wars* film series is littered with leitmotifs, with main characters including Luke Skywalker and Leia and even the Dark Side (The Empire) owning a leitmotif. This musical characteristic signifies to the audience that someone or something important in the film is about to appear on screen. The music becomes linked to that character. When music is linked, or belongs to a specific character, it adds the development of that character as myth. The Bond films are iconic. They have become canonical within cinema, and one of the reasons for this is Bond's leitmotif. Bond, because of his leitmotif, is myth. Bond is seen as a protector, he is the ultimate 00 agent,

defending Britain and her allies against all odds. He is also a mythological figure within cinema and pop culture. The name of Bond is one that
everyone knows within the canon of cinema, and know that when his
theme tune is heard, Bond will soon emerge. Scheurer alludes to this
when he writes of the leitmotif's power in establishing myth: "If popular
myths inform the themes and structure of genre films, it stands to reason
that music will plays a role in generic mythopoesis."[3] Music as a whole,
according to Scheurer, sets up mythology within genre films by bonding
character and iconography together. However, the leitmotif does this as
well by giving a character his or her own signature music, tying character
to music to myth. It is partially down to the James Bond music that the
Bond films have taken on a life of their own, they have cemented themselves as a mythological being within cinema, larger than life, to the point
of sublimity within popular culture.

The figure of James Bond is not only myth within the canon of film,
but the character also occupies a place of myth or legend within his own
filmic landscapes. This can be seen in many of the Bond films where 007
is known about before he arrives and treated with reverence even by his
enemies. This mythic status is also evident within *Diamonds Are Forever*
when Connery's Bond, masquerading as Peter Franks, kills the real
Franks (played by Joe Robinson) and then slips his 007 identity papers
into the dead body of Franks. When Tiffany Case sees Franks, she believes James Bond has just been killed, and she voices her exclamation:
"you just killed James Bond!"[4] She says this line with such shock and
surprise, James Bond is unkillable, he is 007, he is a myth. This is echoed
by James Chapman in who argues that the film "even sends up the myth
of Bond as superman."[5] The character of Bond is a legend, whose very
name brings up shock and awe in his foes. He is treated with respect even
by Ernst Stavro Blofeld, his arch-nemesis.

Of course, James Bond is not the only significant character within
Diamonds Are Forever. The assassins called Mr. Wint and Mr. Kidd are the
main visible villains for the majority of the film. The characters of Mr.
Wint and Mr. Kidd themselves are intriguing, as they are gay assassins.
One of them is also killed by Bond in an allegorical manner, with a bomb
attached to his rear. There is a link between Mr. Wint and Mr. Kidd and
Silva played by Javier Bardem in *Skyfall*. There is the same camp menace,
that despite the time in which *Diamonds Are Forever* is made, there is very
little homophobia woven into the characters, which feels like a blessing
when watching the film with modern-day eyes. There are however
homophobic moments when the villains are killed. Their death scene,
which is woven with metaphor, now thankfully looks very dated. When
Mr. Wint and Mr. Kidd are onscreen the film music uses their own leitmotif, which is very short, only a second or two in length and contains
about 10 notes played on a woodwind instrument. This leitmotif is either
woven into the film music or heard on its own. The ending of this leitmo-

tif is similar to a sting in the music, reminding the cinemagoers that these two are as dangerous as the scorpion we see them with at the start of the film. With the aid of the leitmotif, the characters of Mr. Wint and Mr. Kidd really cling to the imagination of the viewers. In a film that showcased the cinematic excesses of the 1970s and the often kitsch nature of Bond films, Mr. Wint and Mr. Kidd stand the test of time. The music is an integral reason why.

Diamonds Are Forever is one of the most sonically interesting Bond films because of its connection between identity theft and the voice. The majority of the film centers around the figure of Willard Whyte, the mystery of his voice and capitalist empire and whether this is being used for malevolent purposes. The film follows Bond and his search for Blofeld, the head of SPECTRE (Special Executive for Counterintelligence, Terrorism, Revenge and Extortion). *Diamonds Are Forever* was Connery's return to Bond after George Lazenby took over the role of 007 for *On Her Majesty's Secret Service* in 1969. It is this break or change in lead actor that creates an opening sequence full of sonic intrigue. Our introduction to Sean Connery's portrayal of James Bond came in *Dr. No*. In his first appearance in *Dr. No.* film, his face is hidden, the audience only hear the voice of Bond, until he is asked to give his name. The camera cuts to him and his face is seen fully for the first time as he says his name and the classic line: "Bond, James Bond." The now familiar Bond theme music is cued in toward the end of his line. This is reinforcement of the fact that this is Bond's music, whenever the cinemagoers hear it we know Bond is on screen. The start of *Diamonds Are Forever* mimics the introduction to Connery's Bond in *Dr. No*. This introduction does two things: it builds up suspense for when the audience actually sees Bond's face, and it reinforces the move back to Connery's Bond. In these opening scenes, Bond is looking for Blofeld by tracking down some of his associates.

The cinema audience doesn't see Bond's head, only his hands and upper body. The unmistakable voice of Sean Connery is heard, but the mouth is not seen. When the cinemagoer cannot see the mouth, the apparent source of the voice cannot be verified. The audience needs to visibly see the mouth moving and hear the words at the same time to be sure that the actor is speaking those lines. The mouth is the visible source of the voice but not the actual source, that is a combination of organs and bodily parts. However, the mouth is the visual, recognizable source of the voice. When the mouth isn't visible the voice becomes acousmatic. In *A Voice and Nothing More*, Mladen Dolar gives a definition of the acousmatic that can exist in cinema, radio, telephone, anywhere where the voice is hidden: "The acousmatic voice is simply a voice whose source one cannot see, a voice whose origin cannot be identified, a voice one cannot place."[6] The acousmatic voice is also described by Michel Chion, a French composer and theorist, in *The Voice in Cinema* "as when it can't simply be localized to the symbolic place of vocal production which is the mouth;

the answer is, when the mouth isn't visible."[7] Chion, whose writings on film approach the medium as truly audiovisual, analyzes all aspects of the mouth and the voice within cinema, including the acousmatic voice and dubbing. He discusses the fact that the mouth is only the symbolic source, because we can't see the actual combined bodily effort that goes into producing a voice. It is because the mouth is the symbolic source of the voice, that its lack takes on more power. The acousmêtre is the name Chion gives to the acousmatic voice. This voice takes on a powerful role, akin to God. As Chion describes, whenever a voice is acousmatized within cinema it takes on these powers: "The powers are four: the ability to be everywhere, to see all, to know all, and to have complete power. In other words: ubiquity, panopticism, omniscience, and omnipotence."[8] The acousmatic voice carries mystery and power, which is due to the fact that the voice cannot be located but only heard. One example of the acousmatic voice is the narrator, heard speaking to the audience, separate from the main film, guiding the narrative and overseeing all. However, the acousmatic voice also exists within the primary area of the film, as can be seen in *Diamonds Are Forever*. Bond's voice is acousmatic for two fight scenes as he interrogates two suspects on his journey to find the location of Blofeld. For the first 1.07 minutes of the film Bond's face is hidden from the filmic landscape. There are visible fists and kicks flying as he muscles his way to Blofeld, the distinctive voice of Sean Connery is heard saying "where is he?" but the cinemagoer cannot definitely verify that it is Connery.

The reveal of Bond's face means that the voice is deacousmatized. Deacousmatization means that the voice is stripped of the God-like power it had when it was acousmatized. The mystery behind the voice, as Dolar describes, is gone: "The aura crumbles, the voice once located, loses its fascination and power, it has something like castrating effects on its bearer, who could wield and brandish his or her phonic phallus as long as its attachment to a body remained hidden."[9] Fetishization is an easy fit to the Bond films, for one of its primary currencies is sensuality. The removal of power from the voice, according to Chion, is akin to a striptease: "De-acousmatization, the unveiling of an image and of the same time a *place*, the human and mortal body where the voice will henceforth be lodged, in certain ways strongly resembles striptease."[10] In the deacousmatization scene in *Diamonds Are Forever*, there is a double eroticism occurring. The film moves from a striptease for the ears, with the unveiling of the voice's source, to a visual equivalent. When the filmic gaze first sees Bond he is walking toward Marie (played by Denise Perrier). The audience hears and sees Marie ask "who are you?"[11] This line is delivered with most of her body in the cinematic frame and then the camera cuts to Bond who says the now classic line "my name is Bond, James Bond." There is a dramatic shift in the delivery of these lines: gone is the classic look of the tuxedo, it's been replaced by a safari suit, and gone is the slight sense of apathy, or calculated coldness, instead Connery schmoozes his way through the line. The distanced arrogance in *Dr. No* has turned into tacky warmth. Bond lacks the cold, calculating glare and delivery, which has been replaced with casual wit. There is a doubling of eroticism, both visually and aurally. Bond's voice is deacousmatized, this process is a striptease, an unveiling. At the same time, there is a visual equivalent with the outfit of Marie, as she seductively turns to the camera, which lingers on her figure. There follows a visible stripping as Marie's bikini top is ripped from her body and wrapped around her neck, as Bond starts to strangle her and persuade her to reveal the location of Blofeld.

The vocal fixation disappears as we encounter Bond's gaze along with our own cinematic one. It's here that the phonic phallus makes way for the scopophilia we are used to encountering within cinema as a whole, but especially within Bond films. Scopophilia is the sexual pleasure derived from looking; it is essentially voyeurism, which is one of cinema's main stocks in trade. The cinematic gaze is famously discussed by Laura Mulvey in *Visual Pleasure in Narrative Cinema*, where she writes that cinema satisfies a wish for looking at pleasurable things. Cinema, therefore, satisfies an inherent need for looking. Mulvey argues that cinema goes further than this and says that it develops scopophilia, which is defined as pleasure in looking, akin to voyeurism. In her essay, Mulvey develops this further and states that there is an inequality within looking within the world and within cinema. This, as she writes, is split into a gender binary: "In a world ordered by sexual imbalance, pleasure in looking has been split between active/male and passive/female. The determining male gaze projects its fantasy onto the female figure, which is styled accordingly. In their traditional exhibitionist role women are simultaneously looked at and displayed, with their appearance coded for strong visual and erotic impact so that they can be said to connote *to-be-looked-at-ness*."[12] In the film narrative, the women are there to be looked at. Their primary role is to be seen and their secondary role is to aid the narrative. This is slowly changing within the cinematic world, especially Bond, where thankfully the female characters are not quite as problematic, due to their inherent and prescribed passivity, as they were in Connery's time. This shift can be seen in the recent Bond films which have previously had a female M, played by Dame Judi Dench, and an Eve Moneypenny, played by Naomi Harris, who can be in the field firing guns and punching bad guys if she chooses.

As well as Daniel Craig's first appearance as Bond, *Casino Royale* (2006) gives cinemagoers a strong female character Vesper Lynd, played by Eva Green. Lynd wears sensible clothes, a blessing for a woman in a Bond film and can exchange in cutting banter with Bond. She appears to be his match in terms of intelligence and wit. Lynd's character recalls Pussy Galore in *Goldfinger*, portrayed by Honor Blackman. Galore, like

Lynd, matched Bond and was her own independent, smartly dressed woman with goals. However, Lynd's character is nowhere near as problematic as Galore's. Pussy Galore suddenly changes her motivations in the film and even her sexuality shifts after one forced make out session from Bond. This is the stereotype of the women in Bond films, one forced kiss from Bond and a night with him and they'll tell him all their secrets.

This problematic trend is actually mentioned by SPECTRE associate Fiona Volpe, played by Luciana Paluzzi in *Thunderball*. After making love to Bond there is an exchange between Paluzzi's character and Connery's Bond, in which Volpe states "But of course, I forgot your ego, Mr. Bond. James Bond, the one where he has to make love to a woman, and she starts to hear heavenly choirs singing. She repents, and turns to the side of right and virtue."[13] The characters within the film and the audience are made aware of this problem by Volpe, but it still persists throughout the Bond film series. For the women in Bond films, especially in the Connery era, they are there to be looked at, to be visually admired. Mulvey looks at the directorial work of Alfred Hitchcock as a classic example of this cinematic trope, however it also can be seen as the perfect definition of the roles of the majority of women in Bond films.

If we examine many of the Bond films, especially from the pre-Daniel Craig era, we see they have female characters whose function in the narrative is secondary to their role of being looked at. Marie, the first female character the audience sees in *Diamonds Are Forever* exemplifies this. She is an erotic object, there to be looked at. When the audience first sees her, she is revealed fully by the eye of the camera, leaving no aspect of her body out, so that the audience can fully take her in. The fact that she has information vital to the location of Blofeld takes a back seat; the scene becomes choreographed by her looked-at-ness. She is, as Mulvey describes, a functioning object to be looked at by both the cinemagoers and the characters on screen: "Traditionally, the woman displayed has functioned on two levels: as erotic object for the characters within the screen story, and as erotic object for the spectator within the auditorium, with a shifting tension between the looks on either side of the screen."[14] Does Bond actually have to remove Marie's bikini top to partially strangle her and put pressure on her to reveal where Blofeld is, or is this just to satisfy his and the audience's own scopophilia? Her interrogation could take place with her clothes remaining on her body, just like Blofeld's male associates who were also assaulted in the opening scenes. Their scopophilia both merges with Bond's scopophilia and projects the audience's desires onto his own. We identify with Bond, see ourselves within him, he reflects our own visual cravings. According to Mulvey, this gives the cinemagoer a god-like feeling as the desire to look combines with control of the narrative: "As the spectator identifies with the main male protagonist, he projects his look onto that of his like, his screen surrogate, so that the power of the male protagonist as he controls events coincides with the active power of the erotic look, both giving a satisfying sense of omnipotence."[15] Bond controls the narrative, he decides as lead character, where the film goes. He also controls the erotic gaze of the film. Bond always gets the girl, and every girl in his path. The cinemagoer shares in his erotic gaze. Many of the Bond films, including *Diamonds Are Forever*, participate in the scopophilia that exists within films. When the Bond films hit Daniel Craig's era however, they demonstrated that they were slightly more aware of the erotic binary. In *Casino Royale* Daniel Craig emerges from the ocean mimicking Honey Ryder, played by Ursula Andress in *Dr. No*.

The of myth of Echo takes on relevance when discussing the female voice within cinema, as noted by Amy Lawrence in her book *Echo and Narcissus: Women's Voices in Classical Hollywood Cinema*. In her opening paragraph, Lawrence introduces us to the story of Echo and Narcissus. In *Metamorphoses*, Book 3, Ovid writes of a nymph who has been cursed by shielding a cheating god from his wife and has therefore lost the power to speak. Echo's curse is that she is only able to repeat back what is said to her, like an echo. The nymph sees the handsome Narcissus who rejects her attempts at love, with this exchange, according to Lawrence: "May I die before I give you power o'er me." However, Echo turns his words into a loving response through her curse and says "I give you power o'er me."[16] Echo then hides, distraught, in a cave until only her voice remained. The story of Narcissus is familiar as a warning of the seductive power of the image. However, as Lawrence points out, Ovid's original tale is a weaving of audiovision, in which sight and sound collide together. Echo's story is often ignored, dismissed as easily as the nymph herself was by Narcissus. The story of Echo is an ample metaphor through which the problems with the female speech in a lot of films, including the Bond films and *Diamonds Are Forever*, can be dissected.

The primary issue with the retelling and remembering of Echo and Narcissus is that it often becomes the tale of Narcissus with Echo becoming part of the subplot if she is part of the story at all. As soon as Echo's story meets Narcissus, she disappears into his story. In the popular understanding of Narcissus and the danger of looking, Echo is subsumed. This occurs within many of Connery's Bond films. The woman's voice and story are absorbed as soon as they meet James Bond. The classic example is Pussy Galore, in *Goldfinger*, who is committed to the heist and what she intends to do until her story collides with Bond. The female characters within *Diamonds Are Forever* exist in much the same way as Echo. Echo's story begins with desire. However, when she speaks after being cursed she can only repeat words and phrases back. Characters such as Plenty O'Toole—a Las Vegas socialite played by Lana Wood—and Tiffany Case—a link in the diamond smuggling chain played by Jill St. John—vocally exist to repeat phrases back to Bond and to ask questions. Amy Lawrence writes that when Echo speaks it is not

Echo but a reflection of a person: "Even the sound we hear when Echo speaks is not 'Echo' but a representation of sound, not a person speaking but the acoustic reflection of a person. Like the reflection in the pool, an echo is defined but as a fundamental absence: what we perceive is not an entity but an illusion, the reflection of what once was."[17]

When the female characters in *Diamonds Are Forever* speak they reflect whatever is said back. The characters don't add much to the narrative or serve to explain and drive the plot. They are there to aid Bond in his narrative and his control over the narrative. As soon as Case meets Bond her primary vocal role is to ask questions and not to possess and vocalize lines which drive the narrative forward on their own. In the section "Disembodying the Female Voice" from her book *The Acoustic Mirror: The Female Voice in Psychoanalysis and Cinema*, Kaja Silverman writes that the female voice in cinema is considered lesser than the physical appearance of the character: "Woman's words are shown to be less her own than are her 'looks.' They are scripted for her, extracted from her by an external agency, or uttered by her in a trancelike state. Her voice also reveals a remarkable faculty for self-disparagement and self-incrimination—for putting the blame on Mame. Even when she speaks without apparent coercion, she is always spoken from the place of the sexual other."[18] Willard Whyte's prison guards, Bambi and Thumper, played by Lola Larson and Trina Parks respectively, are a prime example of how echo exists within *Diamonds Are Forever* between two female characters, and not only in a male and female scene. Bambi and Thumper are presented as classic Bond erotic objects, dressed and positioned alluringly. They are primarily visual characters, in their looks, clothes, and acrobatic form of fighting. The fight scene is not raw and primal, like the elevator fight between Bond and Franks, instead the characters cartwheel and tumble around Bond, teasing him, forming a sensual fight. Their dialogue contributes very little to this scene, it only introduces the next feat of gymnastics. They echo back to one another: "you're on again Bambi" [. . .] "Thumper."[19] They echo each other's names as a continuous call throughout the fight scene. This fairly minimal dialogue serves as a basic warning for their visual fighting exploits. Their dialogue is not a call and response, it is a continual re-resounding. When a female character speaks in *Diamonds Are Forever* she occupies the space of the erotic object, there to fulfill the scopophiliac urges of Bond and the cinematic audience. These actresses fulfill the cinematic equivalent of the original Echo, they are the sonic reflection of the male lead. Bond starts off the dialogue in the scene, allowing Bambi and Thumper to introduce themselves and then this is all they can say: they must continuously repeat their names in a back and forth. They are the object speaking and as such they can only echo what was said back to them.

Diamonds Are Forever is led by the acousmatic voice and the mouth. After the deacousmatization scene, the next shot we see is a photograph of Blofeld's mouth. This continues the focus on the voice and the visual source of the voice. Blofeld's voice, as the narrative unfolds, is at the heart of the film. For most of *Diamonds Are Forever*, the film focuses on the elusive figure of Willard Whyte, whose voice we hear over the phone and electronic systems but whose face we cannot see. Whyte's voice is acousmatic: he rules over his capitalist empire, including a hotel and casino, but he cannot be seen. However, when Bond scales Whyte's building (the Whyte House in Las Vegas), he finds Blofeld and not Whyte. Blofeld has a voice box inserted in his throat which means that when he presses a button on a machine, he can produce a direct copy of Whyte's voice. To those characters in the film Blofeld masquerades as an already visualized acousmêtre, as he takes on Whyte's voice. An already visualized acousmêtre is a voice which has been previously seen with its appropriate, accompanying body, but is currently acousmatized. With the figures he speaks to within the film, Blofeld uses a stolen voice and therefore they assume it is the familiar, already visualized Willard Whyte.

There is a double doubling within the scene when Whyte's voice is deacousmatized but onto Blofeld's body. Whyte's voice is fully deacousmatized later when the real Willard Whyte, played by Jimmy Dean, is freed. Both Whyte and his voice are freed from imprisonment by Blofeld. Blofeld has successfully doubled himself through surgery, so throughout the scene with Bond at the top of the Whyte House, his voice is doubled as there as two Blofelds. When Blofeld presses the switch his voice changes from his own to Whyte, which is the second doubling. There are two Blofelds, one original and one copy, created through operations to look and sound like Blofeld. Each of them possesses Blofeld's voice and one has a voice box inserted so that he may choose to sound like Whyte, he steals Whyte's voice. Whyte's voice is dubbed onto Blofeld's (played by Charles Gray) body. When there is dubbing, according to Michel Chion, a sonic palimpsest occurs where the new sound is written over the original one: "Dubbing produces a palimpsest beneath which there runs a ghost-text."[20] This palimpsest and ghost text is the dubbing doubling within this scene. The audience sees the lips mouth but hears a different voice. There is a longing for the ghost text underneath to be revealed, especially within this scene. The audience knows the dubbed voice is wrong as the film switches between Dean's and Gray's voices as Blofeld demonstrates the technological grounds he has broken to fool people into thinking he is Whyte. When the dubbed voice is used, the original words that were spoken leave a spectral trace behind in the form of the mouth pronouncing the words. The action undertaken by the mouth is not heard. The audible result from this performative utterance is taken over by another (invisible) voice, the action is claimed by the dubbed voice but it does not own it.

The aim of dubbing in film is to usually go unnoticed and to find a suitable voice to go with a body: an old man's voice to go with an old man, for example. In Blofeld's case the voice of Whyte would fit with his body, however, because of the switch between voices this act of dubbing is malevolent. It jars because cinemagoers know this is not right. This voice has been stolen and misappropriated. This technique is not uncommon as Chion describes: "An actor may be dubbing her own lips or the lips of another, but in any case there is a *doubling*. This is why dubbing may produce disturbing effects of mismatching, where voices seem to waver around bodies (Fellini, Tati), or produce monsters and ghosts (*The Exorcist*). Sound loiters around the image like the voice around the body."[21] As the voice of Whyte doesn't fit Blofeld's body, it floats around the scene, still inside the scene but not quite inside the body. The lips move and the sound emerges but because there is obvious dubbing there is an echo that occurs, a doubling of the sound that is heard and the sound that is wished to be heard. The proper and the improper voice collide, one heard and one not heard, one seen leaving the moving lips and one heard floating in the scene.

Blofeld uses Whyte's capitalist empire and hotel apartment as a base of operations and as a front to run his schemes. Whyte's apartment is at the top of the Whyte House hotel and casino in Las Vegas, where he can look and survey not only the casino and the city but also his business empire. Within the apartment there is a map containing all the locations in Whyte's empire. There Whyte, before he was ousted, and Blofeld sat overlooking everything, closer to the heavens than to the streets of Las Vegas. Whyte's voice, as used by Blofeld, was acousmatic. It was only heard via phones as he relayed instructions down to the staff. This, according to Chion, places Whyte's voice in the realm of the "the radio—acousmêtre" for those filmic characters he spoke to. For cinemagoers, he remained film acousmêtre.[22] Blofeld's voice and Whyte's voice (as used by Blofeld) are acousmatic.

The acousmêtre has similar powers to God, as Chion explains: "*The acousmêtre is everywhere*, its voice comes from an immaterial and non-localized body, and it seems that no obstacle can stop it . . . *The acousmêtre is all-seeing*, it's like the word of God."[23] The acousmêtre is everywhere, it knows all and it sees all. In this respect, the acousmêtre and capitalism possess similar attributes. Capitalism sees all and pervades all. In *Capitalist Realism: Is There No Alternative?* Mark Fisher describes it as an entity which takes over everything it comes into contact with: "This makes capitalism very much like the Thing in John Carpenter's film of the same name: a monstrous, infinitely plastic entity, capable of metabolizing and absorbing anything with which it comes into contact."[24] Mark Fisher was a writer and a theorist, also known as "k-punk" from his blog work. Fisher's most famous book *Capitalist Realism* examines the capitalist and neo-liberalist conditions and that it is easier to imagine the end of the world than it is the end of capitalism.

The capitalist absorption which Fisher describes is visible within *Diamonds Are Forever* as the film begins by showing the diamond smuggling trade ruled by the exchange of money for goods imbued with value. Capitalism is the overarching figure within *Diamonds Are Forever*, haunting the narrative. It's impossible to have a film in Las Vegas, a city ruled by exchange and monetary value (and gambling) and to not have capitalism linger over it like a malevolent and yet seductive God. There is a switch in the film, where the glitz, glamour, and the allure of capitalism is shown to be poisonous. In *Diamonds Are Forever*, we see the seemingly honest intentions of Willard Whyte and his empire turned to the dark side, corrupted and misused by Blofeld, in a not so subtle reminder that capitalism has a very dark side. The cinemagoer witnesses how even Blofeld's schemes are incorporated by capitalism, and we even see how death becomes a business when Bond has to smuggle the diamonds into America. Bond hides the diamonds in the coffin of Franks as he oversees the transportation of the body, acting as a grieving party. The film also demonstrates how capitalism is within everything, even death. How your body is cared for and prepared for funeral, the funeral itself, the flowers. In *Diamonds Are Forever*, death is a business that has become infected with a diamond smuggling chain, which is seen to be the evil form of capitalism, against the good wishes of Britain and its capitalist desires. Capitalism is the overarching baddie within Sean Connery's reign as James Bond. The grand villain in the films is SPECTRE, an evil empire run like a capitalist corporation. Its structure is organized like a gigantic business with board meetings, divisional heads, and a CEO, Blofeld. The hierarchical system and clean, mechanical organization of SPECTRE is a terrifying merger between the villains of cinema and the villainous tendencies of capitalism sitting above it all, overlooking and running a business; the acousmatic voice in *Diamonds Are Forever* is God over the narrative and over the capitalist empire. The capitalism discussed by Mark Fisher and in the many forms on show in *Diamonds Are Forever* is everywhere, seeing everything. *Diamonds Are Forever* takes the omnipresent assets of capitalism and the acousmatic and combines them together. When the cinemagoer witnesses the acousmatic voice emerging from a position of capitalist power, at the top of WW's tower it gives the voice even more allure and dominance. There is an even greater desire to strip the acousmatic voice, to unveil it. Bond also appropriates another's voice using an invention built by Q (played by Desmond Llewelyn). However, this scene differs from Blofeld's misuse of the voice. The implication for Bond is that the borrowing of the voice is merely that, it is temporary and therefore permitted. This is shown through the use of the external technology that Bond uses rather than the inserted device that Blofeld has within his voice box.

Continuing his exploration of capitalism in his seminal work, Fisher explains that films like the *Star Wars* series place capitalism and an evil corporation as the baddie. Much like The Empire in *Star Wars*, the cinemagoer is taught that corporations and capitalism have all the power and used it for evil. In the case of *Diamonds Are Forever* a corporation (Whyte's) is used for evil and is very easily turned for evil deeds. This allows cinemagoers to be anti-capitalistic within the 120 minutes running time: "A film like *Wall-E* exemplifies what Robert Pfaller has called 'interpassivity': the film performs our anti-capitalism for us, allowing us to continue to consume with impunity."[25] We step into a film, which performs anti-capitalism for the audience. However, the irony is that even as the film performs the cinemagoer's anti-capitalism, it is within a capitalist structure of the cinema and the film industry. The audience may perform an anti-capitalist sentiment when watching a film like *Star Wars* or *Diamonds Are Forever*, but it exists within capitalism. The process of going to a cinema is one of continuous exchange and monetary value, the film itself, the ticket, the popcorn, and the adverts. The cinemagoer can safely engage with anti-capitalism but still inside the cocoon of the system. The audience is permitted to be anti-capitalist within *Diamonds Are Forever* but their position is restricted. It is only when recognizable villains, SPECTRE or a diamond smuggling chain that is harmful to Britain's interests, that the shift toward an anti-capitalist sentiment begins. The audience sees how capitalism can be easily misused and misappropriated, like the voice, and it is this element that forms the protest within *Diamonds Are Forever*.

Diamonds Are Forever was nominated for an Oscar for Best Sound. It is a film that is led by its use of sound. Most Bond films are to a certain extent dictated by their sound in the way they individually use Bond's leitmotif and their own title song, which is often repeated and hinted at within the rest of the film score. However, *Diamonds Are Forever* is led by a fascination with the voice, primarily the doubling and ownership of a voice. The acousmêtre is the leading character with *Diamonds Are Forever*. It takes the starring role without ever receiving true credit for its impact upon the film. For the majority of *Diamonds Are Forever*, both Bond and the cinemagoer are obsessed with unveiling this voice and stripping it of its power. The acousmatic voice rules over the narrative of the film, an unseen guide, directing and controlling. It creates intrigue and tension, which is the signature of any spy film. However, the power of the acousmatic voice is controlled purely by the male characters in *Diamonds Are Forever*, as the female characters are reduced to erotic objects, there purely for cinema's scopophiliac tendencies. They can only echo, holding a mirror up to the rest of the film's vocal outpourings.

The cinemagoer is reintroduced to Sean Connery's Bond by mimicking the acousmatic introduction of Bond in *Dr. No*, but it also sets up this sonic thread for the rest of the film. Within this opening sequence, the cinemagoer is not only reintroduced to Connery as Bond but to the acousmêtre. The film uses this to reacquaint the audience to the power and allure that this version of Bond has and the cinematic majesty of his first appearance on screen thanks to the use of the acousmêtre in the casino in *Dr. No*. Through this, the film also showcases the power that the acousmêtre holds. *Diamonds Are Forever* could be perfectly defined as a film about the voice, specifically a hidden voice. The acousmêtre holds suspense and intrigue, it is God-like and yet, the cinemagoer cannot wait to reveal its source, to strip the voice of its power. The audience longs to assign a body to the voice. As we have seen, *Diamonds Are Forever* does not initially present the audience with the right bodily home for the voice. It frustrates this desire for an unveiling, for deacousmatization, by temporarily housing the voice with another body through the means of dubbing. Initially, Whyte's voice belongs to the wrong body, has been taken and abused by Blofeld. Upon hearing this mismatch, the vocal crime, the cinemagoer won't be satisfied until they hear the voice emerging from the right body. The film delays this aural gratification. It finally happens when Whyte is freed by Bond, freeing both his body and his voice. When this happens the acousmatic power that Blofeld had is fully stripped, as we hear Whyte's voice emerging from his own body, from the visible source of vocal production, his mouth. Before this he had a stolen acousmatic voice and even though he was seen, he still wielded its power. After Bond frees Whyte, this is gone. He is just Blofeld and thus slightly more vulnerable than before, ready to be defeated by James Bond. *Diamonds Are Forever* is also led by the acousmêtre. It rules over the film. Bond's task is not just to uncover a diamond smuggling ring and to find Blofeld but to uncover the acousmêtre and strip it of its power. In this film, Bond's true aim is to deacousmatize the voice and return Whyte's voice to its true body. In this way, *Diamonds Are Forever* presents the cinematic fascination and fetishization of the voice and the mouth.

NOTES

1. K. J. Donnelly, *The Spectre of Sound: Music in Film and Television* (London: BFI Publishing, 2005), 63.

2. Timothy E. Scheurer, *Music and Mythmaking in Film: Genre and the Role of the Composer* (London: MacFarland, 2008), 28.

3. Scheurer, *Music and Mythmaking in Film,* 23.

4. *Diamonds Are Forever,* directed by Guy Hamilton (1971; UK: MGM Home Entertainment [Europe], 2000), DVD.

5. James Chapman, *Licence to Thrill: A Cultural History of the James Bond Films* (London: I.B. Tauris, 1999), 158.

6. Mladen Dolar, *A Voice and Nothing More* (London: The MIT Press, 2006), 60.

7. Michel Chion, *The Voice in Cinema,* trans, ed. Claudia Gorbman (New York: Columbia University Press, 1999), 127.

8. Chion, *The Voice in Cinema,* 24.

9. Dolar, *A Voice and Nothing More,* 67.

10. Chion, *The Voice in Cinema,* 28.

11. *Diamonds Are Forever,* directed by Guy Hamilton (1971; UK: MGM Home Entertainment [Europe], 2000), DVD.

12. Laura Mulvey, *Visual Pleasure and Narrative Cinema*, LuxOnline, 1975, http://www.luxonline.org.uk/articles/visual_pleasure_and_narrative_cinema%28printversion%29.html.

13. *Thunderball*, directed by Terence Young (1965; UK: MGM Home Entertainment [Europe], 2000), DVD.

14. Mulvey, *Visual Pleasure and Narrative Cinema*.

15. Mulvey, *Visual Pleasure and Narrative Cinema*.

16. Amy Lawrence, *Echo and Narcissus: Women's Voices in Classical Hollywood Cinema* (Berkeley: University of California Press, 1991), 1.

17. Lawrence, *Echo and Narcissus*, 2.

18. Kaja Silverman, *The Acoustic Mirror: The Female Voice in Psychoanalysis and Cinema* (Indianapolis: Indiana University Press,1988), 54.

19. *Diamonds Are Forever*, directed by Guy Hamilton (1971; UK: MGM Home Entertainment [Europe], 2000), DVD.

20. Chion, *The Voice in Cinema*, 154.

21. Chion, *The Voice in Cinema*, 154.

22. Chion, *The Voice in Cinema*, 21.

23. Chion, *The Voice in Cinema*, 24.

24. Mark Fisher, *Capitalist Realism: Is There No Alternative?* (Ropley, 0 Books, 2009), 6.

25. Fisher, *Capitalist Realism*, 12.

BIBLIOGRAPHY

Campbell, Martin, dir. *Casino Royale*. 2006; UK: Sony Pictures Releasing (Europe), 2006. DVD.

Chapman, James. *Licence to Thrill: A Cultural History of the James Bond Films*. Revised ed. London: I.B. Tauris, 1999.

Chion, Michel. *The Voice in Cinema*, translated by Claudia Gorbman, ed. New York: Columbia University Press, 1999.

Dolar, Mladen. *A Voice and Nothing More*. London: The MIT Press, 2006.

Donnelly, K. J. *The Spectre of Sound: Music in Film and Television*. London: BFI Publishing, 2005.

Hamilton, Guy, dir. *Goldfinger*. 1964; UK: MGM Home Entertainment (Europe), 2000. DVD.

Hamilton, Guy, dir. *Diamonds Are Forever*. 1971; UK: MGM Home Entertainment (Europe), 2000. DVD.

Hunt, Peter, dir. *On Her Majesty's Secret Service*. 1969; UK: Sony Pictures Home Entertainment, 2006. DVD.

Fisher, Mark. *Capitalist Realism: Is There No Alternative?* Ropley, 0 Books, 2009.

Lawrence, Amy. *Echo and Narcissus: Women's Voices in Classical Hollywood Cinema*. Berkeley: University of California Press, 1991.

Mendes, Sam, dir. *Skyfall*. 2012; UK: 20th Century Fox Home Entertainment, 2013. DVD.

Mulvey, Laura. *Visual Pleasure and Narrative Cinema*, LuxOnline, 1975, http://www.luxonline.org.uk/articles/visual_pleasure_and_narrative_cinema%28printversion%29.html.

Scheurer, Timothy E. *Music and Mythmaking in Film: Genre and the Role of the Composer*. London: MacFarland & Company, Inc., Publishers, 2008.

Silverman, Kaja. *The Acoustic Mirror: The Female Voice in Psychoanalysis and Cinema*. Indianapolis: Indiana University Press,1988.

Young, Terence, dir. *Dr. No*. 1962; UK: MGM Home Entertainment (Europe), 2000. DVD.

Young, Terence, dir. *Thunderball*. 1965; UK: MGM Home Entertainment (Europe), 2000. DVD.

THREE

Transforming Bond

Diamonds Are Forever *in Its Contexts*

James Chapman

In 1970 the James Bond film series stood at a crossroads. The first five Bond pictures—*Dr. No* (1962), *From Russia with Love* (1963), *Goldfinger* (1964), *Thunderball* (1965) and *You Only Live Twice* (1967)—had collectively grossed over US $500 million at the box office.[1] The character of the suave but ruthless British secret agent with a licence to kill had become, in *Time* magazine's apt phrase, "the biggest mass-cult hero of the decade."[2] By the end of the 1960s, however, there were signs that Bond's popularity had peaked. The sixth film, *On Her Majesty's Secret Service* (1969), while successful in Britain, had done only around half the business of its predecessor. This had been the first Bond picture without the original star, Sean Connery, whose sardonic performance had done much to define the style of the Bond movies. After five films, Connery had grown tired of the role and his relationship with the producers had become increasingly strained: he decided while shooting *You Only Live Twice* in Japan that it would be his last film as Bond.[3] Moreover, the "new" Bond, a previously unknown Australian model-turned-actor called George Lazenby, had controversially followed Connery's example by deciding that he, too, had had enough of Bond after only one outing and would not be returning for the next film.[4] The end credits of *On Her Majesty's Secret Service* had announced—as was the custom for Bond films at the time—that "James Bond will return in *Diamonds Are Forever*." There was never seriously any question that Bond would *not* return: but the challenge that faced producers Albert R. "Cubby" Broccoli and Harry

Saltzman was how to reinvigorate a franchise that some felt had run its course.

This essay explores some of the contexts—institutional, economic, and cultural—for the production of the seventh Bond film *Diamonds Are Forever*. This represents something of a problematic text for Bond critics and scholars. For many it marks the point at which the Bond films shifted decisively away from their source material in the novels of Ian Fleming and embraced the qualities of parody and camp that came to define the series in the 1970s. For John Brosnan, writing shortly after the release of *Diamonds Are Forever*, "the main flaw in the production, apart from the overly complicated plot, is that everything is played more for laughs instead of thrills and suspense. This has been a growing tendency in the films of late."[5] Raymond Benson, writing in the mid-1980s, concurs: he finds *Diamonds Are Forever* "a very mixed bag . . . The picture has a witty script by [Richard] Maibaum and [Tom] Mankiewicz, but *everything* is played for laughs now. The missing element of authentic suspense is the picture's main flaw."[6] Other critics have been less forgiving of the film's narrative flaws and have also detected unpleasant undertones in its content. Leslie Halliwell, for example, thought it a "[campy], rather vicious addition to a well-worn cycle, with an element of nastiness which big-budget stunts cannot conceal."[7] In particular *Diamonds Are Forever* has drawn criticism for its representation of the homosexual assassins Mr. Wint and Mr. Kidd, who now seem quite offensive gay stereotypes. Stephen Bourne avers not only that "*Diamonds Are Forever* is one of the nastiest Bond films of all" but also considers the deaths of Wint and Kidd—the former is propelled overboard with an exploding cake tied to his coat tails—"one of the most horrific, and homophobic sequences in the history of cinema."[8]

For the cultural historian, however, it does not suffice merely to critique films—or any products of popular culture—for their cultural or ideological shortcomings. It is also incumbent upon us to attempt to explain how and why a film turned out the way it did. *Diamonds Are Forever* makes for a particularly interesting case study in this respect as it seems to me that the content and politics of the film took shape as the consequence of a wide range of institutional and ideological determinants that led the producers and writers to make the decisions they did. In order to demonstrate this, it is necessary to consider the film both in relation to the six Bond films that had come before—especially its immediate predecessor *On Her Majesty's Secret Service*—and to place it in the economic and cultural contexts of the US and British film industries in the early 1970s. I will argue that *Diamonds Are Forever* is a key transitional film for the Bond series: its shortcomings did not prevent it from being a major critical and commercial success—restoring the Bond series to the forefront of popular cinema following the perceived failure of *On Her Majesty's Secret Service* (a film which many Bond aficionados—myself included—regard as far superior to *Diamonds Are Forever*)—while it also set the tone and style that would steer the series through the next decade.

In their pioneering cultural studies analysis of the James Bond phenomenon, *Bond and Beyond* (1987), Tony Bennett and Janet Woollacott argue that "the cultural and ideological currency of the figure of Bond has been changed and adapted to changing circumstances."[9] This has become the dominant trend of much Bond scholarship: Bond has been understood in relation to changing political and social discourses—the decline of the British Empire, the Cold War, the rise of second-wave feminism, and the emergence of international terrorism—while the books and films have been read as mediating texts of these historical processes. Bennett and Woollacott suggest there have been three historical-cultural moments which have defined Bond's place in popular culture. Ian Fleming published his first novel, *Casino Royale*, in April 1953, and thereafter the Bond books appeared regularly at the rate of one a year until Fleming's death in 1964: the last novel, *The Man with the Golden Gun*, and the short-story collection *Octopussy and the Living Daylights* were published posthumously. Sales of the early books were steady rather than spectacular: the first hardback edition of *Casino Royale* published by Jonathan Cape—now a highly prized item for book collectors—had a print run of only 4,750 copies. Nor was Fleming able to interest film or television producers in his work: the only adaptation during the early years was a live studio dramatization of *Casino Royale* by the American CBS network in October 1954 which cast an American actor (Barry Nelson) as Bond. It was in the second half of the 1950s that Bond's popularity really began to grow. Bennett and Woollacott identify 1957—the year in which *From Russia with Love* was serialized in the *Daily Express* (a popular mass-circulation British newspaper) and a "James Bond" cartoon strip began in the same newspaper—as "the first stage in the transformation of Bond from a character within a set of fictional texts into a household name."[10] Sales of the Bond books rose sharply in the late 1950s and early 1960s—combined paperback sales of all the Bond titles in Britain jumped from 105,000 in 1958 to 323,000 in 1960 and 1,315,000 in 1962—and Bond's growing popularity was sufficient for Broccoli (who had been interested in Fleming's books for some time) and Saltzman (who held an option) to persuade United Artists to finance a series of Bond pictures.[11]

The second moment of Bond came in the mid-1960s when the success of the early films—*Dr. No, From Russia with Love, Goldfinger*, and *Thunderball*—"both significantly broadened the social basis of Bond's popular appeal in Britain and extended the horizons of his popularity internationally."[12] *Dr. No*, modestly budgeted at around US $950,000, returned total rentals of $22.1 million worldwide of which nearly three-quarters came from outside North America: from the outset the Bond films were an international rather than a merely local phenomenon.[13] United Artists doubled the budget for *From Russia with Love* ($1.9 million) and were rewarded with total rentals of $29.4 million of which two-thirds came from outside North America. However, it was with the success of *Goldfinger* ($49.6 million rentals against a production cost of $3 million) and *Thunderball* ($56.4 million against a cost of $5 million) that the Bond films became true blockbuster material. It was the third and fourth films that made the breakthrough in the US market with nearly half their revenues accruing in North America. *Thunderball* was the sixth most successful film of the 1960s at the box office and remains the top-grossing Bond movie of all when adjusted for inflation. The mid-1960s was the height of the phenomenon of "Bondmania," which reached across most of the world other than the Iron Curtain and Communist China. As *Time* observed in 1965: "There seems to be no geographical limit to the appeal of sex, violence and snobbery with which Fleming endowed his British secret agent."[14]

"Bondmania" was an international craze: it peaked in 1965–1966 when cinemas were flooded with gimmicky Bond imitation spy movies from both sides of the Atlantic including *The Liquidator, Where the Spies Are, Licensed to Kill, Our Man Flint, The Silencers, Murderer's Row, Deadlier Than the Male, Modesty Blaise, When the Bullets Fly, Agent for H.A.R.M.*, and *The Spy with a Cold Nose*. It also proved to be a short-lived phenomenon: by the late 1960s there was already evidence that Bond's popularity was in decline. In Britain, for example, combined paperback sales of the Bond books fell from a high of 6,782,000 in 1965 to 2,565,000 in 1966, 659,000 in 1968 and 362,000 in 1970.[15] Furthermore, the box-office appeal of the Bond films, which had peaked with *Thunderball* in 1966 (the film was released at the very end of 1965), was on the wane. *You Only Live Twice* saw a slight fall in the box office ($44 million rentals worldwide against a production cost of $9.5 million), but *On Her Majesty's Secret Service* ($24 million rentals against a cost of $7 million) was the least successful since *Dr. No* and was the first Bond film that could be said to have underperformed at the box office. Its "failure" needs to be qualified: by any normal standards *On Her Majesty's Secret Service* was a successful film—it was the leading general release of 1970 in Britain according to *Films and Filming* and second (after the Second World War epic *Battle of Britain*) according to the trade paper *Kine Weekly*—but it was notably less successful than the previous three Bond pictures.[16] The period from 1970 is Bennett and Woollacott's third "moment" of Bond: this was the point at which the nature of Bond's popularity changed from a mass-culture phenomenon to what they describe as an "institutionalised ritual" centered on the production of a new film at regular periods. Bond has now become a familiar institution: a "dormant signifier" which is inactive most of the time but is "periodically reactivated" with the release of each new film.[17] The production of *Diamonds Are Forever* in 1970–1971, therefore, coincided precisely with the transition from the second to the third of the "moments" of Bond: it came following the end of the period of "Bondmania" and marked the start of Bond as "institutionalized ritual."

It was the perceived failure of *On Her Majesty's Secret Service* that to a large extent determined the content and style of *Diamonds Are Forever*. *On Her Majesty's Secret Service* had been the Bond film "with a difference." Debutant director Peter Hunt, who had edited the first five Bond movies, and regular screenwriter Richard Maibaum had taken the introduction of a new Bond actor as an opportunity to revert to something closer to the style of *From Russia with Love*, a straight spy thriller, following the increasing levels of visual spectacle in the previous three films, *Goldfinger*, *Thunderball*, and *You Only Live Twice*. *On Her Majesty's Secret Service* marked a conscious decision to move away from the emphasis on technology and gadgetry in the most recent films—a process that had started with Bond's modified Aston Martin DB5 in *Goldfinger*—and to characterize Bond himself as something other than an indestructible superman. Peter Hunt put it in these terms:

> The James Bond films set the trend for tongue-in-cheek spy spoof movies and, as we know, they were fantastically successful. But there have been so many imitators—not all of them very good by any means—that we were in danger of imitating our imitators . . . We could have stuck to exactly the same formula, but we preferred to progress. Besides, *On Her Majesty's Secret Service* is better without the gadgetry and paraphernalia. It is a marvellous adventure story, with Bond surviving by his own physical skill and ingenuity, and at the same time it is a genuine love story, with 007 falling in love and marrying for the very first time.[18]

On Her Majesty's Secret Service was the closest of the Bond films to Ian Fleming's novel: to this extent it bucked the general trajectory of the series which, following four films that were recognizable to readers of the books, had changed direction with *You Only Live Twice*, which retained only the title, location, and some character names from its notional source text. In the books, *On Her Majesty's Secret Service* had preceded *You Only Live Twice*. However, the films switched around the second and third instalments of the "Blofeld trilogy" in a way that confuses continuity and denies the revenge-driven narrative arc of the original books.

The reasons for the commercial failure (relative to the previous films) of *On Her Majesty's Secret Service* are vigorously debated within Bond criticism. Many critics lay the blame at George Lazenby's door: he lacked Connery's screen presence and was simply too inexperienced to carry the film, especially given that *On Her Majesty's Secret Service* was the one Bond story which demanded a greater emotional range from the actor playing Bond. Alexander Walker felt that Lazenby probably had an impossible task stepping into Connery's shoes: "Another actor who had 'paid his dues' in the same sort of adventure genre as the Bonds might— just *might*—have graduated to the prime role: but the public resented being asked to accept someone who had neither earned his right to be a

contender, nor possessed enough distinctiveness of his own to dim the
memory of his predecessor."[19] In contrast Danny Peary, while conceding
that "it's impossible to ever fully adjust to Lazenby," suggests that his
inexperience was effective in making his Bond a more human and vulnerable hero: "Lazenby's Bond also hasn't the assurance of Connery's
Bond and that is appropriate to the crumbling, depressing world he finds
himself [in]. He seems vulnerable and jittery at times. At the skating rink,
he is actually *scared.*"[20] Another possible reason why *On Her Majesty's
Secret Service* did not match the success of its predecessors is because it
varied the formula: in particular the tragic ending—where a distraught
Bond cradles his dead wife, Tracy, shot by his arch enemy Blofeld as they
drive away on honeymoon—was seen as a deterrent at the box office,
especially for a film released during the Christmas season. As Molly Haskell put it in *The Village Voice*: "If you like your Bonds with happy end-
ings, don't go."[21]

In the United States, moreover, the downturn in the box office for *On
Her Majesty's Secret Service* might also be related to changes in the nature
of film culture. The late 1960s had witnessed a transformation in Holly-
wood with the decline of blockbuster entertainments—a number of big-
budget films between 1968 and 1970, including *Star!, Thoroughly Modern
Millie, Paint Your Wagon, Darling Lili, Ryan's Daughter, Catch-22,* and *The
Adventurers,* failed to recoup their costs—and the emergence of a "New
Hollywood" in the form of films such as *The Graduate, Bonnie and Clyde,
Butch Cassidy and the Sundance Kid, Easy Rider,* and *Midnight Cowboy*
which resonated with the younger adults who now comprised the core of
the diminishing cinema-going audience.[22] The Bond movies, which only
a few years earlier had been in the vanguard of popular cinema, by the
end of the decade seemed to have been overtaken by a new style of film.
Furthermore, the cultural impact of wider world events should not be
ignored. A feature article in the *New York Times* in February 1970 suggested that the Bond movies, with their Manichean ideological frame-
works of Good and Evil, had become anachronistic in the aftermath of
Vietnam and Mai Lai:

> Spectre—that diabolical world organization of sin and corruption—
> seems less corrupt than Bond himself, not to mention his heartless
> superiors who license 007 to kill. Meanwhile, the enemy is an enigma.
> We aren't told why we should hate the enemy, but only that we must at
> all costs HATE the enemy. But it doesn't work. We are enlightened
> young men and women who have learned the importance of *knowing*
> the enemy—and we have learned to know him well in real life. In fact,
> we are downright intellectual about the enemy. And we aren't buying
> any hate propaganda; so the evil that lurks behind the guillotine shad-
> ows of childhood doesn't frighten the activist-oriented kids of the
> seventies. We don't get our jollies from sitting in dark theaters and
> hating prescribed enemies.[23]

For all his embracing of the permissive society and his irreverent attitude toward authority, the screen Bond was fundamentally a loyal corporation man: he is endowed with his lethal authority (his "licence to kill") by the state. The very title of *On Her Majesty's Secret Service*—redolent with its code of patriotism and endorsement of monarchical authority— seems ideologically anachronistic at a time that witnessed the emergence of screen anti-heroes exemplified by Clint Eastwood's "Man with No Name" and Dirty Harry.

All these factors mandated that *Diamonds Are Forever* would be a very different kind of Bond film to its predecessor. Indeed there is a sense in which *Diamonds Are Forever* is the very antithesis of *On Her Majesty's Secret Service*: rarely has there been such a radical shift of style and tone between two successive Bonds. (The closest parallels are *Moonraker* and *For Your Eyes Only* and *Die Another Day* and *Casino Royale*: in both those cases the switch was from a more spectacular and fantasy-oriented Bond to a more "realistic" spy adventure.) It was decided to abandon the greater psychological realism of *On Her Majesty's Secret Service* and to return to the visual spectacle and narrative excess of *You Only Live Twice*. It is particularly significant in this regard that Ken Adam, the production designer of *Dr. No*, *Goldfinger*, *Thunderball*, and *You Only Live Twice*, returned to the series for *Diamonds Are Forever*. Adam had developed a unique combination of modernism and expressionism in his set designs for previous Bonds: the "look" of *Diamonds Are Forever*—exemplified in the extravagant sets of Blofeld's apartment and the interior of Willard Whyte's desert retreat—is markedly different from Syd Cain's more naturalistic interiors for *On Her Majesty's Secret Service*. The return of Guy Hamilton as director also signaled that this was likely to be a more light-hearted Bond than its predecessor. Hamilton had previously directed *Goldfinger* and had been responsible for injecting more visual humor into the film: nowhere is this better exemplified than in the moment in the pre-title sequence where Bond removes his wetsuit to reveal an immaculate white tuxedo beneath. This was the sort of visual humor that Peter Hunt, an action specialist, had largely eschewed for *On Her Majesty's Secret Service*.

Diamonds Are Forever also differed from its predecessor in distancing itself from its source material. Five of the six Bond movies of the 1960s had been recognizably adapted from Fleming's books—the exception was *You Only Live Twice*—but these had also been the most recent books. *Dr. No*, for example, was produced four years after the book (1958), *From Russia with Love* six years later (1957), *Goldfinger* five years later (1959), *Thunderball* four years later (1961) and *On Her Majesty's Secret Service* six years later (1963). (Ironically the shortest gap of three years between novel and film was for the least faithful adaptation: *You Only Live Twice*.) However, Fleming had died in 1964 and the remaining available titles were becoming older. Other than *The Spy Who Loved Me*, an atypical story that did not focus on Bond, and *The Man with the Golden Gun*, generally regarded as one of the weaker books, the remaining Fleming novels had all been published in the 1950s. *Diamonds Are Forever* had been Fleming's fourth Bond novel and was published in 1956: it had pitted Bond against American gangsters rather than the Soviet counter-intelligence organization SMERSH (a contraction of *Smiert Spionam*—"Death to Spies") which featured directly or indirectly in all the other Bond novels published during the 1950s. The novel sees Bond travel from London to New York in the guise of a smuggler called Peter Franks in order to penetrate the diamond smuggling pipeline; his contact is a "Miss Tiffany Case" who works for a gang known as the Spangled Mob. In New York Bond meets his old friend Felix Leiter, formerly of the Central Intelligence Agency and now working as a private investigator for Pinkerton's. They travel to Saratoga Springs, where they conspire to upset the mob's attempt to fix a horse race, and from there first to Las Vegas and then to a Western ghost town called Spectreville where Bond and Case escape on a railroad push-cart. They return to London on the RMS *Queen Elizabeth* where they survive an assassination attempt by the mob's enforcers Wint and Kidd. A coda sees Bond in Sierra Leone, where he kills Jack Spang, the mastermind behind the smuggling operation, by shooting down his helicopter.

The film of *Diamonds Are Forever* would maintain certain elements of the novel—the diamond smuggling motif, the Las Vegas location, several character names, and the fight on the ocean liner in the film's coda—but to all intents and purposes it was an original screenplay. With the Fleming content diluted, the producers evidently took previous Bond movies as their template. In particular *Diamonds Are Forever* was very strongly influenced by *Goldfinger*: indeed in most key respects *Diamonds Are Forever* seems like nothing so much as a highly programmed attempt to make another *Goldfinger*. This made commercial sense insofar as *Goldfinger* was widely regarded as the film that had perfected the Bond formula and had also marked the series' breakthrough in the American market. Accordingly the narrative of *Diamonds Are Forever* recalls *Goldfinger* in being mostly set (and this time actually shot) in the United States with much of the action taking place in and around Las Vegas. There was even a suggestion that Gert Frobe should be invited back to play Goldfinger's twin brother. According to regular Bond screenwriter Richard Maibaum: "This fellow is supposed to say to Bond at one point, 'Oh, my brother Auric—mother always said he was a bit retarded.' We were going to cast Gert Frobe again, but it didn't work out."[24] In the event it was decided to bring back Bond's arch enemy Blofeld—who does not feature in the novel—for the third film in succession. This creates a number of continuity problems for the series: not so much on account of the recasting of Blofeld each time—played in turn by Donald Pleasence (*You Only Live Twice*), Telly Savalas (*On Her Majesty's Secret Service*) and Charles Gray (*Diamonds Are Forever*)—but rather because the revenge motif that might have been expected following the end of the previous film was entirely lost.

Maibaum wrote a first draft of *Diamonds Are Forever*, which was then revised by Tom Mankiewicz, a young (28-year-old) writer recruited on the strength of his screenplay for the surfing movie *The Sweet Ride* (1968) and the short-lived musical *Georgy!* Mankiewicz was part of a Hollywood dynasty: his father Joseph L. Mankiewicz had directed *All About Eve* (1951) and *Cleopatra* (1963), while his uncle Herman J. Mankiewicz had written *Citizen Kane* (1941) in collaboration with Orson Welles. Mankiewicz came onto the Bond movie because he was deemed able to write dialogue appropriate for both a British and an American idiom. In his autobiography, Mankiewicz averred that "the Mankiewiczes have had a proclivity for writing. It's something in our DNA. Every Mankiewicz has good dialogue. Mankiewiczes are not as good at structure. But you can learn structure. You can't learn to write good dialogue."[25] It was Mankiewicz who was responsible for injecting more humor into *Diamonds Are Forever* and who wrote the film's more risqué lines such as the meeting between Bond and casino shiller Plenty O'Toole (the ample-bosomed Lana Wood):

Plenty: Hi. I'm Plenty.

Bond: I'd be foolish to deny —

Plenty: Plenty O'Toole.

Bond: Very penetrating. Named after your father, no doubt.[26]

(The exchange is slightly different in the finished film: Bond's "I'd be foolish to deny" has become "But of course you are" and the line "Very penetrating" has been removed.)

As the screenplay of *Diamonds Are Forever* took shape during the course of 1970, attention turned to the casting of the key role: James Bond. With George Lazenby having ruled himself out, the field was open. Here there is evidence of some disagreement between Broccoli and Saltzman on the one hand and United Artists on the other. Broccoli always maintained that it was the character of Bond rather than the actor who was the real star: he resisted casting major stars such as Clint Eastwood or Paul Newman (both of whose names were mentioned in relation to *Diamonds Are Forever*) and would later resist demands to cast Mel Gibson in the role. In the event the producers' choice was American actor John Gavin, whose screen test suggested that he would be able to play Bond as British but who did not have an established screen persona. However, United Artists wanted Sean Connery back, to the extent that UA's president David Picker personally negotiated a deal that would bring Connery a then-record fee of US \$1.25 million (which the actor used to establish a charity for Scottish artists and writers) in addition to a percentage of the box-office receipts and an undertaking to produce a further two films of Connery's choice. (In the event, one of these films was made—Sidney Lumet's *The Offence*: the second project—a film of *Macbeth*—was abandoned when Roman Polanski made his version of the Scottish play.) Broccoli was ambivalent about Connery's return: "Sean had turned his back on Bond. He was clearly a restless actor, anxious to discover whether he could repeat his triumph as Bond in other roles . . . Harry and I had misgivings about taking him back. But we couldn't ignore UA's insistence, nor overlook Sean's strong hold on the world box office."[27]

It had been four years since Connery had last played Bond: a gap that seems normal in the Daniel Craig era but at the time a long hiatus between films. He was heavier in build and graying at the temples in comparison with his appearance in *You Only Live Twice*. Alexander Walker wrote, somewhat unfairly, that "*Diamonds Are Forever* revealed a Connery who was now packing flab as well as a Walther PPK. His style resembled an elder statesman of espionage with an implanted pace-maker."[28] However, Connery's relaxed, droll performance drew much praise from critics who almost universally welcomed his return to Bondage. *Esquire*'s Thomas Belger, for one, felt that "Connery's thickened figure is all to the good, contributing solidity to his imposture [*sic*], as well as a slight weariness which is usefully evident when two young women give him a savage drubbing in bare-handed combat."[29] The self-parodic quality that some critics would later find a deterrent to Roger Moore's portrayal of Bond was fully evident in Connery's performance in *Diamonds Are Forever*. The idea of Bond as superman is mocked following Bond's fight with smuggler Peter Franks:

Tiffany: My God, you've just killed James Bond!

Bond: Is that who it was? Well, it just goes to show, nobody's indestructible.

Moments such as this anticipate the (often derided) Roger Moore Bond films: indeed there is a sense in which *Diamonds Are Forever* is the first Moore Bond (just without Moore).

There seems to have been a conscious narrative strategy in *Diamonds Are Forever* to erase the memory of *On Her Majesty's Secret Service*. There are no references to the death of Bond's wife in the previous film (such references would feature in some of the Roger Moore films, including *The Spy Who Loved Me* and *For Your Eyes Only*) and no obvious revenge motif. The pre-title sequence has Bond pursuing Blofeld and (apparently) killing him in a pit of boiling sulphur, but even Bond's "Welcome to hell, Blofeld" is delivered with a self-satisfied smirk rather than the vengeful relish one might expect from a psychologically realistic Bond. Elsewhere the film takes every opportunity to acknowledge Connery's return to the series, as in the exchange between Sir Donald Munger (Laurence Naismith) and Bond:

Sir Donald: You've been on holiday, I understand. Relaxing, I hope?

Bond: Oh, hardly relaxing, but most satisfying.

This might (or might not) be read as a reference to the four non-Bond films—*Shalako*, *The Molly Maguires*, *The Red Tent*, and *The Anderson Tapes*—that Connery had made in the four years since *You Only Live Twice*. In narrative terms the film plays as if the events of *On Her Majesty's Secret Service* had never happened: to all intents and purposes it picks up where *You Only Live Twice* had finished. (The Bond series would use this technique again in the hiatus between Timothy Dalton and Pierce Brosnan: the pre-title sequence of *GoldenEye* is set nine years before the main narrative—therefore locating the pre-title sequence in 1986, the year that Brosnan lost out on the Bond role when he was unable to secure release from his contract for the television series *Remington Steele*.)

The term that best describes the style of *Diamonds Are Forever* is camp. It is a film replete with ostentation and excess. *Diamonds Are Forever* includes a succession of bizarre narrative situations that would not have been out of place in later episodes of *The Avengers*: Bond nearly cremated at a funeral parlor, Bond escaping from a secret desert research facility in a comically cumbersome moon buggy, Bond using a piton-gun to climb around outside his hotel while clad immaculately in a black dinner jacket, and Bond knocked around by two athletic women calling themselves Bambi and Thumper. The cinematic Bond had always been a larger than life character, but *Diamonds Are Forever* was the first film where this was taken to excess. Consider, for example, Mankiewicz's description of Bond's appearance on the floor of the Whyte House casino: "BOND enters, takes in the room. He is impeccably dressed: white dinner jacket, red carnation, every hair in place—four cuts better looking than anything else in the casino. CAMERA FOLLOWS as he walks through, drawing appreciative glances from many, especially the women."[30] (The script as written has Bond seen from the point-of-view of "a well-known CELEBRITY (à la Sammy Davis or Dean Martin):" Sammy Davis Jr did indeed film a cameo which was not included in the finished film.)

The camp aesthetic of *Diamonds Are Forever* should be seen not as an aberration but rather as a conscious strategy to position the film within popular culture. This was a period when camp was becoming an increasingly familiar mode in popular film and television: it was exemplified variously in television series such as *The Avengers* (1961–1969) and *Batman* (1966–1968) and in films including Dino de Laurentiis's *Barbarella:*

Queen of the Galaxy (1968) and the same producer's remake of *King Kong* (1976). Its role in *Diamonds Are Forever* can be understood in two particular ways. First it represents a form of product differentiation: *Diamonds Are Forever* sets out to be different from the realistic style of American "cop" films of the early 1970s such as *The French Connection* (1971), *Dirty Harry* (1971), and *Serpico* (1973). This differentiation would become increasingly important for the Bond films in the 1970s and beyond: there were now more contemporary action thrillers (and therefore more competition) than there had been at the time of the early Bond movies in the 1960s. And secondly the camp strategy of *Diamonds Are Forever* can be seen as an attempt to distance the film from some of the more culturally problematic aspects of Fleming's books. The Bond films of the early 1970s were adapting stories whose social politics were rooted in a previous era. Fleming's description of the homosexual killers Wint and Kidd makes a clear association between homosexuality and sadism. Leiter tells Bond:

> They're the top torpedoes for the Spangs. Wint is a mean bastard. A real sadist. Likes it. He's always sucking at that wart on his thumb. He's called "Windy." Not to his face, that is. All these guys have crazy names . . . Kidd's a pretty boy. His friends call him "Boofy." Probably shacks up with Wint. Some of these homos make the worst killers. [31]

Instead the film turns Wint and Kidd—played by Bruce Glover and Putter Smith—into a more comic pairing who demonstrate none of the sadism of Fleming's villains. It is a sign of how far social attitudes toward homosexuality have evolved that the film's association of queerness with comic relief is now also deemed problematic by some commentators. What is important to stress here is that the characterization of Wint and Kidd in the film—as so far as can be ascertained from the reviews—does not seem to have troubled contemporaries.

On a more general level the camp qualities of *Diamonds Are Forever* may also be seen to be rooted in the genre of the spy adventure. Most histories of spy fiction distinguish between two main trends: Michael Denning, in his book *Cover Stories* (1987), identifies these as the "magical" and "existential" lineages of the thriller. The "magical" thriller—exemplified by the adventure stories of John Buchan and "Sapper" (H. C. McNeile) in the early twentieth century and by Fleming's Bond novels after the Second World War—is one "where there is a clear contest between Good and Evil with a virtuous hero defeating an alien and evil villain." The "existential" thrillers—exemplified by the more realistic spy novels of Graham Greene and Eric Ambler in the 1930s and John le Carré and Len Deighton in the 1960s—"play on a dialectic of good and evil overdetermined by moral dilemmas, by moves from innocence to experience, and by identity crises, the discovery in the double agent that the self may be evil." [32] A common motif of both the magical and existential variants of the spy thriller is that of impersonation and masquerade: the secret agent—whether an amateur such as Buchan's Richard Hannay or a professional such as Bond—is able to disguise his real identity and to move across a range of different social identities. *Diamonds Are Forever* is preoccupied with the theme of impersonation: Bond—at various points in the film—assumes the identity of a diamond smuggler (Peter Franks) and a minor bureaucratic functionary ("Klaus Hergesheimer—G Section"), while Blofeld has two "doubles" whom Bond dispatches before the "real" Blofeld apparently meets his end at the film's climax. Moreover, the motif of impersonation extends to the performances. Charles Gray's Blofeld is posited on a vocal impersonation of Noël Coward, while at one point Blofeld makes his escape from the Whyte House by dressing as a woman. Blofeld's appearance in female drag is the most obviously camp moment of *Diamonds Are Forever* and tends to be regarded as an aberrational moment by Bond aficionados: but in truth it is no more an aberration than Bond's impersonation of Sir Hilary Bray ("Call me, Hilly") in *On Her Majesty's Secret Service* or—to take another particularly notorious example—Roger Moore's clown disguise in *Octopussy* (1983).

Yet for all its camp qualities, there are other aspects of *Diamonds Are Forever* that serve to anchor the film in some sort of reality. It is widely acknowledged that the inspiration for the character of reclusive billionaire property tycoon Willard Whyte (Jimmy Dean) was Howard Hughes. Blofeld has imprisoned Whyte and is using his business empire as a cover for his scheme to launch a laser satellite into space. As Bond remarks: "The ideal kidnap victim. No-one's seen the man in five years, so who's going to miss someone who's already missing?" The association between Blofeld/Whyte and Hughes anticipates later Bond films, particularly *Tomorrow Never Dies* (1997) and *Quantum of Solace* (2008), where the villains are, respectively, a media tycoon and the chief executive of a global corporation. The parallel with *Quantum of Solace*, an otherwise entirely dissimilar Bond film, is particularly notable: Blofeld masquerades as an idealist in order to secure the co-operation of the pacifist Dr. Metz (Joseph Furst), while Dominic Greene (Mathieu Amalric) in *Quantum of Solace* is ostensibly the chief executive of an organization promoting economic and environmental development. The other aspect of *Diamonds Are Forever* that suggests a more realistic—in a geopolitical sense at least—outlook is the film's acknowledgment of the decline of British power. This is exemplified by Blofeld's comment when Bond arrives at the oil rig: "Don't tell me you've come to negotiate, Mr. Bond. Your pitiful little island hasn't even been threatened."

To this extent, *Diamonds Are Forever* exemplifies the ideological processes through which the films modernized Fleming's material. Fleming's Bond was an ideological product of the "end of empire": David Cannadine highlights the symbolism in the fact that the first Bond novel, *Casino Royale*, was published in 1953, coinciding with the coronation of Queen Elizabeth II—which Cannadine describes as "a retrospectively un-

convincing reaffirmation of Britain's continued great-power status" —
whereas Fleming's last novel, *The Man with the Golden Gun*, was published in 1965, the year that marked the passing of Sir Winston Churchill,
whose state funeral represented "not only the last rites of the great man
himself, but was also self-consciously recognised as being a requiem for
Britain as a great power."[33] It has been argued that the ideological project
of Fleming's books is to deny the decline of British power by presenting a
world in which the *Pax Britannica* still operates. This was also evident to a
degree in the early Bond films but was becoming increasingly anachronistic by the 1970s. The threat in *Diamonds Are Forever* is not directed specifically against Britain: Blofeld's conspiracy is to use his laser satellite to
destroy military installations belonging to the United States, the Soviet
Union, and Red China in order to hold "an international auction—with
nuclear supremacy going to the highest bidder." *Diamonds Are Forever*
was the first Bond film to suggest the hubris of Britain's continued world-
power ambitions.

To the extent that it was both a commercial and a critical success, the
strategy of *Diamonds Are Forever* for refreshing the Bond series can be
adjudged to have succeeded. It earned worldwide rentals of $45.7 million
(more or less equivalent to *You Only Live Twice*) of which $19.7 million
came from North America. Even allowing for inflation, it had nearly
doubled the box-office revenues of *On Her Majesty's Secret Service*. Critics
who previously had written the Bond movies off now looked for all sorts
of reasons to explain the success of *Diamonds Are Forever*. In Britain the
Monthly Film Bulletin felt that "the latest Bond film impresses as probably
the most efficient and enjoyable since *Goldfinger*. The style has become
genuinely distinctive, shaped partly by Connery's idiosyncratic hero
with his impeccable grooming and throwaway innuendoes, partly by
Ken Adam's highly inventive set designs."[34] The *New York Times*—which
only two years earlier had argued that Bond was an ideological anachro-
nism—attributed its success to a form of cultural nostalgia: "Simply, the
Bond brand of escapist fantasy—to a world where the two eternal verities
are money and power and the two foregone conclusions are violence and
sex—scratches an itch that nothing else in the emotionally torpid Nixon
era can reach as directly."[35] Andrew Sarris, the influential film critic of
the *Village Voice*, felt that *Diamonds Are Forever* "demonstrates how to
enrich an established genre by digging into the sociological subconscious
of the audience." He concluded his review thus:

> [The] major positive virtues of the movie seem to originate from the
> cockily contemporaneous screenplay . . . which manages to relate to
> recent headlines without being oppressively relevant to the in-depth
> continuations on the back pages. This process can be described as hav-
> ing your cake and eating it. Thus, we get tantalizing glimpses of the
> Howard Hughes empire with its invisible emperor, the ecological
> nightmare of oil rigs off the Californian coast, spoofs of moon men and

their dune buggies, Russian nuclear subs and Red Chinese nuclear missiles, a Los Angeles mortuary out of "The Loved One," jokes about the dullness of Kansas as a nuclear target and about the deterioration of Great Britain into a third-rate power.[36]

The Bond films had often featured topical references (if not intended entirely seriously): in *Dr. No*, for example, Bond notices Goya's portrait of the Duke of Wellington, which had been recently stolen from the National Gallery, in the villain's lair. The *Washington Post* sounded a slightly less rhapsodic note: it anticipated the later view among Bond critics that "in terms of tempo and the quality of the action sequences, *Diamonds* seems unaccountably slack . . . For once the production team appears content to deliver just enough to amuse us rather than more than ever."[37] But the consensus was that Bond was back at the top of his form.

The success of *Diamonds Are Forever* ensured the future of the Bond film series as it moved into its period of "institutionalized ritual." Guy Hamilton and Tom Mankiewicz would both remain on board for the first two Roger Moore films: *Live and Let Die* (1973) and *The Man with the Golden Gun* (1974). These films were both produced on a less spectacular scale than *Diamonds Are Forever*—they reverted to the standard Academy aspect ratio last used for *Goldfinger* and the extravagant set designs of Ken Adam are noticeably absent—but their employment of parody and camp was indebted to *Diamonds Are Forever*. Mankiewicz received a sole screenplay credit for *Live and Let Die*, and—as he had with *Diamonds Are Forever*—updated Fleming's second Bond novel to the film culture of the 1970s. *Live and Let Die* made some nods to the "blaxploitation" cycle of the early 1970s in its representation of African American villains, though this has also prompted accusations of racism.[38] The influence of *Diamonds Are Forever* is apparent in the American locations—the narrative concerns a conspiracy to flood the United States with heroin—and in the characterization of the redneck Sheriff J. W. Pepper (Clifton James), who can be seen as an expanded version of the Las Vegas sheriff in *Diamonds Are Forever*. *Live and Let Die* earned worldwide rentals of $48.7 million—more or less comparable to *Diamonds Are Forever* when inflation is taken into account—though it was less successful in America ($15.9 million) and more successful in the international market ($32.8 million). Maibaum and Mankiewicz shared the writing credit for *The Man with the Golden Gun* which mirrored *Live and Let Die* structurally while including rather more photogenic locations in the Far East. *The Man with the Golden Gun* is one of the more uneven Bond films: Christopher Lee's excellent villain Scaramanga marks a significant improvement on the book, but the topical solar-energy plot lacks the sense of global threat that characterized other Bond movies. It was less successful at the box office, with worldwide rentals of $37.2 million. It marked the last collaboration between Broccoli and Saltzman, whose partnership ended amidst much acrimony in 1977.

The Spy Who Loved Me (1977)—the first Bond movie produced by Broccoli alone—marked the series' return to the level of spectacle seen in *You Only Live Twice* and *Diamonds Are Forever*. It was directed by Lewis Gilbert (*You Only Live Twice*) from a screenplay by Christopher Wood and Richard Maibaum: Mankiewicz performed an uncredited revision.[39] It was also Ken Adam's first film since *Diamonds Are Forever*: his designs for Stromberg's super-tanker and underwater city again reassert the fantasy element of the Bond films that had been less evident in the previous two films. *The Spy Who Loved Me* was even further detached from Fleming: instead its sources were previous Bond films from which it borrowed all the most successful elements including a ski chase (*On Her Majesty's Secret Service*), Bond's specially equipped car (*Goldfinger*), a train-compartment fight (*From Russia with Love*), underwater action (*Thunderball*), and a set-piece battle in the villain's headquarters (*You Only Live Twice*). It earned worldwide rentals of $87.7 million—over twice as much as its predecessor—including $33 million from North America. The critical reception of *The Spy Who Loved Me* recalled *Diamonds Are Forever* in emphasizing its nostalgic escapism. As Frank Rich argued in the *New York Times*: "The continued appeal of the Bond movies is a real phenomenon—particularly when you consider what a dated cultural artefact James Bond is . . . Maybe we no longer need James Bond to defend the honor of the free world, but how lucky we are that he's survived to defend the increasingly endangered traditions of the well-made commercial film."[40]

NOTES

1. "The James Bond Dossier," *The Hollywood Reporter*, 19 November 2002: S-14.
2. "Bondmania," *Time*, 11 June 1965: 59. For further discussion of "Bondmania," see Drew Moniot, "James Bond and America in the Sixties: An Investigation of the Formula Film in Popular Culture," *Journal of the University Film Association* 28, no.3 (Summer 1976): 25–33; James Chapman, *Licence to Thrill: A Cultural History of the James Bond Films* (London: I. B. Tauris, 1999), 111–48; and Alexis Albion, "Wanting to Be James Bond," in Edward P. Comentale, Stephen Watt, and Skip Willman (eds.), *Ian Fleming and James Bond: The Cultural Politics of James Bond* (Bloomington: Indiana University Press, 2005), 202–20.
3. *New York Times*, 14 June 1967: 40.
4. *Los Angeles Times*, 1 February 1970: D-18.
5. John Brosnan, *James Bond in the Cinema* (London: Tantivy Press, 1972), 152.
6. Raymond Benson, *The James Bond Bedside Companion* (London: Boxtree, 1988), 206.
7. Leslie Halliwell, *Halliwell's Film Guide*, 6th ed. (London: Grafton Books, 1987), 268.
8. Stephen Bourne, *Brief Encounters: Lesbians and Gays in British Cinema 1930–1971* (London: Cassell, 1996), 228.
9. Tony Bennett and Janet Woollacott, *Bond and Beyond: The Political Career of a Popular Hero* (London: Macmillan, 1987), 26–27.
10. Bennett and Woollacott, *Bond and Beyond*, 24.
11. Bennett and Woollacott, *Bond and Beyond*, 26–27.
12. Bennett and Woollacott, *Bond and Beyond*, 29.

13. "James Bond 25th Anniversary," *The Hollywood Reporter*, 14 July 1987 (Supplement).

14. "Bondmania," 59.

15. Bennett and Woollacott, *Bond and Beyond*, 26–27.

16. Sue Harper and Justin Smith, *British Film Culture in the 1970s: The Boundaries of Pleasure* (Edinburgh: Edinburgh University Press, 2012), 269.

17. Bennett and Woollacott, *Bond and Beyond*, 38.

18. Quoted in Herb A. Lightman, "The 'Cinemagic' of 007," *American Cinematographer*, 51, no.3 (March 1970): 204.

19. Alexander Walker, *National Heroes: British Cinema in the Seventies and Eighties* (London: Harrap, 1985), 56.

20. Danny Peary, *Cult Movies 3 50 More of the Classics, the Sleepers, the Weird, and the Wonderful* (New York: Simon & Schuster, 1988), 175.

21. *The Village Voice*, 24 December 1969: X.

22. David A. Cook, *Lost Illusions: American Cinema in the Shadow of Watergate and Vietnam, 1970–1979* (Berkeley: University of California Press, 2000), 496–97.

23. *New York Times*, 1 February 1970, S2: 19.

24. "Richard Maibaum: 007's Puppetmaster," *Starlog*, 68 (March 1983): 27.

25. Tom Mankiewicz and Richard Crane, *My Life as a Mankiewicz: An Insider's Journey through Hollywood* (Lexington: University of Kentucky Press, 2012), 135.

26. British Film Institute Unpublished Script Collection S6502: *Diamonds Are Forever*. Final Draft Screenplay by Tom Mankiewicz, no date.

27. Albert R. Broccoli, with Donald Zec, *When the Snow Melts: The Autobiography of Cubby Broccoli* (London: Boxtree, 1998), 221–22.

28. Walker, *National Heroes*, 57.

29. *Esquire*, June 1972: X.

30. BFI S6502: *Diamonds Are Forever*.

31. Ian Fleming, *Diamonds Are Forever* (Las Vegas: Thomas and Mercer, 2012 [1956]): 119.

32. Michael Denning, *Cover Stories: Narrative and Ideology in the British Spy Thriller* (London: Routledge & Kegan Paul, 1987): 34.

33. David Cannadine, "James Bond and the Decline of England," *Encounter*, 53, no. 3 (November 1979): 46.

34. *Monthly Film Bulletin*, 39, no.457 (February 1972): 30.

35. *New York Times*, 28 December 1971: X.

36. *Village Voice*, 16 December 1971: X.

37. *The Washington Post*, 24 December 1971: D-1.

38. Chapman, *Licence to Thrill*, 170–71.

39. Mankiewicz, *My Life as a Mankiewicz*, 162.

40. *New York Times*, 21 August 1977: S2–11.

BIBLIOGRAPHY

Albion, Alexis. "Wanting to Be James Bond." In Edward P. Comentale, Stephen Watt, and Skip Willman (eds.), *Ian Fleming and James Bond: The Cultural Politics of James Bond* (Bloomington: Indiana University Press, 2005), 202–20.

Bennett, Tony, and Janet Woollacott. *Bond and Beyond: The Political Career of a Popular Hero*. London: Macmillan, 1987.

Benson, Raymond. *The James Bond Bedside Companion*. London: Boxtree, 1988.

Bourne, Stephen. *Brief Encounters: Lesbians and Gays in British Cinema 1930–1971*. London: Cassell, 1996.

Broccoli, Albert R., with Donald Zec. *When the Snow Melts: The Autobiography of Cubby Broccoli*. London: Boxtree, 1998.

Brosnan, John. *James Bond in the Cinema*. London: Tantivy Press, 1972.

Cannadine, David. "James Bond and the Decline of England." *Encounter*, 53, no.3 (November 1979): 46–55.

Chapman, James. *Licence to Thrill: A Cultural History of the James Bond Films*. London: I.B. Tauris, 1999.

Cook, David A. *Lost Illusions: American Cinema in the Shadow of Watergate and Vietnam, 1970–1979*. Berkeley: University of California Press, 2000.

Denning, Michael. *Cover Stories: Narrative and Ideology in the British Spy Thriller*. London: Routledge & Kegan Paul, 1987.

Fleming, Ian. *Diamonds Are Forever*. Las Vegas: Thomas and Mercer, 2012 [1956].

Halliwell, Leslie. *Halliwell's Film Guide*, 6th ed. London: Grafton Books, 1987.

Harper, Sue, and Justin Smith. *British Film Culture in the 1970s: The Boundaries of Pleasure*. Edinburgh: Edinburgh University Press, 2012.

Lightman, Herb A. "The 'Cinemagic' of 007." *American Cinematographer*, 51, no.3 (March 1970): 204–5.

Mankiewicz, Tom, and Robert Crane. *My Life as a Mankiewicz: An Insider's Journey Through Hollywood*. Lexington: University Press of Kentucky, 2012.

Moniot, Drew. "James Bond and America in the Sixties: An Investigation of the Formula Film in Popular Culture." *Journal of the University Film Association*, 28, no.3 (Summer 1976): 25–33.

Peary, Danny. *Cult Movies 3: 50 More of the Classics, the Sleepers, the Weird, and the Wonderful*. New York: Simon & Schuster, 1988.

"Richard Maibaum: 007's Puppetmaster." *Starlog*, 68 (March 1983): 23–27.

Walker, Alexander. *National Heroes: British Cinema in the Seventies and Eighties*. London: Harrap, 1985.

FOUR

James Bond, Meet John Blaize

Identity Theft and Intertextuality in Ian Fleming's
Diamonds Are Forever *and* The Diamond Smugglers

Oliver Buckton

In April 1957, *The New Statesman* lamented the apparent death of James Bond at the end of Fleming's most recent novel, *From Russia with Love*, published on April 8. At the end of this novel, Bond has apparently been fatally stabbed by the concealed shoe blade, tipped with poison, administered by Colonel Rosa Klebb of SMERSH, the Soviet spy agency. Fleming's novel concludes with the ominous words, "Bond pivoted slowly on his heel and crashed headlong to the wine-red floor."[1] Fleming's dissatisfaction with writing James Bond adventures had been growing in the last year, following the publication of *Diamonds Are Forever* (*Diamonds*), his fourth novel. Fleming expressed his growing discontent with his literary hero in a letter of April 27 to Raymond Chandler: "probably the fault about my books is that I don't take them seriously enough . . . If one has a grain of intelligence it is difficult to go on being serious about a character like James Bond."[2] Chandler had publicly praised Fleming with an endorsement which Fleming hoped would increase his visibility, and drive up his sales in America.[3] But Chandler had also advised Fleming in July 1956 that he ought to aim higher, stating of *Diamonds*: "I simply don't think it is worthy of your talents."[4]

It was in a despondent frame of mind that Fleming planned to kill off his spy hero, thereby bringing the Bond novels to a conclusion, and track a new course as a writer. Yet the enthusiastic reception of *From Russia with Love* changed his mind, leading Fleming to recognize that his shaking up of "the usual Bond formula" had lent his hero a new lease on life.[5] The problem remained however that—in the eyes of his reading public— James Bond was deceased. In a desperate rearguard action, Fleming wrote *The New Statesman* on April 29 about "The Late James Bond"—to reassure the magazine and its readers that his hero was alive and kicking.[6]

Bond had therefore been saved, for future adventures in *Dr. No*, but Fleming was nonetheless on the lookout for new avenues of literary adventure. In the same month that saw the publication of *From Russia with Love*, Fleming grasped just such an opening for an escape from James Bond when he was invited to cover the real-life smuggling operation, led by Sir Percy Sillitoe, the former head of MI5.[7] Fleming would inject all the elements of espionage and intrigue—from a "cover address" to the mysterious phone call from an unnamed friend and the offer to meet an agent—to launch his new narrative, which he originally envisaged titling "The Diamond Spy."[8]

Intriguingly, the interest shown by this "unnamed spy" in Fleming's James Bond books—specifically *Diamonds Are Forever*—prompts him to select Fleming as the author of "his story." The spy thus offers himself as a potential substitute for James Bond, and invokes a self-reflexivity and intertextuality that punctuates the narrative throughout. Moreover, the new project offers Fleming the opportunity himself to take center stage in a spy story, rather than being merely the subordinate "biographer" of James Bond, on whom he depends for the fame of his own name.

The Diamond Smugglers was based on Fleming's extensive interviews with "the Diamond Spy," which took place in Tangier, a city Fleming disliked as he made clear in a letter to his wife, Ann, from the Hotel El Minzah Tangier on April 20, 1957.[9] Fleming usually wrote his novels in the exotic tropical surroundings of Goldeneye, in Jamaica, a far cry from the degraded picture of Tangier. Despite these unpromising surroundings, however, Fleming was thrilled with the story he was hearing: "it has been very exciting and the story is sensational—at least I think so. Please don't say a word about it or we may be stopped publishing."[10]

Thus from the outset, Fleming insisted the "Diamond Spy" story was shrouded in secrecy, even though Fleming had incorporated material about the actual operation in his recent novel and thus drawn public attention to it. His wish to dramatically highlight the secrecy of the new book can perhaps be recognized as a kind of publicity stunt. His stress on the "sensational" elements of the story places it in the same category as his thrilling novels, but with the added "thrill" that the story was based on fact.[11]

One of Fleming's key decisions in writing *The Diamond Smugglers* was to invent a pseudonym for his "Zulu" or accomplice—the leading agent in Sir Percy Sillitoe's anti-smuggling operation—whose real name was John Collard. In doing so, he creates the more exotic (or at least fiery) name of John Blaize, thus introducing another (partly) fictional spy character boasting the initials J.B. Fleming's intention to exploit Blaize as a substitute for Bond is made apparent, with the shared initials and covert identity of "The Diamond Spy." Fleming would re-use the diamond smuggling story, but in a manner that returns it to the context of the Cold War—a context that is so conspicuously lacking in his novel. Fleming in effect "steals" Collard's identity and story in order to create a thrilling adventure for his new spy hero. In doing so, he repeats a pattern of identity theft that had already been established and immortalized in the James Bond novels from their very inception.

As is well known, Ian Fleming, while writing his first novel *Casino Royale* at his Jamaica retreat Goldeneye, was seeking a name for his newly created spy hero. His eye fortunately fell on one of his "bibles" on his bookshelf, *Field Guide of Birds of the West Indies*, whose author was an American ornithologist named James Bond. Fleming lifted this name—without asking the permission of its owner—for his fictional secret agent, little imagining how long and successful the flight of his bird-inspired spy would be. The attraction of this name was simple: Fleming wanted to avoid the kind of upper-class, flamboyant names of past spy heroes (Fleming gave "Peregrine Maltravers" as an example of the kind of name he wanted to avoid) because "I wished him to be unobtrusive. Exotic things would happen to and around him but he would be a neutral figure—an anonymous blunt instrument wielded by a Government Department." [12] Identity theft, or impersonation, may be described as one of the central motifs in Fleming's fiction. In *Casino Royale*, the first novel, Bond arrives at Royale-les-Eaux under an assumed identity: "Bond knew Jamaica well so he asked to be controlled from there and to pass as a Jamaican plantocrat whose father had made his pile in tobacco and sugar and whose son chose to play it away on the stock market and casinos." [13] In choosing this cover for 007, Fleming cryptically reveals Jamaica as the "origin" for his spy hero, where all the James Bond novels were written. Bond's cover is soon blown, and an attempt to assassinate him by bomb is not long in following. [14] In the second novel, *Live and Let Die* (1954), Fleming takes this identity theft further, by stealing the last name of his oldest friend Ivar Bryce for Bond's cover when he travels with Solitaire down to St. Petersburg, Florida, traveling as Mr. and Mrs. Bryce on the Silver Phantom train. [15] These assumed identities lead to mayhem after Bond and Solitaire leave the train, as Felix Leiter (whose first name is also the middle name of Ivar Bryce) reports: "Your compartment was tommy-gunned and bombed. Blown to bits." [16] Nor do the assumed names prevent the kidnapping of Solitaire by Mr. Big's henchmen, or the capture and shark attack on Felix Leiter. The signs are ominous in these early novels that Bond's assumption of cover identities is unlikely to end well.

In the third novel, *Moonraker*, Bond does not change his name—although he impersonates a new security officer sent by the Ministry of

Supply to replace the murdered Tallon, shot by one of Hugo Drax's German engineers. The masterstroke of identity theft in *Moonraker* is, however, accomplished by the villain, Sir Hugo Drax, who triumphantly announces to a captive Bond: "My real name . . . is Graf Hugo von der Drache. My mother was English and because of her I was educated in England until I was twelve. Then I could stand this filthy country no longer."[17] Following the friendly fire incident in which his face is seriously damaged, Drache fortuitously stole another man's identity: "From the identities they offered me so helpfully I came upon the name of Hugo Drax. What a coincidence! From Drache to Drax!"[18] Remarkably, this rabid Nazi has become a national hero in Britain, savior of its independent nuclear deterrent, and knighted as Sir Hugo Drax. Drax's impersonation of a patriotic—if ill-mannered—English millionaire is initially spectacularly successful compared to Bond's own identity thefts. Yet ultimately even Drax's master disguise unravels, leading to his—and his plot's—demise.

While each of Fleming's previous novels had involved Bond or his enemies assuming false, cover identities none of them feature identity theft as centrally as Fleming's fourth, *Diamonds Are Forever*. The theme of impersonation is introduced in a non-human context, as Bond's first appearance in the novel shows him being fooled by a fake diamond. Comparing the genuine diamond to the fake, Bond "could understand the passion that diamonds had inspired through the centuries, the almost sexual love they aroused among those who handled them and cut them and traded in them."[19] Hence Bond's ability to discriminate between a genuine and a fake diamond is essential to the plot of the novel.

Of equal importance to the mission is Bond's willingness to assume, again, a false identity. In preparation for visiting the House of Diamonds under the false identity, Bond is given a makeover at Scotland Yard resulting in "someone who certainly wasn't James Bond."[20] Though this disguise is fairly short-lived, it introduces an instability into Bond's identity that influences the ensuing novel.

Bond's next change of identity is more substantial. In trying to cut off a diamond smuggling pipeline originating in Africa, M advises Bond that he must himself follow the pipeline to America.[21] And the best way to insert Bond into this pipeline is for him to steal the identity of a small-time crook and diamond smuggler, Peter Franks. Thus disguise and false identity are pivotal to Bond's mission, despite the fact that the SMERSH zapiska (file) on Bond—revealed in the next novel *From Russia with Love*—notes that Bond "does not use disguises."[22] Posing as Franks, Bond works with the American smuggler Tiffany Case, and we learn that Case also has traveled to Britain "under a different name."[23] Although Case readily accepts Bond as "Peter Franks"—her only concern being how he is to smuggle the diamonds into America—Bond admits to Case that his passport is "in my real name . . . James Bond."[24] This abrupt offloading of his alias suggests that false identities are so common in the world of smugglers, there is no point in maintaining the fiction. In Fleming's novel, Franks and Bond are seemingly interchangeable: the picture of Franks is described by Vallance of Scotland Yard as "near enough like you to pass with someone who's only got his description." [25]

In Guy Hamilton's film version of *Diamonds Are Forever*, the conflict over the identity of "Peter Franks" is much more dramatic and extensive. In contrast to the easy replacement of Franks by Bond in Fleming's novel, the film introduces an extended scene in which the "real" Peter Franks (Joe Robinson)—after being detained at British customs at Dover—escapes from the police, then goes to his meeting with Tiffany Case (in Amsterdam), after Bond has already introduced himself as Franks. Bond (Sean Connery), learning of Franks's escape, anticipates his arrival at Case's apartment, leading Bond into a memorable fight-to-the-death with the real Franks inside an elevator, to determine who will keep the identity. As the victor, Bond then "switches" identity documents with the corpse of Franks, leading Case (Jill St. John) to exclaim in amazement: "You've just killed James Bond!" Bond's reply—"Is that who it was? Well it just proves no one's indestructible"—both points to and mocks the myth of Bond's invincibility. [26] Indeed, *Diamonds Are Forever* joins the group of several Bond films starring Sean Connery in which a character who is called, or looks like, James Bond is apparently killed but then returns from the dead (*From Russia with Love* and *You Only Live Twice* being other examples).

The cases of identity fraud continue to pile up in Fleming's novel, as Bond discovers that the man known as Rufus B. Saye, proprietor of the House of Diamonds in London (whom Bond investigates with Sergeant Dankwaerts, of the Special Branch of Scotland Yard), is also a fake: exposed by his failure to recognize that "Yellow Premier and Cape Unions" are not really types of diamond. [27] Saye's deception goes deeper than this imposture as proprietor of a diamond store: he is really Jack Spang, one of the villainous brothers who lead the Spangled Mob, the American end of the diamond smuggling pipeline. Another of his aliases is "A B C," the mysterious contact that all operatives within this smuggling network have to call in order to receive their instructions. Along with such colorful yet unlikely monikers as Shady Tree, Wint and Kidd, and Tingaling Bell, the reader gets the impression that all identities in this novel are—like the fake diamond that Bond examines through an eyeglass in chapter 2—likely to be exposed as forgeries.

The further Bond delves into his mission, the deeper the deception goes. Hence, having smuggled diamonds into America using Franks's identity, Bond goes to the superficially elegant town of Saratoga, New York, in order to receive his payment by betting on a horse named Shy Smile in a fixed race. But as Felix Leiter—now working for Pinkerton's rather than the CIA—is eager to point out, this air of gentility is merely a front for various rackets going on in town. The horse Bond is instructed to bet on, "Shy Smile," is in fact an imposter: the real "Shy Smile" having been shot and disposed of.[28] As they observe the horse in training, Leiter's proposal is to bribe the corrupt jockey "Tingaling" Bell to throw the race, thus thwarting the Spangled boys' attempt to make a fortune.[29] Hence the jockey becomes a double imposter—hired by the Spangled Mob to ride a fake horse, he is bribed by the other side (law enforcement) to renege on his earlier deal. Ironically, the methods of the "good guys" are thus indistinguishable from those of the gangsters—involving bribery, coercion, and corruption.

With such widespread episodes of subterfuge, Fleming highlights the idea that the two "sides" are mirror images of each other: if Bond can convince the gangsters he is a diamond smuggler, then what is the difference between Bond and a real smuggler? Moreover, what are the ethical implications of involving an SIS agent directly in an illegal contraband operation with no immediate bearing on Britain's national security? Such issues are left unexplored and would hardly belong in the partly unreal world of *Diamonds*. For, as Fleming admitted to Raymond Chandler, the America portrayed in *Diamonds* is "an America of much more fantasy than I allowed myself in *Live and Let Die*."[30] Such "fantasy" is apparent in one of the more bizarre scenes of the novel, in which Wint and Kidd—the homosexual hitmen of the Spangs—arrive at the Acme Mud and Sulphur Baths to mete out punishment to Tingaling Bell for his betrayal. The men are disguised in a sinister outfit of black hoods, giving them the appearance of executioners.[31] They point a loaded pistol at Tingaling—trapped in his "coffin" of a mud-box—before pouring boiling-hot mud over the jockey's face.[32] The dodgy ethics of Bond and Leiter's methods are highlighted by the description of the scalded Bell, who has paid the price for conspiring with 007.[33] The hideous transformation of Bell's face is another variant of the theme of identity change in *Diamonds Are Forever*, in which the distinction between heroes and villains—like the authenticity of diamonds—can be hard to verify.

One reason for this blurring of identities and functions between protagonists and antagonists is that Fleming has abandoned (for this novel) his established Cold War opposition of SMERSH—the Soviet spy organization against whose agents Bond did battle in the previous three novels—and the SIS/CIA alliance. While Bond works for SIS, Leiter is no longer with the CIA (following his injuries from the shark attack in *Live and Let Die*), but a private detective working for Pinkerton's.[34] More significantly, SMERSH is conspicuous by its absence from *Diamonds*. The revelation expected by experienced readers of Fleming that the Spangled Mob will turn out to be another front for SMERSH activity—like Le Chiffre's prostitution racket, Mr. Big's gold smuggling operation, or Drax's Moonraker project—never occurs. Without the anchor of Soviet antagonism, the clear opposition between hero/villain begins to fade.

This anomaly has been noted by Umberto Eco in his seminal essay, "Narrative Structures in Fleming." In discussing the formula usually followed by Ian Fleming to create the Bond villains, Eco notes one significant exception in the canon: "Only the evil characters in *Diamonds Are Forever* have no connections with Russia. In a certain sense the international gangsterism of the Spangs appears to be an earlier version of Spectre. For the rest, Jack and Seraffimo possess all the characteristics of the canon."[35] The organization SPECTRE—the Special Executive for Terrorism, Revenge, and Extortion—would of course supplant SMERSH as the chief antagonist for Bond and the SIS in Fleming's later novels, starting with *Thunderball* in 1961. Eco's suggestion that SPECTRE is already present in embryonic form in *Diamonds*, might plausibly have been seized upon by Fleming's defense in the legal case brought by Kevin McClory, the Irish film producer who alleged—in 1963—that Fleming had stolen this identity for his exclusive use in the novel *Thunderball*. This novel—McClory's case claimed—was based on a screenplay written by McClory, Fleming, and Jack Whittingham. Described by Fergus Fleming as "a perfect storm of evil, combining veterans from every violent organization in the world . . . under the overall control of Ernst Stavro Blofeld," SPECTRE demonstrated Fleming's determination to raise his game and increase the global implications of his villain's plots.[36] Yet in the eyes of McClory, Fleming himself was the villain, and the 1963 court case was settled in his favor.[37]

The obvious objection to Eco's suggestion that the Spangled Mob is a nascent version of SPECTRE, is that the mob is not headed by Ernst Stavro Blofeld, the organization's mastermind and Bond's arch enemy. The Eon Productions Bond films made good this lack, by introducing SPECTRE as the enemy from the very first installment—*Dr. No*, in 1962—where the Chinese-German villain declares his allegiance to SPECTRE. Blofeld would first appear in the second film, *From Russia with Love*, in 1963, his face concealed but shown stroking his familiar white cat. By 1971, the SPECTRE machine was so well established as a screen presence that Blofeld was smuggled into the adaptation of *Diamonds Are Forever*, usurping the Spangled Mob altogether as the central villain.

Yet in Fleming's novel, in light of Eco's argument, it is the Spangs themselves who can be considered imposters, usurping the role of villain formerly taken by the Soviet spy agency SMERSH. In each of his previous novels, Fleming had linked the chief villain—however unique, bizarre, or grotesque in role and appearance—to SMERSH. At the end of *Casino Royale*, following Bond's discovery that his lover and SIS colleague Vesper Lynd was a double agent for the Russians, Bond made his strong vow to vengeance against SMERSH: "Here was a target for him, right to hand. He would take on SMERSH and hunt it down . . . He would go after the threat behind the spies, the threat that made them spy."[38] By jettisoning this mission of Bond's in *Diamonds*, Fleming risked diluting his hero's purpose as a professional spy.

Identity theft goes beyond the purloining, exchanging, or disguising of individual identities in *Diamonds*, to become manifest as the blurring between fact and fiction that destabilizes the boundary between the "fantasy" of the novel and the actuality of the smuggling operation on which it was based. As the pretext for Bond's entrance into the diamond smuggling pipeline, Fleming imports the details of an actual spy operation to identify and close down rampant diamond smuggling from the mines of Africa. This real life operation—headed by the retired former chief of MI5, Sir Percy Sillitoe—lends authenticity to Fleming's sometimes far-fetched plot.[39] In an additional ironic twist, Sillitoe was himself a substitute for the man the Diamond Syndicate originally wanted to stem the smuggling from its African mines: Sir William Stephenson, formerly head of the British Security Coordination (BSC) based in the Rockefeller Center in New York during World War II. The covert purpose of the BSC—to produce propaganda (often involving deception) that would induce the United States to join the Allies in the war against Germany and the Axis powers—was embraced by Ian Fleming, who made frequent trips to New York and the BSC, along with Admiral Godfrey, to coordinate with Naval Intelligence.[40] Stephenson—known as "little Bill" or "the quiet Canadian"—had the experience of espionage and intrigue that would have made him ideal as the head of the anti-smuggling racket. As H. Montgomery Hyde writes in his biography of Stephenson, "In 1953, Stephenson was approached by Jon Archer Dunn . . . [who] came on behalf of the members of the Diamond Syndicate, who were extremely worried about the consistent thefts of diamonds from the South African mines and the smuggling of these stones . . . into America. The Syndicate's emissary was authorized to offer Stephenson the sum of one million pounds sterling, together with an additional blank cheque to be filled in by Stephenson in any sum he wished if he could provide a satisfactory solution of the leak."[41] As Hyde relates, Stephenson declined the offer and so the job was offered to Sillitoe, a less expensive substitute: "It was eventually undertaken as a police operation by Sir Percy Sillitoe, the former Director-General of the Security Service (MI5), though not for the sum offered to Stephenson. The subject later formed the background to one of the best of Ian Fleming's James Bond thrillers, *Diamonds Are Forever* (Fleming took his title from the Diamond Syndicate's slogan)."[42] As Hyde's parenthetical comment indicates, the title of the novel—like the name James Bond—was acquired through theft. In a sense, Fleming pays for his appropriation of the slogan—itself a valuable commodity—by the publicity he gives to their operations in his novel.

Perhaps suitably, the plot of *Diamonds* is launched by the failure of Sillitoe as a substitute for Stephenson (though Stephenson himself is never mentioned in Fleming's novel). Fleming referred to Sillitoe dismissively as "Blaize's old friend and booby."[43] In the novel, Sillitoe's official "report" on the diamond smuggling doesn't solve the problem, which is why the intervention of James Bond becomes necessary.[44] Using this foundation of the Diamond Syndicate's actual operation, then, Fleming constructs a fantasy-plot involving beautiful diamond smugglers, American gangsters, corrupt gambling operations, identity theft, and the bizarre Wild West town, Spectreville, where Seraffimo Spang lives out his own "pillow fantasy"—all of which involve illusion and deception.[45]

Fleming's use of Sillitoe's real-life operation as the basis for his fictional plot exemplifies what intelligence historian Nigel West has described as "faction"—a blend of fiction with factual events, reflecting that "even what is purported to be copper-bottomed fact, from an ostensibly reliable source, can fall into the realms of fiction, or a potentially confusing mixture of the two, faction."[46] Despite Fleming's emphasis on the "fantasy" elements of the novel, he insists on the realism of the story's premise—as he would do in the next novel, *From Russia with Love*, in which Fleming's prefatory "Author's Note" claims "a great deal of the background to this story is accurate."[47] Yet West was not the first to note this blend of fact and fiction in spy novels. It had been detected many years earlier in Kingsley Amis's classic study *The James Bond Dossier*, in which Amis notes the pattern of incorporating elaborate detailed information about gadgetry, locations (such as the Royal St. Marks golf course in *Goldfinger*), and technical specifications. Amis coined the term "the Fleming Effect" for this technique. As he writes, "This might be called the imaginative use of information, whereby the pervading fantastic nature of Bond's world, as well as the temporary, local, fantastic elements in the story, are bolted down to some sort of reality, or at least counterbalanced . . . I don't see why it shouldn't be called the Fleming effect."[48]

While Fleming's mixture of fact and fiction is a feature in *Diamonds*, it becomes even more pronounced in *The Diamond Smugglers* (1957). Fleming's original plan to title this work "The Diamond Spy," highlights his desire to create a new spy hero to supplement—or, perhaps, replace—James Bond. The timing of the book, with its use of the same actual smuggling case as *Diamonds*, results in the blurring between Fleming's fictional narrative and his nonfiction account, also suggested by the linking of this text to Fleming's fourth and fifth Bond novels.[49]

The question is, why would Fleming—having already used key elements of the De Beers smuggling operation in the plot of *Diamonds*—decide to recycle this story in a new book? The first answer is that Fleming was a journalist before he became a novelist—working for Reuters in the 1930s (when he reported on the Metro-Vickers espionage trials in Moscow), and for Kemsley Newspapers at the *Sunday Times* from 1945. This meant that the invitation to cover the John Collard story for the *Sunday Times* was an offer he could not refuse. By way of a more complex answer, we should recall that Fleming, by the time he wrote his fourth novel, was growing weary of James Bond, and already looking about for other literary avenues to explore. Fleming was eager to find a more "serious" outlet for his literary talents. The solution to this conundrum, it appeared, would be "John Blaize."

In fact, Fleming had recently written to defend his novels from attack in the *Manchester Guardian*, explaining how "I chose the *pseudonym* of James Bond for my hero."[50] Calling Bond a "pseudonym" emphasizes the fictional status of the name, but also implies there is another "real" identity beneath the assumed name. Such playing with names may lend weight to the theory that "James Bond" is a code name, rather than the actual name of any of the 00 agents who assume it.[51] Alternatively, the reference to a pseudonym might suggest that Fleming saw *himself* as the true hero of the novels, for which "James Bond" was merely a cover that he would eventually dispense with. From the beginning, then, we observe a confusing of identities between Fleming and Bond, which is intensified in *The Diamond Smugglers* itself.

Into this narrative, Fleming "smuggles" another fictional identity bearing the initials J.B.—in this case "John Blaize." Fleming's pseudonym for the agent—whose real name was John Collard—reveals his determination to import the duplicity and intrigue of the spy game into his new book. Just as the details about the real-world anti-smuggling operation launched Fleming's novel, the presence of fiction becomes tangible early on in *The Diamond Smugglers*. Even the substitution of *The Diamond Smugglers* for the more sensational title of "The Diamond Spy" (Fleming was still using this title in correspondence with William Plomer as late as May 1957), does not mitigate the role of fabrication in the story. "Blaize's" own preface to the book introduces him as a narrator before Fleming himself and warns the reader that the story is incomplete: Fleming "had to tone down a few of my rather critical opinions and some interesting names and details had to be withheld altogether."[52] Blaize's subsequent remarks surely bring a cautionary note into the proceedings, stating "I had brought with me a private diary of my own activities which I had been compiling in idle moments over a long period, and it was these notes and my memories which [Fleming] has *most skillfully forged* into a connected narrative."[53] Identifying Fleming's role as a "forger," Blaize reminds us that Fleming is first and foremost a fabricator of popular adventure stories. Beyond the practical purpose of disguising the actual identity of the agent used by Percy Sillitoe (John Collard), the use of a pseudonym allows Fleming to take creative license with the character, making him into a more dynamic and thrilling protagonist. Fleming is keen to emphasize Blaize's status as a "secret agent" working with the "Diamond Detectives branch of the South African Police":[54] Blaize, "like all Britain's best secret agents . . . had common sense, a passion for accuracy and a knowledge of men and how to use them."[55] Fleming also invents other dramatic escapades for his hero, informing Plomer that "Blaize had a very unfortunate time at Monte Carlo. I gave him an infallible system which nearly broke him and when he did get a number 'en plein' a French tart pinched his stake and he practically started a riot."[56] Fleming's need for romantic, dramatic incident indicates that his brief was more than simply tell the truth about the smuggling pipeline. The intertextuality between Fleming's novel, *Diamonds*, and his nonfictional account of diamond smuggling is highlighted as Blaize shows awareness of the fictional hero whom he was designed to supplant. For example, Blaize points out that his role in Sillitoe's mission mirrored the plot of Fleming's novel: "putting a spy in at one end [of the pipeline] in the hopes that he'd work his way up it till he got to the top . . . Rather like that book you wrote last year, but the girls don't come quite so pretty around the diamond fields."[57] There is a metafictional dimension to this work, as one (at least partly factual) character comments on his resemblance to the fictional James Bond.

Further highlighting the intertextuality of *Diamond Smugglers*, Fleming includes reflections on the art of spy fiction that might be taken as an implied critique of his own novels, noting "Even in fiction there is very little good spy literature. There is something in the subject that leads to exaggeration . . . perhaps only Somerset Maugham and Graham Greene and Eric Ambler have caught the squalor and greyness of the Secret Service."[58] Hoping to join this distinguished company of serious spy novelists, Fleming felt he had to abandon the glamor and "exaggeration" of the Bond novels and attempt a grittier portrait of the "squalor" of spies. Notably, *The Diamond Smugglers* lacks the kind of sexual adventure that Fleming made a hallmark of the Bond novels, such as Bond's first glimpse of Tiffany Case "half naked, astride a chair in front of the dressing table."[59] Fleming, as narrator, attempts to lead his new hero Blaize into confessions of amorous adventure: a risqué anecdote about Blaize's exploits in a night club, "was my cue to ask Blaize if he had come across many women in the smuggling racket—beautiful couriers, glamorous shills in the mining towns, and so on. Blaize said sadly that the only beautiful girls he had come across had been on the side of the angels."[60] Fleming's hope for Blaize to imitate Bond's sexual escapades—part of the popular appeal of the 007 novels—is further dampened by Blaize's disclosure that "in general diamond smugglers didn't trust women. They had found that the stones were too much of a temptation."[61]

Yet if *Diamond Smugglers* could afford to dispense with the sparkle of "Bond girls," it could not do without a larger-than-life villain. Here, in fact, Fleming sought to improve on the somewhat theatrical malefactors of the Spangled Mob in *Diamonds*. In *Diamond Smugglers*, indeed, Fleming turns away from the gangsterism of the Spangled Mob and uses Blaize to establish the principal villain of the piece: "the biggest [operator] of all, whom I'll call 'Monsieur Diamant.' Of course this isn't his real name, but it's the name, or rather title, we gave him."[62] Like Auric Goldfinger (the eponymous villain of Fleming's seventh novel, published two years after *Diamond Smugglers*), this villain's name embodies the precious commodity he covets, hoards, and smuggles, and he can be placed in the company of SMERSH operatives like Dr. No and Mr. Big, or even the biggest Bond villain of all, Ernst Stavro Blofeld.

Assisting in Fleming's plot to go Bond one better, Blaize places this villain as the zenith of Fleming's line of fictional baddies, observing: "'You've written about some pretty good villains in your books, but truth is stranger, etc, and none of your villains stands up to Monsieur Diamant. I should say he's the biggest crook in Europe, if not in the world.'" [63] Blaize even warns Fleming that were he to publish the whole truth about Monsieur Diamant, "'he'd have you bumped off.'" [64] Diamant's excesses include "endless champagne and caviar and half a dozen girls that some agent used to procure for him. . . . Monsieur Diamant had peculiar ways with girls—not a very attractive man, really." [65] Like various Bond villains, Diamant's evil nature is manifested in his exploitation, abuse, and mistreatment of women, consuming them like champagne and caviar. Yet as Monsieur Diamant reminds us, the most potent passion evidenced in both fiction and nonfiction works, is the lust for diamonds themselves. Having studied the authentic jewel proffered by M in *Diamonds Are Forever*, Bond "could understand the passion that diamonds had inspired through the centuries, the almost sexual love they aroused among those who handled them and cut them." [66] Various characters in both the novel and nonfiction book fall victim to this "passion," becoming enthralled by what Fleming terms "the myth of diamonds." [67]

But M. Diamant is not simply a diamond-obsessed smuggler but, like Goldfinger, an agent for the Russians, smuggling diamonds extensively behind the Iron Curtain. [68] *Diamond Smugglers* thus exploits the Cold War conflict that is conspicuously missing from *Diamonds Are Forever*: Blaize tells Fleming that the proposal to buy illicit diamonds in Liberia with Government money is approved by Whitehall: "Thanks to the importance of the diamond trade to Britain, Whitehall needed very little persuading. They were particularly influenced by the fact that industrial stones being sold in Monrovia were being bought up by an agent for Russia and were going via Antwerp and Zurich through the Iron curtain to be used in the Russian armaments industry." [69] Indeed, the two narratives share a preoccupation with the international security and prestige of Britain, which is threatened by the diamond smuggling: in the novel, M's original brief to Bond notes that "most of what they call 'gem' diamonds in the world are mined on British territory." [70]

Blaize, like Bond, is "On Her Majesty's Secret Service," a hero required for Britain's economy to hold its own in a post-imperial age. Yet Blaize's disenchantment with the life of a spy echoes Bond's sentiments in *From Russia with Love*, (published the same year), where he was "disgusted to find that he was thoroughly bored with the prospect of the day ahead."[71] Similar to his fictional counterpart, Blaize complains "I'm sick of crooks and sick of spying on them. All I want is a nice quiet job as a country lawyer or administrator."[72] To back up his disdain for his trade of espionage, Blaize ends the book by quoting back Fleming's own words: "'As you said in the last sentence of one of your books: "It reads better than it lives."[73] There are no glittering prizes for guessing the novel whose closing words Blaize repeats: it is, of course, *Diamonds Are Forever*.

In support of the idea that Blaize was intended as a replacement for 007, Fergus Fleming notes the author hoped that "'John Blaize' would emerge as a new Bond-like character."[74] Such hopes were also founded on Fleming's long-standing desire to bring a spy hero to film: a project in which Bond had not yet achieved success. Alexander Korda—the British agent and film producer—had enjoyed reading *Live and Let Die* but declined the option to film it. He then encouraged Fleming to write a story specifically for film, which Fleming attempted with *Moonraker*, but again this prospect did not materialize.[75] Hence the "glittering prospect" of a deal was enticing when the film rights to *The Diamond Smugglers* were purchased by the Rank organization—several years before Eon Productions began the official Bond film series in 1962—and even after Fleming's death, plans to film *The Diamond Smugglers* remained active, though ultimately unrealized.[76] Fleming wrote, in an "author's note" in his privately bound copy of *The Diamond Smugglers*, "It was a good story until all the possible libel was cut out."[77] Bound by libel laws—as he was not in the Bond novels—Fleming wrote Plomer about *The Diamond Smugglers*, "it is all absolutely true with the exception of the man's name."[78] It was the "man's name," however, that made the James Bond novels and films such a valuable commodity. For all his misgivings, it turned out Fleming needed Bond more than he cared to admit.

NOTES

1. Ian Fleming, *From Russia with Love* (Las Vegas: Thomas and Mercer, 2012), 268.

2. Fergus Fleming (ed.), *The Man with the Golden Typewriter: The James Bond Letters* (London: Bloomsbury, 2015), 228.

3. Fleming (ed.), *Golden Typewriter*, 224.

4. Fleming (ed.), *Golden Typewriter*, 231.

5. Fleming (ed.), *Golden Typewriter*, 120.

6. Fleming (ed.), *Golden Typewriter*, 128–29.

7. Ian Fleming, *The Diamond Smugglers* (Las Vegas: Thomas and Mercer, 2013), 1.

8. Fleming, *The Diamond Smugglers*, 1.

9. Fleming (ed.), *Golden Typewriter*, 170. In *Golden Typewriter*, the letter to Ann is dated Saturday [Easter 1957]. As Easter Sunday fell on April 21 in 1957, one can assume that the letter was written on Saturday, April 20, the day before. The letter is given the same date in *The Letters of Ann Fleming*, ed. Mark Amory (London: Collins, 1985), 196.

10. Fleming (ed.), *Golden Typewriter*, 169.

11. Fleming (ed.), *Golden Typewriter*, 172. In his introduction, "Blaize" notes that "some interesting names and details had to be withheld altogether"(Fleming, *Diamond Smugglers*, xi).

12. Fleming (ed.), *Golden Typewriter*, 185.

13. Ian Fleming, *Casino Royale* (Las Vegas: Thomas and Mercer, 2012), 21.

14. Ian Fleming, *Live and Let Die* (Las Vegas: Thomas and Mercer, 2012), 84.

15. Fleming, *Live and Let Die*, 89.

16. Fleming, *Live and Let Die*, 118.

17. Fleming, *Moonraker*, 204.

18. Fleming, *Moonraker*, 207, 208.

19. Fleming, *Diamonds Are Forever* (Las Vegas: Thomas and Mercer, 2012.), 11.

20. Fleming, *Diamonds Are Forever*, 25–26.

21. Fleming, *Diamonds Are Forever*, 15–16.

22. Fleming, *From Russia with Love*, 50.

23. Fleming, *Diamonds Are Forever*, 23. In dealing with her question, "So you're Peter Franks," Bond switches the attention from his assumed name to hers: "I've been wondering what T stands for" (Ibid, 35).

24. Fleming, *Diamonds Are Forever*, 36.

25. Fleming, *Diamonds Are Forever*, 20.

26. *Diamonds Are Forever*, directed Guy Hamilton (Eon Productions, 1971).

27. Fleming, *Diamonds Are Forever*, 31.

28. Fleming, *Diamonds Are Forever*, 91.

29. Fleming, *Diamonds Are Forever*, 90.

30. Fleming (ed.), *Golden Typewriter*, 225

31. Fleming, *Diamonds Are Forever*, 114.

32. Fleming, *Diamonds Are Forever*, 111, 117.

33. Fleming, *Diamonds Are Forever*, 118.

34. Fleming, *Diamonds Are Forever*, 66.

35. Umberto Eco, "Narrative Structures in Fleming," *The Role of the Reader: Explorations in the Semiotics of Texts* (Bloomington: Indiana University Press, 1984), 153.

36. Fleming (ed.), *Golden Typewriter*, 237.

37. Fleming (ed.), *Golden Typewriter*, 238.

38. Ian Fleming, *Casino Royale*, 178.

39. Fleming, *Diamonds Are Forever*, 15.

40. See Andrew Lycett, *Ian Fleming* (London: Phoenix, 1996), 127–28. It was on one of these trips that Fleming and Godfrey stopped in Estoril, Portugal, where Fleming played in the casino and so gained the idea of the epic card battle in *Casino Royale*.

41. H. Montgomery Hyde, *The Quiet Canadian: The Secret Service Story of Sir William Stephenson* (London: Hamish Hamilton, 1962), 240.

42. Hyde, *Quiet Canadian*, 241.

43. Fleming (ed.), *Golden Typewriter*, 172.

44. Fleming, *Diamonds Are Forever*, 15.

45. Might the "earlier version of Spectre" noted by Eco, be indicated by the name of Seraffimo Spang's fantastic recreation of a Wild West frontier town, "Spectreville"? In any case, the origin of SPECTRE became a controversial issue during the notorious court case in which Kevin McClory took legal action against Fleming and his friend Ivar Bryce for breach of copyright over *Thunderball*, in 1963. Among other claims, McClory alleged that Fleming, in publishing the novel *Thunderball* under his own name, had stolen a shared idea: in the words of Andrew Lycett, "McClory remained adamant that SPECTRE was a 'cumulative idea,' the product of their joint endeavours" (Lycett, *Ian Fleming*, 354).

46. Nigel West, "Fiction, Faction, and Intelligence," *Intelligence and National Security* 19/2 (2004), 276.

47. Fleming, "Author's Note," *From Russia with Love*, ix.

48. Kingsley Amis, *The James Bond Dossier* (London: Jonathan Cape, 1965), 111.

49. See the cover of Fleming, *The Diamond Smugglers*, 1957 Jonathan Cape edition.

50. Fleming (ed.), *Golden Typewriter*, 185.
51. One piece of evidence that has been cited in support of this theory is George Lazenby's opening line in *On Her Majesty's Secret Service*. After his attempt to save Tracy from commiting suicide and then from a group of attackers, he watches as she drives away and remarks: "This never happened to the other fellow." Implying that the previous "James Bond"—i.e., Sean Connery—would have been more successful with the woman, Lazenby also opens up the idea that "James Bond" is merely an assumed name used by different 00 agents.
52. Fleming, *Diamond Smugglers*, xi
53. Fleming, *Diamond Smugglers*, xi (emphasis added).
54. Fleming, *Diamond Smugglers*, xiii.
55. Fleming, *Diamond Smugglers*, 27.
56. Fleming (ed.), *Golden Typewriter*, 172.
57. Fleming, *Diamond Smugglers*, 28.
58. Fleming, *Diamond Smugglers*, 13.
59. Fleming, *Diamonds Are Forever*, 33.
60. Fleming, *Diamond Smugglers*, 59.
61. Fleming, *Diamond Smugglers*, 60.
62. Fleming, *Diamond Smugglers*, 93.
63. Fleming, *Diamond Smugglers*, 93.
64. Fleming, *Diamond Smugglers*, 93.
65. Fleming, *Diamond Smugglers*, 94.
66. Fleming, *Diamonds Are Forever*, 11.
67. Fleming, *Diamonds Are Forever*, 11. Fleming's nonfiction account also dwells on the "temptation" of diamonds, which lead to the corruption of numerous officials in the Diamond syndicate, as well as the smuggling rings themselves (*Diamond Smugglers*, 15–17).
68. Fleming, *Diamond Smugglers*, 94.
69. Fleming, *Diamond Smugglers*, 66–67.
70. Fleming, *Diamonds Are Forever*, 14.
71. Fleming, *From Russia with Love*, 95.
72. Fleming, *Diamond Smugglers*, 100.
73. Fleming, *Diamond Smugglers*, 100.
74. Fleming, *Diamond Smugglers*, ix.
75. Fleming (ed.), *Golden Typewriter*, 53.
76. Fleming (ed.), *Golden Typewriter*, 51.
77. Fleming (ed.), *Golden Typewriter*, 167.
78. Fleming (ed.), *Golden Typewriter*, 172.

BIBLIOGRAPHY

Amis, Kingsley. *The James Bond Dossier*. London: Jonathan Cape, 1965.
Amory, Mark, ed. *The Letters of Ann Fleming*. London: Collins, 1985.
Diamonds Are Forever, directed Guy Hamilton (Eon Productions, 1971).
Eco, Umberto. "Narrative Structures in Fleming." *The Role of the Reader: Explorations in the Semiotics of Texts*. Bloomington: Indiana University Press, 1984. 144–72.
Fleming, Fergus, ed. *The Man with the Golden Typewriter: Ian Fleming's James Bond Letters*. London: Bloomsbury, 2015.
Fleming, Ian. *Casino Royale*. Las Vegas: Thomas and Mercer, 2012.
———. *Diamonds Are Forever*. Las Vegas: Thomas and Mercer, 2012.
———. *The Diamond Smugglers*. Las Vegas: Thomas and Mercer, 2013.
———. *From Russia with Love*. Las Vegas: Thomas and Mercer, 2012.
———. *Live and Let Die*. Las Vegas: Thomas and Mercer, 2012.
———. *Moonraker*. Las Vegas: Thomas and Mercer, 2012.
———. *Thrilling Cities*. Las Vegas: Thomas and Mercer, 2013.

Hyde, H. Montgomery. *The Quiet Canadian: The Secret Service Story of Sir William Ste-phenson*. London: Hamish Hamilton, 1962.

Lycett, Andrew. *Ian Fleming*. London: Phoenix, 1996.

West, Nigel. "Fiction, Faction, and Intelligence." *Intelligence and National Security* 19/2 (2004).

2

Gender and Sexuality in
Diamonds Are Forever

FIVE

My Adversary, Myself

*An Examination of James Bond and How Wint and Kidd
Reflect His Own Psyche in* Diamonds Are Forever

Grant C. Hester

With all the villains James Bond has conquered and killed, all the women he has seduced, all the drinks he has guzzled back, and the gadgets he has employed, arguably, nobody has done it better. Yet, the question remains, how is it that he does it better? There is a simple answer and a much more complicated one. The simple answer is he is written that way—where he does whatever necessary to come out on top. However, Eve Moneypenny says to Bond in the film *Spectre,* "You've got a secret. Something you can't tell anyone, because you don't trust anyone."[1] As such, an examination of said secret can lead to the more complicated answer: that he is written that way with a subtext that belies the heteronormative text one views in a casual reading or viewing of the film.[2]

Undoubtedly, Bond exists in a heteronomative world. In fact, Ian Fleming who authored the novels and short stories upon which most of the films were based (as is the case with *Diamonds Are Forever*), died in 1964 three years before homosexuality was decriminalized in England and Wales as part of the Sexual Offences Act of 1967. As a result, when I speak of the subtext of the novels, it should be noted that the subtext—coded language used by the author—would have been the only possible way to communicate such a revelation about a character who was known to serve in "Her Majesty's secret service." In looking at the "coded" language of the novel (or novels), one should consider that Fleming was known for his use of colorful language which is readily accepted. Consider the names of the Bond girls: Plenty O'Toole (self-explanatory), Tiffany Case (a character involved in solving a case of diamond smuggler and an obvious reference to the famed jeweler), and Pussy Galore (an openly lesbian character though she ultimately succumbs to and is seduced by Bond). Each of these names blatantly points to aspects of the character. Contemplating such an action, Fleming's use of other coded language seems entirely probable.

This is not the first bit of research I have done to trouble the assumptions of Bond's heteronormative existence and position him in queer domain.[3] I have done other research drawing on numerous theorists and applied them to various films. In fact, I will be utilizing some of that research as I consider *Diamonds Are Forever*. The Bond *oeuvre* provides many elements that contribute to an over-arching argument supporting a theory of Bond as a repressed homosexual or as a character who I would classify as a potentially queer individual including a camp sensibility (especially from the earlier films). In her "Notes on Camp," Susan Sontag obviously aligns her definition of the camp sensibility with a homosexual male sensibility.[4] Additionally, gender and sexuality performativity as put forth by Judith Butler (building on Sigmund Freud) can contribute, illustrating how Bond performs a hypermasculine role to mask an inward femininity even from himself.[5] My research has also led me to examine the typical male gaze put forth by Laura Mulvey and consider how it is subverted to a gay male gaze in the Bond films.[6] But, ultimately, much of my research stems from Freud's theory of repressed sexuality. In short, Bond has proven to be a rich character for an examination of the psyche of the repressed homosexual male and frankly, both the novel and film *Diamonds Are Forever* contain elements which incorporate all of my previous research.[7] Further, while I think it is near impossible to have this discussion without examining the other novels and films, I will try to do so sparingly and only when it directly relates to my analysis of Bond's portrayal in this novel and film.

With this in mind, it seems appropriate to examine the character of Bond in *Diamonds Are Forever* with particular interest given to his interactions with the openly homosexual characters of Wint and Kidd.[8] Wint and Kidd are an interesting pair for Fleming to introduce in the novel given their sexual orientation in a time when it was literally outlawed in the United Kingdom, and their sexual identity provides a unique parallel and vantage point for an examination of Bond himself.

Fleming certainly did not shy away from the depiction of gay characters. Pussy Galore, with her band of lesbians, in *Goldfinger* (1959) is a prominent example. Still, Fleming seemingly shows her as a lesbian whose entire character—including her sexuality—is "redeemed" upon her encounter with Bond. Yet, arguably Fleming uses Pussy Galore to give insight into the character of Bond in the novel version of *Goldfinger*. Galore says to Bond, "You know what, Mister Bond? I got a feeling there's something phoney about you. I got instincts, see?"[9] The coded language is barely that. The lesbian character is calling Bond out on his false existence. She does not say that he is gay, but she points to an aspect of his personality that was not openly discussed at the time. In fact, when the novel was adapted to film five years later in 1964, the filmmakers chose to downplay Galore's lesbianism. In another example, Fleming depicts Bond, M, and others discussing the possibility that the villainous Francisco Scaramanga in Fleming's last novel—the posthumously published *The Man with the Golden Gun* (1965)—has "homosexual tendencies."[10] Fleming's depiction of these characters (and others) invites an open discussion about the stereotypes that exist about the vilification of gay characters. However, as a gay critic myself, I posit that specifically Wint and Kidd merely represent another aspect of Bond's psychological makeup: his gay self.

Vito Russo addresses the obviously relevant argument of homosexuality and the Bond villain in his groundbreaking work *The Celluloid Closet*: "Popular sex farces and James Bond spy thrillers used sissies and dykes to prove the virility of cartoon heroes and to stress the sterility of homosexuality."[11] However, that seems to merely scratch the surface of the subject. Wint and Kidd are shown to have an almost asexual existence together. While they hold hands as they walk off into the sunset, there is no kiss shared between them nor any scene of the two men in bed discussing their exploits or plotting their next attempt to destroy Bond. Their relationship reflects the sterility Russo mentions. The two of them could have just as plausibly been portrayed as heterosexual characters attempting to kill Bond. However, as villains, Fleming and the filmmakers show the characters as gay to demonstrate a perceived weakness on the part of gay individuals and how that weakness would allow Bond to overtake them in any encounter. Yet, I would argue that their weakness has nothing to do with homosexuality. Rather, the two of them are simply outmatched by the training and fortitude of Britain's master spy.

To explore this, I point to the work of Chuck Klosterman and his exploration of villainy in *I Wear the Black Hat*.[12] He begins by asking, what is the most villainous move one can make? He overrules such things as murdering a bunch of people stating that that "seems obvious" and notes that "rape is vile, human trafficking is disturbing, and blowing up the planet and blotting out the sun are not for the innocent." He even points out in a sad and non-ironic fashion that "electrocuting helpless dogs for the sake of convenience seems almost diabolical, but not diabolical enough to keep you off the NFL Pro Bowl Roster." Instead, he posits the "most villainous move on the market" as he terms it is tying a woman to the railroad tracks, thus creating a damsel in distress as an "unadulterated expression of evil."[13] While Bond presumably has not tied an actual woman to a railroad track, he has certainly been in the position of seeing the woman with whom he has become embroiled being then captured, bound, tortured, and ultimately used to ensnare him into whatever exploits his adversary has decided to mastermind. However, Klosterman puts forth, "In any situation, the villain is the person who knows the most, but cares the least."[14] Considering this assertion, who is the real villain—Bond's adversary or Bond himself? Bond's rival may be the one who has captured the film's so-called "Bond girl" and is now using her against 007 himself, but how many times has it happened in the course of the books and films? How has Bond never learned that his romantic entanglements never work out well for the woman? Perhaps, it is he simply does not care due in large part to his never actually forming a true emotional attachment to said woman.

Whether Bond is a villain or not is really a secondary argument to be considered. Klosterman points out, paradoxically, that there are certain villains who are not villains. He even provides a list of what he considers "anonymous people who—in theory—are bad people and social pariahs." He lists: men who hijack airplanes, con artists, funk narcissists, drug dealers, and athletes who use race as a means for taunting an opponent. However, Klosterman then asks us to consider charismatic people who under what he terms "special circumstances" with a "high dose of false emotional attachment" can never be considered villains. The lists are the same.[15] This proves interesting when looking at Bond. What have the villains he encounters done that he has not? They have killed people. So has he. They have exploited others—especially women—for their own gain. So has he. They have broken laws or manipulated them to suit their own needs. So has he. Do we simply have a "high dose of false emotional attachment" because we are told Bond is the hero? I would argue yes, we do. In many ways, Bond is merely a mirror image of his own adversaries. They have done nothing worse than he has. He just happens to be able to justify his actions by the fact that he is a government agent working to protect the interests of the Queen. Considering this, Mr. Wint and Mr. Kidd leave us with an interesting question to ponder. If Bond in many ways reflects his own adversaries and their deeds, does he also then serve as a reflection of Wint and Kidd in their deeds? If so, does that include their own homosexual activities?

Obviously, on the surface of the film and novel, the answer to that question is simply no. However, in examining the subtext of the books and film, evidence points to a different conclusion. As mentioned, homosexual activity was outlawed in Great Britain at the time Fleming's novel was written. With that knowledge, consider the following passage from the novel in which Bond feels the elevator operator "watching him" after he gets off the elevator and proceeds to his room. Basically, he is being cruised. However, Fleming points out that Bond was not taken aback as this hotel is known for "petty crime."[16] Is Fleming referring to petty crime only—thievery and such? Or, is his description also serving as coded language to indicate Bond is entering a place where he believes homosexual activity (illegal at the time) regularly takes place? If one argues the latter to be the case, then many other instances in the book and film can be viewed in a different way. The liftman (elevator operator for us Americans) is watching him. Why is he watching him? Is Bond being cruised and admired by the liftman in a place known for gay cruising? Arguably, the text can indicate that.

Additionally, the scene provides a disruptive view of Bond as the apex of masculinity when one considers the work of Laura Mulvey in her seminal article "Visual Pleasure and Narrative Cinema." Mulvey examines the image of the woman on film. In her argument, she asserts of film, "Traditionally, the woman displayed has functioned on two levels: as erotic object for characters within the screen story, and as erotic object for the spectator within the auditorium, with a shifting tension between the looks on either side of the screen."[17] Mulvey bases her work on an argument made by Sigmund Freud where, she points out, he "associated scopophilia with taking other people as objects, subjecting them to a controlling and curious gaze."[18] Mulvey notes that Freud's theory of scopophilia centers largely on children and their desire to actively use their voyeurism to investigate things that are typically not readily discussed with them such as genitals and bodily functions. Just as Mulvey adapts Freud's theory for her examination of the female form in cinema, the same argument can be subverted for those persons existing outside the heteronormative world to claim that a queer individual (particularly a gay man) can exist to be viewed or "gazed" upon in a similar fashion.[19]

Further demonstrating this point is that when Bond first encounters Mr. Wint and Mr. Kidd, the encounter takes place in "Acme Mud and Sulphur Baths." The gay bathhouse is a now legendary part of gay culture and history where in another time when homosexuality was less socially accepted, men who sought such things would go to "the baths" to seek other men to among other things, "gaze" at them. I put forth an argument that with London having its own gay baths such as the Savoy Turkish Baths (which was open from 1910 to 1975), Fleming was signaling readers to recognize certain things about Bond's character. He even goes as far as pointing out the sign for the bus that transported clients to and from the bathhouse reads, "Every hour on the hour." This again would not be an uncommon phrase for men, seeking such an activity, to also seek a place for their clandestine meetings that rented hourly rather than daily.[20] Additionally, Fleming describes inside the bathhouse with each room housing a man who had already rid himself of his clothing. He continues, describing how they would look out into the room "through a veil of water" with "mouths gulping for air" while their hair was covering their eyes.[21] The description does not exactly depict a scene from the typical heteronormative experience but instead shows how the activities inside the Acme Mud and Sulphur Baths could have taken on what was, at the time, considered to be a more nefarious activity.

Frankly, the subtext of the novel and film is not *that* simple or *that* obvious. As Nikki Sullivan points out in her book *A Critical Introduction to Queer Theory*, "If there is no single correct account of sexuality, then contemporary views of particular relationships and practices are not necessarily any more enlightened or any less symptomatic of the times than those held by previous generations."[22] She continues with the importance of remembering that point in the examination of texts. As the novel *Diamonds Are Forever* was first published in 1956 and the film was released in 1971, this chapter examines sources from roughly the past sixty years, each of which is arguably a representation of its time's own respective zeitgeist. Moreover, as Fleming himself states in *On Her Majesty's Secret Service* (1963), "homosexual tendencies" were considered to be something that could be successfully treated with hypnosis at the time.[23] So, with my position on Bond being cruised in the hotel, was this merely the only way Fleming could allude to Bond's behavior in a way that readers who were privy to such coded language would pick up? I think it certainly creates an interesting point to consider. Also, in the sixty years since the publication of the novel, the films of the Bond canon have been allowed to be "less coded" and more frank in their descriptions and allusions as will be discussed later.

In an effort to explore the queer subtext of *Diamonds Are Forever* more fully, I employ the theoretical framework set forth by Sigmund Freud in his article "Certain Neurotic Mechanisms in Jealousy, Paranoia, and Homosexuality" first published in 1922.[24] In his article, Freud sets forth three layers of jealousy, which he feels mask a repressed homosexuality. Those three types are *competitive* (or normal) *jealousy, projected jealousy*, and *delusional jealousy*.[25] However, he notes that in a delusional case, the subject will show indications of jealousy of all three types and never just the delusional subset.[26] To be explored later, the three types of jealousy in conjunction with paranoia lead to Freud's recognition of homosexuality—often repressed—and its effect on a subject. Similarly, I will employ this methodology to examine the character of James Bond in his various incarnations to determine the queer subtext, which underscores Bond's repressed homosexuality.

Freud plainly states about his theory of competitive jealousy, "It is noteworthy that in many persons it is experienced bisexually; that is to say, in a man the suffering in regard to the loved woman and the hatred against the male rival, grief in regard to the unconsciously loved man and hatred of the woman as a rival will add to its intensity."[27] As a result, he posits that it is not rare that an individual will have underlying feelings for the same sex. "Many persons" possess the desire for the same sex whether or not it is ever physically acted upon. Secondly, Freud describes projected jealousy as being one that is derived from men and women either from actual unfaithfulness on their part or from impulses toward unfaithfulness, which have been suppressed by them. Freud describes how a person who represses such an action will still be provoked strongly in the direction of infidelity such that he will ultimately be relieved to use his unconscious alleviation of the situation. He states, "This relief—more, absolution by his conscience—he achieves when he projects his own impulses to infidelity to the partner to whom he owes faith."[28] Freud's third layer of jealousy, delusional jealousy, also has its origin in the repressed impulses of infidelity. However, Freud notes that in this case, the object of the impulse is of the same sex as the subject. He states, "Delusional jealousy represents an acidulated homosexuality, and rightly takes its position among the classical forms of paranoia."[29] To be clear, it is repressed homosexuality that is being termed a form of paranoia and not acknowledged homosexuality.

Ultimately, Freud describes the case study of one of his patients. The description could practically be that of James Bond himself. Freud details,

> The homosexuality of this patient was easily surveyed. He had made no friendships and developed no social interests; one had the impression that the delusion had constituted the first actual development of his relations with men, as if it had taken over a piece of work that had been neglected. The fact that his father was of no great importance in the family life, combined with the humiliating homosexual trauma in early childhood, had forced his homosexuality into repression and barred the way to its sublimation.[30]

Freud's description may as well be that of James Bond. Bond, the character, has no friends or lasting relationships.[31]

As revealed in other later Bond films (such as *Skyfall*[32] and *Casino Royale*[33]), Bond's family life was lacking, and like many British boys he was then educated in a boarding school situation. Simply, this patient could be the prototype for Bond's personality. His only continuing relationship is with M who—although later recast as a maternal figure for Bond and the other Double-0s when portrayed by Judi Dench in more recent films culminating in *Skyfall*—is depicted as a male character in the novels, with whom Bond has a somewhat friendly, but very respectful relationship on the part of Bond.[34]

Still, Fleming does leave the reader with a few innuendos regarding their relationship. For example, he begins chapter 2 of *DAF* with M saying to Bond, not to "push" it in but instead, he should "screw" it in. While they were in fact talking about how to wear a jeweler's loop on one's eye, a more sexual reading of the sentence can certainly be considered before the reader advances in the chapter. And, Fleming continues with the arguably coded language in the scene. M also says in the exchange, "So don't think you are going to have the pleasure of shovelling that lot into my in-tray."[35] M finishes the scene by lighting up a smoke (a pipe in his case), which has long been portrayed as the afterglow period following a sexual encounter. Also, as Bond is leaving the office, the secretary points out, his tie is crooked.[36] While seemingly insignificant, it could also be interpreted as a fairly common disheveled appearance following redressing after a sex act. Finally, Fleming also alludes to what could be a deeper relationship between the two in the scene, where Fleming notes that Bond holds "a great deal of affection" along with his "loyalty and obedience" for M who reciprocates the feelings.[37] While it is certainly not a frank depiction of a sexual encounter, the codified language exists which can lead to another, deeper interpretation in the subtext of the novel.

Additionally, one could also point to an interchange later in the novel between Bond and Tiffany Case where they discuss the state of their love lives and romantic entanglements. Bond himself jokes (or declares depending on your interpretation), that he is married to M and that he would have to divorce him before he could be married to a woman.[38] Though decades before the subject of legally recognized same-sex marriage was anywhere near common discourse, it is somewhat telling that Fleming would write Bond—his hyper-masculine character—as a man who seems comfortable or even resigned to a life with another man as his companion. Whatever the true terms of their relationship, such an admission clearly points to Bond's affection for M.

With this observation (or, more accurately, theory) of Bond's personality, another consideration of Wint and Kidd is in order. As in the novel, the two are minor characters in the film adaptation. When first introduced to the characters they kill a character with a scorpion and plant a bomb in a box to blow up another character in a helicopter. However, it should be noted that they each address the other as "Mr." and following the helicopter explosion are seen walking hand-in-hand across the desert to the mountains. However, despite addressing each other as Mister, the filmmakers also chose to address a feminine side of the characters by constantly showing Wint with an atomizer spritzing himself—a more feminine trait. In fact, following the first scene showing Wint spritzing himself, the filmmakers almost immediately show Tiffany Case spritzing an atomizer on Bond's drinking glass to obtain his fingerprints. The parallel is clear.

While the filmmakers certainly portray Bond in other scenes which can be viewed under the guise of a queer interpretation that are worth mentioning, Wint and Kidd with their expressed sexuality distinctively add to the queer interpretation of those scenes. For example, Bond encounters Peter Franks in an elevator while on his way to visit Case in Amsterdam. Franks attacks Bond and a fight erupts between the two. However, the fight is more of a wrestling match within the confines of the elevator. Finally, at the conclusion of the entanglement, Bond sprays Franks with a fire extinguisher to finish him off. The comparison of a fire extinguisher expelling its contents and male ejaculation is not a hard one to make. However, the scene can also be viewed in terms of camp as defined by Sontag. She describes camp as, "the essence of the unnatural:

of artifice and exaggeration. And Camp is esoteric—something of a private code, a badge of identity even." Further Sontag posits (note 16) that the camp sensibility is "one that is alive to a double sense in which some things can be taken." Additionally, she posits in note 50 that camp is in many ways defined by a self-elected class: homosexuals who deign themselves as arbiters of taste.[39]

In another scene, an associate of Wint and Kidd passes Bond in a hotel hallway. He immediately does a double take and turns to gaze at Bond. The depiction is very indicative of a gay male cruising scene and is easily viewed with that perception. The scene also subverts the work of Mulvey's theory of the male gaze. Her theory addresses the way men view women in film as the viewer of the film, the director of the film, and those interacting in the scene (all presuamably male) objectify the female present in the scene.[40] Bond—being viewed or even gawked upon by the other male in the scene—one with an identity already troubled to be outside the heteronormative world because of his association with Wint and Kidd—is himself the object of the male gaze. That gaze sexualizes Bond in the same way a woman would be, thus placing him as the object of an arguably homosexual contemplation.

However, perhaps the film's strongest hints as to Bond's personality reflecting that of Wint and Kidd comes in the villains' scenes together and their interactions with Bond. First, Wint describes Case as being very attractive "for a lady" much to his partner's chagrin.[41] However, the seemingly throwaway line, as Jill St. John who portrayed Tiffany Case is indeed quite beautiful, serves another purpose. It shows that one can find their designated or declared object of sexual desire to be less limited than it appears. If that is true for Wint and Kidd, it can also be true for Bond.

Yet, the most compelling and arguably most telling allusions come from the manner in which Wint and Kidd try to kill Bond. In one scene, they place him into a pipeline to be buried alive. An analysis considering the traditionally masculine Bond being inserted to an orifice (the pipeline) by another man can clearly be made. The other two attempts on Bond's life are more obvious, but even more troubling. Part of the troubling derives from the use of the word "flaming" to describe a stereotypically feminine gay male. In an early encounter, Wint and Kidd assault Bond with a cremation urn, put him "to bed" in a coffin, and then send him into the crematorium indicating Bond's own "flaming" nature. Then, in their final confrontation on board the cruise liner, near the end of the film, the two are posing as waiters serving a private dinner to Bond and Case. Bond recognizes the scent of Wint's cologne—something that traditionally would happen between lovers rather than adversaries—before Kidd begins to attack Bond with skewers of meat which he has set on fire. Literally, he is attacking Bond with flaming phallic-shaped meat—the examination of the scene is too rich and frankly a bit too ribald for this paper. Bond, of course, tosses wine on Kidd so he literally dies as a flaming homosexual and then turns his attention to Wint who he manages to castrate with Wint's own arm (as demonstrated by Wint's high-pitched squeal) and then wraps the bomb the two had intended for Bond around his hand giving Wint one more explosion/ejaculation in that area—only this time resulting in Wint's death.

Still, it is not lost on me that until James Bond is depicted actively engaging in homosexual sex acts in officially sanctioned books or films, detractors to the exploration of his repressed homosexuality will remain. On October 24, 2015, the *Daily Mail* in the United Kingdom published an interview that was subsequently picked up by other media outlets throughout the world with actor (and former Bond) Sir Roger Moore who stated unequivocally a narrow view of the character. He put forth, "I have heard people talk about how there should be a lady Bond or a gay Bond. But they wouldn't be Bond for the simple reason that wasn't what Ian Fleming wrote. It's not about being homophobic or, for that matter, racist—it is simply about being true to the character."[42] However, I would argue that Moore either has not read the books in a while or is unaware of the subtext of the novels indeed written by Ian Fleming (they were adapted by other writers for the screen). And the filmmakers clearly feel differently than Moore. For example, in the 2012 film *Skyfall* (though not based on one of Fleming's novels), Bond (Daniel Craig) is being intimidated by Silva (Javier Bardem), a former Double-0 who is now seeking to destroy the organization. The scene plays out as follows:

> **Raoul Silva:** (Caresses James Bond's thighs as Bond is tied to a chair) Well there's always a first time.
>
> (Bond Smiles)
>
> **Raoul Silva:** Yes?
>
> **James Bond:** What makes you think this is my first time?
>
> **Raoul Silva:** (sits back) Oh, Mr. Bond[43]

To me, that says it all. Even Bond himself admits it is more than possible he has been with a man before. Until the filmmakers choose to show a frank and actual depiction of Bond engaged in homosexual activity, that coy pronouncement may have to be enough.

NOTES

1. *Spectre*. Dir. Sam Mendes. Columbia Pictures and Metro Goldwyn Mayer, 2015.
2. Lauren Berlant and Michael Warner, "Sex in Public," *Critical Inquiry* 24.2 (1998), 547–66. www.jstor.org/stable/1344178. In using the term "heteronormativity," I use the

definition put forth by Lauren Berlant and Michael Warner. They define heteronormativity as follows:

> By heteronormativity we mean the institutuions, structures of understanding, and practical orientations that make heterosexuality seem not only coherent—that is, organized as sexuality—but also privileged. Its coherence is always provisional, and its privilege can take several (sometimes contradictory) forms: unmarked, as the basic idiom of the personal and social; or marked as a natural state; or projected as an ideal or moral accomplishment. It consists less of norms that could be summarized as a body of doctrine than of a sense of rightness produced in contradictory manifestations—often unconscious, immanent to practice or to institutions.

3. Alexander Doty, *Making Things Perfectly Queer* (Minneapolis: University of Minnesota Press, 1993). For the purpose of this paper, I will employ the definition of "queer" that Alexander Doty notes in his book *Making Things Perfectly Queer*. He states, "When I use the terms 'queer' or 'queerness' as adjectives or nouns, I do so to suggest a range of nonstraight expression in, or in response to, mass culture. This range includes specifically gay, lesbian, and bisexual expressions; but it also includes all other potential (and potentially unclassifiable) non-straight positions" (xvi). Further, Doty theorizes that the queerness of mass culture develops in three areas:

1. Influences during the production of texts (or films in the case of this paper)
2. Historically specific cultural readings and uses of texts by self-identified gays, lesbians, bisexuals, and queers
3. Adopting reception positions that can be considered "queer" in some way, regardless of a person's declared sexual and gender allegiances (xi).

Additionally, I intersperse the use of the words "homosexual" and "homosexuality" with similar regard and meaning. Basically, the use of the words is to mean non-heterosexual. Any of the terms falling under the "queer umbrella" are understood to be part of the analysis.

4. Susan Sontag, *Against Interpretation and Other Essays* (New York: Picador, 1966).

5. Judith Butler, *Gender Trouble* (New York: Routledge, 1990).

6. Laura Mulvey, "Visual Pleasure and Narrative Cinema," *Screen* 16.3 (Autumn 1975): 6–18.

7. *Diamonds Are Forever*. Dir. Guy Hamilton. Columbia Pictures and Metro Goldwyn Mayer, 1971.

8. Ian Fleming, *Diamonds Are Forever* (Las Vegas: Thomas & Mercer, 2012).

9. Ian Fleming, *Goldfinger* (Las Vegas: Thomas & Mercer, 2012), 244.

10. Ian Fleming, *The Man with the Golden Gun* (Las Vegas: Thomas & Mercer, 2012), 29.

11. Vito Russo, *The Celluloid Closet: Homosexuality in the Movies* (New York: Harper and Row, 1987), 154–55.

12. Chuck Klosterman, *I Wear the Black Hat* (New York: Scribner, 2014).

13. Klosterman, *Black Hat*, 9.

14. Klosterman, *Black Hat*, 14.

15. Klosterman, *Black Hat*, 39.

16. Fleming, *Diamonds Are Forever*, 32.

17. Mulvey, "Visual Pleasure," 8.

18. Mulvey, "Visual Pleasure," 6.

19. James Keller, "Does He Think We Are Not Watching?: Straight Guys and The Queer Eye Panoptican," *Pop Culture Association in the South* 26:3 (April 2004), 49–60.

20. Fleming, *Diamonds Are Forever*, 106.

21. Fleming, *Diamonds Are Forever*, 115.

22. Nikki Sullivan, *A Critical Introduction to Queer Theory* (New York: New York University Press, 2003), 1.

23. Ian Fleming, *On Her Majesty's Secret Service* (Las Vegas: Thomas & Mercer, 2012), 199.

24. Sigmund Freud, "Certain Neurotic Mechanisms in Jealousy, Paranoia, and Homosexuality," in *Sexuality and the Psychology of Love* (New York: Simon and Schuster, 1963). Critic Robin Wood employs a similar argument in his examination of the character Jake La Motta in Martin Scorsese's film *Raging Bull*. See Robin Wood, *Hollywood: From Vietnam to Reagan . . . and Beyond* (New York: Columbia University Press, 1986).

25. Freud, "Neurotic Mechanisms," 150 emphasis in text.

26. Freud, "Neurotic Mechanisms," 152.

27. Freud, "Neurotic Mechanisms," 151.

28. Freud, "Neurotic Mechanisms," 151.

29. Freud, "Neurotic Mechanisms," 152.

30. Freud, "Neurotic Mechanisms," 154.

31. An argument can be made that Bond has a lasting friend with Felix Leiter, his counterpart from the CIA. However, while the two have many work assignments that they coordinate over the course of the novels and films, their relationship is merely that: a work relationship. The two are never shown interacting outside of their assignments in a way that friends would. As such, I would say they are merely familiar business associates who each go their own way at the end of their joint missions.

32. *Skyfall*. Dir. Sam Mendes. Columbia Pictures and Metro Goldwyn Mayer, 2012.

33. *Casino Royale*. Dir. Martin Campbell. Columbia Pictures and Metro Goldwyn Mayer, 2006.

34. Jack Halberstam, *Female Masculinity* (Durham: Duke University Press, 1998). Halberstam also explores the recasting of M with Judi Dench and the effects of said recasting on the character in *Female Masculinity*. She posits, "There's something curiously lacking in *Goldeneye*, namely, credible masculine power" (3). Yet, she has other declarations for Judi Dench's M. She states, "Bond's boss, M, is a noticeably butch older woman who calls Bond a dinosaur and chastises him for being a misogynist and a sexist" (3). According to Halberstam, Bond's masculinity is prosthetic and has little to do with "biological maleness" but feels M is the character that most exemplifies masculine performativity and that performance is at the expense of Bond's "sham" of masculinity (3–4).

35. Fleming, *Diamonds Are Forever*. 13.

36. Fleming, *Diamonds Are Forever*. 13.

37. Fleming, *Diamonds Are Forever*. 13.

38. Fleming, *Diamonds Are Foever*. 199.

39. Sontag, "Notes on Camp," 290.

40. Mulvey, "Visual Pleasure," 17.

41. Hamilton, *Diamonds Are Forever*.

42. Tim Walker, "Bond Row Looms as Roger Moore Says 007 Can't Be Gay—Or a Woman: Star, 88, Says 'Political Correctness' Should Not Be Considered," *Daily Mail*. Oct. 24, 2015.

43. Mendes. *Skyfall*.

BIBLIOGRAPHY

Berlant, Lauren, and Michael Warner. "Sex in Public." *Critical Inquiry* 24.2 (1998): 547–66. www.jstor.org/stable/1344178.

Doty, Alexander. *Making Things Perfectly Queer*. Minneapolis: University of Minnesota Press, 1993.

Fleming, Ian. *Diamonds Are Forever*. Las Vegas: Thomas & Mercer, 2012.

Freud, Sigmund. *Sexuality and the Psychology of Love*. New York: Simon and Schuster, 1963.

Halberstam, Jack. *Female Masculinity*. Durham: Duke University Press, 1998.

Klosterman, Chuck. *I Wear the Black Hat.* New York: Scribner, 2014.

Mulvey, Laura. "Visual Pleasure and Narrative Cinema." *Screen* 16.3 (Autumn 1975): 6–18.

Skyfall. Dir. Sam Mendes. Columbia Pictures and Metro Goldwyn Mayer, 2012.

Sontag, Susan. *Against Interpretation and Other Essays.* New York: Picador, 1966.

Spectre. Dir. Sam Mendes. Columbia Pictures and Metro Goldwyn Mayer, 2015.

Sullivan, Nikki. *A Critical Introduction to Queer Theory.* New York: New York University Press, 2003.

Walker, Tim. "Bond Row Looms as Roger Moore Says 007 Can't Be Gay—Or a Woman: Star, 88, Says 'Political Correctness' Should Not Be Considered." *Daily Mail.* Oct. 24, 2015.

Wood, Robin. *Hollywood: From Vietnam to Reagan . . . and Beyond.* New York: Columbia University Press, 1986.

SIX

The Devolution of Tiffany Case

Jennifer L. Martinsen

Of the heroines in Ian Fleming's James Bond novels, Tiffany Case in *Diamonds Are Forever* is one of the most complex, independent, and resourceful. Such a dynamic female character enhances Bond's character, too, because it provides opportunities for him to develop. Readers discover that Bond can admire and respect a woman for her brain—not just her body. Unfortunately, Guy Hamilton's 1971 cinematic adaptation of *Diamonds Are Forever* reduces Tiffany Case to a stereotypical, cardboard floozy and portrays James Bond as a mere domineering chauvinist. As a fictional character that has permeated our cultural consciousness for over sixty-five years, Bond works as a "cultural reference" capable of "producing meaning";[1] therefore, his attitudes and behaviors toward women provide a model as to how gender dynamics can function. While the 1956 novel seems to adhere to the standard formula of Bond meets a beautiful woman, saves her, and then sleeps with her, Fleming gives Tiffany Case more personal agency, and, as a result, the story presents a more complex example of gender relations. On the other hand, the 1971 film takes a step back in time. Not only does it recast Sean Connery in the leading role, it returns to treating women as bed-warmers rather than as partners. Reverting to a more traditional gender paradigm and presenting Tiffany Case as a bimbo weakens the franchise by reducing the growing complexity of Bond's relationship to women and diminishing his relevance as a social icon able to adapt to a more progressive era for women.

The figure of the "Bond Girl" is almost as famous as the character of James Bond himself. What makes her distinctive is not simply her appearance but her function within the narrative. It is easy to label Fleming's Bond novels as sexist (even misogynist) and reactionary not only for

105

his depictions of women but also because Bond espouses many troubling claims about how women are simply for "recreation."[2] The novels also regularly convey a specific view of women that suggests that their "proper" place is in Bond's bed.[3] Yet, as Kingsley Amis rightly points out, the "Bond Girl" is "inside the plot rather than a sexy or status-conferring appendix to it."[4] That is, there are enough examples of strong heroines throughout Fleming's texts to suggest that the "Bond Girl" is not simply there to look pretty and warm Bond's bed. In fact, she often helps Bond and serves as an asset to his mission and to the story.[5] Her ability to act as a helpmeet—not just a bedmate—accounts for why critics have occasionally claimed that a number of Fleming's female characters demonstrate more independence than their cinematic counterparts.[6] When discussing the gender politics of Fleming's Bond, for example, James Chapman insists that "the Bond novels are paradoxically more sexist in their attitudes yet at the same time allow greater narrative agency for their female characters than most of the films that have been spun from them."[7] The narrative arc for Tiffany Case in Fleming's novel repeatedly positions her as a "Bond Girl" that has the potential to be a valuable partner—on a mission as well as in bed. By illustrating how a woman can be an asset to a character such as Bond, Fleming provides a model for gender relations in which women are respected for both their beauty and their brains.

Throughout the novel, each major scene in which Tiffany Case appears builds her character and/or develops Bond's admiration for her. For instance, when Bond first glimpses Case, Fleming describes how she is wearing only a bra and panties while straddling a chair and looking into a mirror. With her arms crossed over the top of the chair and her back slightly curved, Bond can't help but notice a certain "arrogance" about her.[8] Her position and lack of clothing "whip[s] at Bond's senses."[9] Fleming's description of her near nakedness makes it clear that Case was comfortable with her body and her authority. She does not bother to change position to answer the door when Bond knocks nor does she bother to stop the music she has playing or throw on something to cover herself up. She stays put because it suits her purposes. She uses her body as a weapon to assert her power over men. The move aims to throw Bond off his guard and put him in his place. He is not someone worth getting dressed for because he is simply part of her job. He is the new diamond smuggler, while she is his handler. Although some may find Fleming's description of her figure prurient and unnecessary, Boel Ulfsdotter insists that readers have a choice: they can understand the scene as either "an expression of mere voyeurism when related to her forthcoming performance in the narrative," or they can "admit that Case is a woman who is in complete control of her own integrity."[10] Fleming continues to build the image of Case as a confident woman comfortable within her own skin by stating how her beauty seems almost nonchalant as if she doesn't care what anyone thinks of her appearance. The only opinion that matters is her own.[11] Fascinated and intrigued by her, Bond concludes that this is a woman used to being in control of her body and her actions. Thus, from the outset, Bond clearly recognizes Case's power and her autonomy, which encourages readers to do the same.

In some respects, Case's initial appearance within the narrative seems to follow the traditional "Bond Girl" formula; however, the way in which Fleming uses this introduction to establish her character starts to set her apart from other Bond heroines. Many critics have discussed the narrative elements that feature systematically in every Bond work.[12] The "Bond Girl" is an indispensable and predictable part of Fleming's text. Indeed, there is little deviation in the language Fleming uses to refer to his female characters, their physical appearance, or their role within the story.[13] For instance, Amis points out how the "circumstances" surrounding the "Bond Girl's" first appearance "are often ritualistic" because if she was "not introduced in a furiously driven car . . . [she] shows a strong tendency to make her debut naked or half-naked. She will not have expected a man to come by then or . . . will have expected exactly that."[14] While the experienced Bond reader would not be surprised at Case's near-nakedness, what stands out is how Fleming positions her character as a strong, independent woman in control of her own body. Honeychile Rider in *Dr. No* and Tatiana Romanova in *From Russia with Love*, for example, are near-naked or naked during their first encounter with Bond. However, Honeychile immediately attempts to cover up parts of her body which signifies her insecurity,[15] while Tatiana Romanova's body "belongs to the State" which denotes her lack of real independence.[16] By emphasizing Case's self-assurance and showing Bond's respect for it and her, Fleming begins to establish a compelling character that readers can admire.

Fleming doesn't present Tiffany Case as Bond's convenient pawn, and, in fact, Bond's increasing esteem for her becomes clearer during their dinner once they reach New York. Thanks to Felix Leiter, Bond now knows that Case was gang-raped when she was sixteen; therefore, when she informs him that she won't be having sex with him, he doesn't interpret her pronouncement as a challenge.[17] Instead, he perceives her as someone who doesn't want to be hurt and with whom he will need to be careful.[18] Moreover, he's starting to actually like her personality.[19] Liking Case is dangerous because developing feelings for her would potentially interfere with his mission. Bond's orders are to work his way up the pipeline of the Spangled Mob's diamond smuggling operation, and, as his handler, she is the first stop. Even so, at the end of their dinner, while Bond realizes that deceiving Case is necessary, he vows never to manipulate her emotionally.[20] This decision highlights how Case will be more than a mere tool or sexual playmate for Bond. Bond's attitude and behavior toward Case evolve the more he gets to know her. At this point, he views her as wounded and fragile, as someone to protect—even from himself. Therefore, his resolution not to seduce her reveals that he is going to be a gentleman rather than a cold-hearted or domineering cad. Thus, Case's complexity provides Fleming with an opportunity to further develop Bond's character.

Bond's ever-evolving reactions to and attitude toward Tiffany Case elevate her to a more equal footing as a potential partner. His admiration continues to build when he next observes her dealing blackjack at the Tiara. Again, Fleming's attention to detail is telling. He writes that Case "snapped the pack with a fluid motion of the hands, broke it and put the two halves flat on the table and executed what appeared to be a faultless Scarne shuffle."[21] As she performs the move a second time and presents Bond with a chance to cut the deck of cards, he admires how she then deals "the difficult single-handed Annulment, one of the hardest gambits in card-sharping."[22] Case has the skills to make dealing cards—not-to-mention cheating with them—look effortless. Fleming establishes Bond's gambling credentials at the beginning of the series in *Casino Royale*; therefore, when Fleming informs readers that Bond recognizes and approves of her skills in executing one of the most challenging tricks in cheating cards, they can trust Bond's assessment. Fleming doesn't leave it there, though. He relates that Case's manipulation of the cards is a masterclass in brilliance that Bond can't help but respect.[23] Confidence and competence are what attract Bond—not merely how she looks in her Western uniform with its short skirt, grey blouse, sombrero, black boots, and nude stockings.[24] Her skills leave such an impression, in fact, that during their return voyage to England, Bond takes the time to ask her how she got to be so good. He tells her that the way she handled the cards was phenomenal and that he believes she could go far with skills like that.[25] Bond readers know that the master spy does not give compliments lightly nor does he cajole as a means of seduction. His sincere admiration emphasizes Case's significance as a "Bond Girl" worthy of respect and distinction.

Furthermore, she proves her worth when she rescues them both from the clutches of the Spangled Mob. After Seraffimo Spang has captured Bond and ordered Wint and Kidd to torture him, Bond becomes aware of Case's effort to help him regain consciousness. She tells him that they need to jump on a handcar to get out of Spectreville in the Nevada desert. Case is the one that encourages him to move. She's the one that helps him to limp along, and she's the one that plans the details of their escape. While they do run out of gas and must deal with Spang's pursuit, they end up victorious because Case keeps Bond focused on getting away and getting to safety. Critics tend to emphasize that it is Case's knowledge about how to use the handcar that places her among such "Bond Girls" as Domino Vitali in *Thunderball* and Kissy Suzuki in *You Only Live Twice* who are given more narrative agency because they save Bond.[26] Yet, Case's resourcefulness extends beyond simply knowing how to use a handcar. Her attention to detail is what helps them to escape because she not only fills the handcar up with gas but also remembers Bond's Beretta. Even when the gas is gone, she's the one who thinks to run down the track and find the branch line. That information gives Bond the idea to divert Spang's train toward its final and deadly destruction. Fleming presents Tiffany Case as capable, brave, and quick on her feet.

It is significant that Fleming makes sure Bond gives Case due credit because it encourages readers to do the same. At the end of the scene, the narrator asserts that even though he is out of it, Bond still has the where-withal to realize that Case is responsible for saving him. If it wasn't for her, he would have wandered around the desert aimlessly until he was overwhelmed by exhaustion and the grueling heat of the sun.[27] Since she saves Bond's life, he perceives her as a teammate on whom he can depend. Her forethought and ability to keep her wits about her contributes to Bond's respect and solidifies her position as a savvy, independent "Bond Girl."

At the end of the novel, after Bond and Case have finally consummated their relationship and survived a last assassination attempt by Wint and Kidd, Bond reflects on how this mission evolved. He recognizes that "he had had luck and three good friends, Felix and Ernie and Tiffany."[28] Word choice matters here. Bond considers Case a "friend" on par with Felix Leiter for whom Bond feels genuine affection and who functions as Bond's partner in multiple novels. That is, Case is no mere damsel in distress. She saves him as much as he saves her, and Fleming draws attention to that by having Bond consider her as more than just a sexual conquest. In addition, the novel concludes with Bond and Case living together and contemplating marriage. Readers only discover at the beginning of the next novel, *From Russia with Love,* that their relationship has ended and that Case has returned to the United States. The fact that Tiffany Case and her relationship with Bond survives beyond one novel highlights her unique position within the "Bond Girl" consortium. Friendship, complexity, resourcefulness, intelligence, and wit are all strengths Fleming gives to his heroine, but that director Guy Hamilton utterly denies her in the film version.

Unfortunately, from the 1956 novel to the 1971 film, Tiffany Case goes from being an asset to a liability. Tony Bennett and Janet Woollacott contend that the Bond films of the 1970s increasingly portrayed "the Bond Girl" as "'excessively independent'" whose "destiny . . . is to meet her come-uppance in her encounter with Bond. The main ideological work thus accomplished in the unfolding of the narrative is that of a 'putting-back-into-place' of women who carry their independence and liberation 'too far' or into 'inappropriate' fields of activity."[29] For Bennett and Woollacott, this "narrative organisation clearly constituted a response . . . to the Women's Liberation movement, fictitiously rolling back the advances of feminism to restore an imaginarily more secure phallocentric conception of gender relations."[30] Hamilton's *Diamonds Are Forever* marks the beginning of this trend.

At times, the movie flirts with the idea of maintaining the independent and resourceful character that Fleming originally created, but a combination of script changes, costuming, and camerawork ultimately deny that possibility. Some critics, as well as Fleming's readers, lament the fact that the Bond film adaptations often leave much to be desired, especially regarding their portrayals of "Bond Girls."[31] The changes that occur with *Diamonds Are Forever* are particularly troubling since the characters of both Tiffany Case and James Bond suffer as a result. Viewers of the 1971 picture—unlike readers of the 1956 novel—are left with a banal bimbo who lacks substance and an overbearing sexist who is happy to knock a woman around if it suits his purpose. Rather than demonstrating how a multifaceted woman can help a man adapt and grow, the movie presents an outdated and regressive gender paradigm.

The first scene in which Tiffany Case appears teases viewers with the idea that this representation will be like Fleming's original by initially presenting her as a strong, confident woman fully in charge of her world.[32] As the scene progresses, however, the movie starts to undermine her power and establish her as simply a trollop that Bond must outwit, seduce, and control. Viewers first glimpse Case's scantily clad backside as she walks into a bedroom (a view that the audience will be *very* familiar with by the end of the film.) Throughout the scene, actress Jill St. John walks around in her underwear and appears as a blond, a brunette, and finally, the red-head she remains. She clearly uses her body as a weapon to establish authority and put Bond in his place, especially when she declares that she doesn't go out of her way to impress underlings.[33] This opening encounter between Bond and Case mirrors Fleming's original. Both versions present Case as a confident and self-assured woman who knows how to use her body as a source of power. Furthermore, unlike in the novel when Case cautiously agrees to meet Bond for dinner after they smuggle the diamonds into the United States, this scene makes it clear that the cinematic Case's near-nakedness does not necessarily connote her potential sexual availability. In fact, St. John's Case immediately shoots down Bond when he asks her to dinner. Her refusal when combined with St. John's costuming is unsettling. As Ulfsdotter explains:

> Given the implications underpinning her image, it takes a minute for the audience to realize that Case is not wearing this particular outfit because she intends to lure Bond into the bedroom, an important signal of her unique standing in the narrative since the audience would be expecting this to happen given that *Diamonds Are Forever* is a Bond film after all. On the contrary, Case remains in control of her identity and her costuming becomes nothing less than a statement of power.[34]

These factors—her confidence, self-possession, and willingness to display her body for power—imply that the screen version of Tiffany Case not only will stay true to Fleming's original but might even surpass her as a strong and independent heroine.

Their first encounter gets more interesting and complicated when she goes to take Bond's fingerprint because it begins the movie's systematic process of destabilizing Case's power. Offering to get him more ice for his drink, Case takes Bond's glass into her bedroom. There, she dusts the glass for a print and takes a picture of it. When the photo's ready, she reveals that she has a machine hidden in her closet which will blow up images and allow her to compare Bond's print to that of the real smuggler, Peter Frank. This moment seems to suggest that Case is a modern woman using technology to her advantage and a potential opponent not to be taken lightly. When Bond realizes that she has taken a copy of his print, however, he smirks, undermining that impression. Afterward, the scene immediately cuts to a phone conversation between Bond and Q during which Bond expresses his admiration for Q's cleverness in coming up with a way to outsmart the machine and, consequently, Case. As in the novel, the movie audience is encouraged to identify with Bond as the leading male protagonist, but the camera angle compounds this identification process by capturing the scene from Bond's perspective. As Laura Mulvey argues, when a "woman performs within the narrative, the gaze of the spectator and that of the male characters in the film are neatly combined without breaking narrative verisimilitude."[35] Thus, Bond's assessment of and reactions to Case influence how audiences respond to her too. In allowing Bond (with the help of Q) to appear the victor in their first encounter, the picture encourages viewers to perceive Tiffany Case not as a potential partner for Bond, but rather as merely a means to an end, a woman who couldn't hope to compete with the cleverness of her more cunning male counterpart. This scene further reminds us that, as a man, it is Bond who has more access to the resources and institutions of power.[36]

Tiffany Case's next major appearance in the film not only marks another sharp contrast between the novel and picture but also continues to diminish her capability within the narrative. More importantly, it viciously undercuts the impression that St. John's Case will be an independent, professional woman immune to Bond's sexual allure. While the literary Case does sleep with Bond at the end of the novel, she is never portrayed as a floozy. The same cannot be said for her character in the film. For example, the next time that Bond and Case meet is after successfully smuggling the diamonds into the United States, in his hotel room. As part of his investigation into the diamond smuggling ring, Bond has replaced the real diamonds with fake ones. In the hopes of finding out where the real diamonds are, Case proposes that they partner up . . . to steal the diamonds for themselves. Since this is a Bond movie, the best place to propose such a partnership is, of course, in a bedroom; conse-quently, St John appears wearing only a negligée and is carefully, strate-gically, posed in the center of the bed. She's clearly on display for Bond's, and the viewer's, pleasure. With Case maintaining her "come hither" pose, she and Bond begin to play a cat and mouse game. As Bond strips, he confidently admits that he obviously realizes that she simply wants to know where the diamonds are, etc. This implies that while he has no intention of providing her with this information, he still assumes—cor-rectly as it turns out—that she will nevertheless give him full access to her body. Case makes herself visually and sexually available because in a heteronormative male-dominated world, her body seems to be the most reliable way to get what she wants. According to Laura Mulvey, both men and women are conditioned to understand how this process works:

> In a world ordered by sexual imbalance, the determining male gaze projects its phantasy onto the female figure, which is styled according-ly. In their traditional exhibitionist role women are simultaneously looked at and displayed, with their appearance coded for strong visual and erotic impact so that they can be said to connote *to-be-looked-at-ness*.[37]

Thus, the pose, the negligée, and the naked shoulders, are all signs that enable Bond and the audience to know what will happen without having to be told. Jill St. John's body, her *"to-be-looked-at-ness,"* is all that they need.

While it is part of the cinematic Bond formula, the commencement of Bond and Case's sexual relationship damages Case's character.[38] From the beginning, Fleming's works drew critical attention because of how he depicted human sexuality. Some critics considered the sexual content immoral and indecent, while others saw it as signifying the dawn of a new era when both men and women could enjoy more sexual freedom without censure.[39] Nevertheless, for women in 1956, in 1971, and still today there's perhaps a fine line between coming across as sexually liber-ated and sexually debased. Fleming carefully positions his original hero-ine into the first category because she and Bond have sex before marriage but only after they have fallen in love, whereas the cinematic version falls into the second category because Case uses her body without compunc-tion to manipulate Bond to get what she wants. Such a narrative shift highlights how the film's problematic gender paradigm operates. The movie bombards audiences with example after example of Case acting as an opportunistic floozy; therefore, how could they read her as anything else? The post-coitus scene between Case and Bond illustrates this point. Once Case and Bond start to converse, she tries to warn him that he is going to need to divulge the location of the diamonds because her bosses will not take no for an answer.[40] Therefore, she's the one to propose a 50/50 split. Bond has the diamonds, but she can get them out of the city. She then suggests that they run away together. Since Bond's being watched, she offers to get the diamonds. From her facial expressions and the smile that she gives Bond behind his head, it is clear that she thinks she's being cunning and pulling one over on him. However, viewers quickly learn that just the opposite is true.

The subsequent scene immediately shows that instead of using Bond, Case is the one being used. As the camera pans away from Case walking the floor of the circus waiting to pick up the real diamonds, the focus shifts to Bond and Felix Leiter sitting in a room spying on her. When Leiter asks Bond why he's continuing to go through with the plan Case suggested, Bond states that the odds are even because it will be Case's love of money against his irresistible charisma.[41] Here, Bond reveals that he considers Tiffany Case as just a thief: nothing more, nothing less. Again, as opposed to the novel, there's no indication that Bond feels any respect or admiration for her. She is simply a woman to be used and kept under control.

The power imbalance in Bond and Case's relationship increases significantly in the following scene. After easily slipping away from the incredibly inept CIA agents who are supposed to tail her once she has the diamonds, Case finds Bond at her house hanging out by the pool. Immediately, he begins to simply give orders. In fact, almost every verbal exchange between the two now consists of him telling her what to do or making demands. The scene opens with Bond commanding her to remove some clothing and relax.[42] There's no salutation, no real attempt to be personable or particularly courteous. There's just an imperative. The scene quickly comes to a head once Case realizes that the dead woman floating in the pool is supposed to be her, and Bond begins his interrogation. When she delays in responding to his demand that she disclose her connection, he slaps her with his tie. He then repeats the question. She continues to ask for more information about him, but he's the only one that gets to ask questions and to receive answers. He's clearly in charge physically and verbally. There are no repercussions for his willingness to use violence to get what he wants either.

By this point, the picture has firmly established Case as a woman that acts solely in her own self-interest. Bond knows her well enough to realize that she's no martyr; therefore, he does not have to give her a real choice: she can either do what he says or face the violent consequences. Bond and the viewer both know that she won't put up a fight and will give him what he wants. It doesn't matter if it's information, her car, or her body. This moment puts Bond's dominance front and center and effectively squashes any idea that there would be a connection between the two based on a sense of teamwork, let alone respect. It also signifies that the movie has now utterly and irrevocably abandoned any sense of fidelity to either the characters or how their relationship works within Fleming's original text.

Just as the action on Blofeld's oil rig serves as the film's climax, it also functions as the culmination of the devaluation of Tiffany Case's character. Throughout each scene, the objectification of Tiffany Case reaches its apex. She appears for the first time in a purple bikini. Her costuming matters here because having St. John wear a small bikini turns her character "into an object of the male gaze by Blofeld . . . despite the fact that she is [about to be] involved in an action sequence."[43] Furthermore, this costuming decision "works to limit her narrative agency since she can do little to help Bond fight the bad guys wearing such a skimpy outfit."[44] As opposed to previous scenes in which the character is scantily clad, her near-nakedness "now connotes her own state of powerlessness."[45] Clothing (or the lack thereof) is just the opening gambit in the character's increasing debasement during this action sequence.

The script, costuming, and camerawork all come together to discredit her. After viewers first glimpse Case sunbathing on the deck of the oil rig, they see her next when she enters Blofeld's cabin office. Bond and Blofeld are the primary speakers. Case is simply an object for them to talk about—not talk to. In response to Bond's question about how Blofeld lured Case to his rig, Blofeld says that Case's approach to her current situation is quite rational because "Like any sensible animal, she is only threatening when she's threatened."[46] Bond then tells Blofeld that he seems to hold "all the aces. Right down to Dragon Lady over here."[47] Case's silence signifies her insignificance, for previously she was incredibly talkative and did not hesitate to share her opinions (regardless of whether anyone was interested in them). Robert A. Caplan concurs when he states that the "'animal' is . . . relatively quiet, as if she has been muzzled, a clear and stark contrast to her previous obnoxious loquaciousness."[48] Thus, she no longer speaks or acts. After this male-dominated riposte concludes, Blofeld proposes that he and Bond tour the facilities so that Bond can fully appreciate Blofeld's genius in using the diamonds in the satellite to hold the world hostage. At this point, Case gets up from the couch on which she was lounging, grabs the dummy cassette case, and holds it behind her back.

The screen shot here is worth discussing because it marks the moment when the camerawork becomes overtly sexist and demeaning. Case and Bond are standing next to each other with their backs to the camera. He's dressed in a black suit, and no real details of his body are discernible. Case's back is visible as well; but, since she's wearing a bikini, much more of her body is on display. Only Blofeld faces the camera; consequently, the audience can observe his face and most of his body. The profile of an anonymous guard fills the right side of the screen. Since Case is in the foreground, viewers can observe more of her; therefore, their gaze is drawn to her gesture when she taps Bond's backside to give him the tape. On the one hand, Case's attempt to exert some agency and help Bond sabotage Blofeld suggests that she is not double-crossing Bond like he believes. Yet, the camerawork problematizes this reading. By focusing so much on her scantily clad body, especially her bottom, the camera encourages the audience to view her as just that—a body, an object. Theoretically, the camera functions as a third person objective witness as the action unfolds. However, the cinematic gaze is rigidly controlled and biased. This control directs not only what the audience literally sees but also how they understand the story being told and a performer's role within it. Moments like these early scenes on the oil rig demonstrate how "Going far beyond highlighting a woman's to-be-looked-at-ness, cinema builds the way she is to be looked at into spectacle itself."[49] The camera reveals that what matters is how Tiffany Case looks—not what she thinks, what she has to say, or how she acts. This attention to her body, particularly her buttocks, only gets more pronounced in the scenes that follow.

Word choice and camerawork continue to demean Case when she joins Bond and Blofeld in the control room. While they were still in his office, Blofeld gave Case permission to join his tour with Bond on the condition that she wear more clothes because, as he informs Bond, he does not want his crew distracted by "a pretty body."[50] In response to his injunction, she has simply covered up her shoulders and arms. As Bond gets ready to be put in a holding cell, he comes up to Case and says, "Bitch."[51] This insult serves as a pretext for Bond to approach Case, stick the cassette tape down her bikini bottom, and tell her that her troubles "are all behind" her.[52] Viewers are encouraged to interpret this interlude as merely a performance for Blofeld. They know that Bond and Case are supposedly working together to thwart Blofeld's diabolical plans. Yet, Case has now been called an "animal," a "Dragon Lady," a "body," and a "bitch." Bond will soon call her a "stupid twit" once she reveals that she accidentally put the real tape back in the machine. The men's language clearly demonstrates their lack of respect for her. In addition, the camerawork continues to reinforce the idea that Case lacks any worth beyond her figure. During this short scene, there's a close-up on her bottom as Bond eases the cassette case into her bikini and another close-up once the tape is firmly in place. So far, there have been three close-ups on Jill St. John's bikini-clad derriere.

By repeatedly showing Tiffany Case as an easily outwitted and inept ditz who gets in the way and often needs rescuing, the film negates any power she may have ever possessed. Viewers witness her failure every time she attempts to exert some form of agency. The camera never gives the audience a chance to perceive Case positively. All of this makes her last scene in the control room noteworthy. In an effort to correct her mistake, Case goes up to the satellite control machine and leans in for a closer look. For the fourth time now, the focus is on St. John's bottom. Immediately, the camera pans to Blofeld's face. The audience watches Blofeld as he watches Case. He then states, "Tiffany, my dear, [pause] we're showing a bit more cheek than usual aren't we?"[53] During Charles Gray's pause, the camera obviously zooms in on St. John's behind *for the fifth time!* The camera stays focused on her backside until Gray is done delivering the line. Once he's finished, the camera cuts up to St. John's face, and she gives a slow smile. After she returns the tape to Blofeld, he states, "What a pity. And, such nice cheeks, too. If only they were brains."[54] Both Bond and Blofeld treat Tiffany Case as a brainless bimbo. How can the audience avoid doing the same?

Interestingly, viewers do not actually know for certain whether or not she succeeded in switching the tapes back because the camera stays focused on Blofled's face while he watches her. Based on how Bond and Blofeld and even the camera have treated Case throughout the film, however, audiences are led to assume that she failed. She has clearly failed at everything else; therefore, why would she do differently at this moment? The scene's ambiguity ultimately continues to undermine her power. By not allowing viewers to see what she did (or didn't) do, the director denies her an equal role as a protagonist. Her success in switching the tapes would negate the need for the final violent destruction of the oil rig because the satellite would no longer work. But, she cannot be the one who saves the day. The only way to minimize the threat of Tiffany Case proving everyone wrong is to deny her any witnesses.

This was Case's last opportunity to redeem herself. It was the one moment where she could contradict the story that Bond and Blofeld were creating for and about her. However, Hamilton denies her the chance to be an equal player in helping to save the world. Her role is essentially over now. Viewers watch as she ineptly fires an assault rifle and jiggles her way off the oil rig platform, and they watch as she helplessly looks on while Bond is attacked by Wint and Kidd during their third unsuccessful assassination attempt. The fact that she has the last words is irrelevant because the film has made sure she ends up properly in her place—in the arms of Bond.

At the box office, *Diamonds Are Forever* did quite well. Audiences welcomed the return of Sean Connery and found the picture enjoyable. Curiously enough, many reviewers commended the movie for its contemporary feel: "While some critics thought the film provided escapism from the problems of the present," Chapman states, "others argued that *Diamonds Are Forever* had caught the mood of American cinema-goers not because it offered a nostalgic escape into the past but because it offered a commentary on contemporary issues and concerns."[55] Andrew Sarris in the *Village Voice*, for instance, claims that the picture's "major positive virtues . . . seem to originate from the contemporaneous screenplay . . . which manages to relate to recent headlines without being oppressively relevant."[56] Sarris specifically highlights "the ecological nightmare of oil rigs off the California coast, spoofs of moon men and their dune buggies, Russian nuclear subs and Red Chinese nuclear missiles . . . jokes about the dullness of Kansas as a nuclear target and about the deterioration of Great Britain into a third-rate power."[57] Tellingly, nowhere in his review does Sarris discuss Tiffany Case. While the references Sarris spotlights were current in 1971 and helped give the movie a modern feel, the same cannot be said about how it presents Tiffany Case. The trajectory of her character is anything but modern, updated, or progressive. Besides, it makes the picture less appealing. James Hovey states it well: "When Bond seduces women who are not his equals . . . things are not nearly so interesting" as is the case with "Tiffany Case in *Diamonds Are Forever*, who offers an interesting challenge to Bond" at first but then "becomes far less compelling—as does the film—when she turns into a plaintive, lobotomized bimbo running around an oil rig in a bikini."[58] In other words, characters and movie audiences all suffer when a Bond film perpetuates outdated gender dynamics.

In the novel, Ian Fleming presents Tiffany Case as a strong counterpart for Bond. Unfortunately, in the film, Guy Hamilton depicts her as a ludicrous and ineffectual ass, an ass to enjoy looking at, or a pain in the ass to be controlled. By looking to the past, the director and producers weakened the franchise by flattening the main female character. This trend would continue until 1977's *The Spy Who Loved Me*, when audiences can finally enjoy a strong female character in Anya Amasova who is not only cunning and competent in her own right but far sexier because she isn't just a throw-away bimbo. No doubt, James Bond is the character that keeps fans returning to the books and the movies time and time again, but he is at his best when confronted by villains and women alike who challenge him, force him to adapt, and, yes, grow.

NOTES

1. Tony Bennett and Janet Woollacott, *Bond and Beyond: The Political Career of a Popular Hero* (New York: Methuen, Inc., 1987), 14.

2. After learning that a woman would be assisting him in *Casino Royale*, Bond (in)famously thinks, "Women were for recreation. On a job, they got in the way and fogged things up with sex and hurt feelings and all the emotional baggage they carried around. One had to look out for them and take care of them" (Ian Fleming, *Casino Royale* [New York: Penguin Books, 2002], 27).

3. For further discussion of the traditional gender paradigm in Fleming's novels see, Bennett and Woollacott, *Bond and Beyond*; Jeremy Black, *The Politics of James Bond: From Fleming's Novels to the Big Screen* (Lincoln: University of Nebraska Press, 2005), 105–11; Christine Bold, "Under the Very Skirts of Britannia': Re-reading Women in the James Bond Novels," in *The James Bond Phenomenon: A Critical Reader*, ed. Christoph Linder, 2nd ed. (Manchester: Manchester University Press, 2009), 205–19; Robert A. Caplan, *Shaken & Stirred: The Feminism of the James Bond Films* (Bloomington, IN: Xlibris Corporation, 2010); James Chapman, *Licence to Thrill: A Cultural History of the James Bond Films*, 2nd ed. (London: I.B. Tauris, 2007), 22–48; James Chapman, "'Women Were for Recreation': The Gender Politics of Ian Fleming's James Bond," in *For His Eyes Only: The Women of James Bond*, ed. Lisa Funnell (London: Wallflower Press, 2015), 9–17; Michael Denning, *Cover Stories: Narrative and Ideology in the British Spy Thriller*,

(London: Routledge & Kegan Paul, 1987), 107–13; and Ben Macintyre, *For Your Eyes Only: Ian Fleming + James Bond* (London: Bloomsbury, 2008), 121–37.

4. Kingsley Amis, *The James Bond Dossier* (New York: The New American Library, 1965), 46.

5. For further discussion of "Bond Girls" helping Bond, see Amis, *Dossier*, 43–51; Bold, "Re-reading Women," 207–8; Caplan, *Shaken & Stirred*, 53; Chapman, *Licence*, 32; and Chapman, "Gender Politics," 15.

6. For more detail about how Fleming's contemporaries compared the literary "Bond Girls" to their cinematic counterparts, see Bennett and Woollacott, *Bond and Beyond*, 143–44 and Macintyre, *For Your Eyes*, 124. For more recent analytical comparisons, refer to Chapman, "Gender Politics," 15; James Hovey, "Lesbian Bondage, or Why Dykes Like 007," in *Ian Fleming & James Bond: The Cultural Politics of 007*, ed. Edward P. Comentale, Stephen Watt, and Skip William (Bloomington: Indiana University Press, 2005), 52; Boel Ulfsdotter, "The Bond Girl Who Is Not There: The Tiffany Case," in *For His Eyes Only: The Women of James Bond*, ed. Lisa Funnell (London: Wallflower Press, 2015), 18–27; and Janet Woollacott, "The James Bond Films: Conditions of Production," in *The James Bond Phenomenon: A Critical Reader*, ed. Christoph Linder, 2nd ed. (Manchester: Manchester University Press, 2009), 128–29.

7. Chapman, "Gender Politics," 9.

8. Ian Fleming, *Diamonds Are Forever* (Las Vegas: Thomas & Mercer, 2012), 33.

9. Fleming, *Diamonds Are Forever*, 33.

10. Ulfsdotter, "The Tiffany Case," 21.

11. Fleming, *Diamonds Are Forever*, 35.

12. For extensive analysis of Fleming's Bond formula, refer to Amis, *Dossier*; Bennett and Woollacott, *Bond and Beyond*, 44–142; and Umberto Eco, "Narrative Structures in Fleming," in *The James Bond Phenomenon: A Critical Reader*, ed. Christoph Linder, 2nd ed. (Manchester: Manchester University Press), 34–55.

13. For discussion of Fleming's "Bond Girl" formula specifically, see Amis, *Dossier*, 43–51; Bennett and Woollacott, *Bond and Beyond*, 114–27; and Eco, "Narrative," 44.

14. Amis, *Dossier*, 44.

15. Ian Fleming, *Doctor No* (New York: Penguin Books, 2002), 79.

16. Ian Fleming, *From Russia with Love* (New York: Penguin Books, 2003), 82.

17. Fleming, *Diamonds Are Forever*, 71.

18. Fleming, *Diamonds Are Forever*, 73.

19. Fleming, *Diamonds Are Forever*, 74.

20. Fleming, *Diamonds Are Forever*, 77.

21. Fleming, *Diamonds Are Forever*, 145.

22. Fleming, *Diamonds Are Forever*, 145.

23. Fleming, *Diamonds Are Forever*, 146.

24. Fleming, *Diamonds Are Forever*, 144.

25. Fleming, *Diamonds Are Forever*, 198.

26. For further discussion of how Tiffany Case fits amongst "Bond Girls" such as Domino Vitali and Kissy Suzuki, see Bold, "Re-reading," 207–8; Chapman, *Licence*, 32; and Chapman, "Gender Politics," 15.

27. Fleming, *Diamonds Are Forever*, 184.

28. Fleming, *Diamonds Are Forever*, 228.

29. Bennett and Woollacott, *Bond and Beyond*, 39.

30. Bennett and Woollacott, *Bond and Beyond*, 39.

31. As Ben Macintyre explains, "Readers who liked the Bond women in the books looked askance at the parade of almost characterless beauties being loved and left in each successive film" (*For Your Eyes*, 124).

32. *Diamonds Are Forever*, directed by Guy Hamilton, performances by Sean Connery, Jill St. John, and Charles Gray, Ultimate Edition, (1971; Beverly Hills and Los Angeles: MGM and Twentieth Century Fox, 2006), DVD.

33. *Diamonds Are Forever* (1971).

34. Ulfsdotter, "The Tiffany Case," 24.

35. Laura Mulvey, *Visual and Other Pleasures*, 2nd ed. (London: Palgrave Macmillan, 2009), 20.

36. Dennis W. Allen provides insight into how technology functions within this scene by stating, "Because *Diamonds* omits the standard expository scene with Q so that we encounter many of the gadgets for the first time as Bond uses them, an inherent principle of Bondian technology is clearer here than it usually is: Bond always has precisely the device necessary for the situation he encounters even if there was no way of knowing in advance that such a situation would occur. Thus, although Tiffany's fingerprint scanner comes as a surprise, it turns out that the fake fingerprints Q thought 'might come in handy' are in fact exactly what the situation requires." ("'Alimentary, Dr. Leiter': Anal Anxiety in *Diamonds Are Forever*," in *Ian Fleming & James Bond: The Cultural Politics of 007*, ed. Edward P. Comentale, Stephen Watt, and Skip Willman, (Bloomington: Indiana University Press, 2005), 34).

37. Mulvey, *Visual*, 19.

38. The length of time the camera spends focusing on St. John's seduction pose illustrates Mulvey's point that the "presence of woman is an indispensable element of spectacle in normal narrative film, yet her visual presence tends to work against the development of a story-line, to freeze the flow of action in moments of erotic contemplation" (*Visual*, 19–20).

39. For a discussion of contemporary critical responses to Fleming's novels (especially the harsh critiques by Bernard Bergonzi and Paul Johnson in 1958), see Chapman, *Licence*, 24–29; Chapman, "Gender Politics," 10; and Macintyre, *For Your Eyes*, 135. Denning offers a historical analysis of the prominence of sex in the Bond novels (*Cover*, 107–13); however, he contends that the books exemplify an early form of "mass pornography" with Bond representing a "voyeur" (*Cover*, 110). Bennett and Woollacott (in *Bond and Beyond*) as well as Chapman (in *Licence*) provide a historical and more favorable explanation of how Fleming's novels anticipated the changing sexual mores of the 1950s and 1960s.

40. *Diamonds Are Forever* (1971).

41. *Diamonds Are Forever* (1971).

42. *Diamonds Are Forever* (1971).

43. Ulfsdotter, "The Tiffany Case," 24.

44. Ulfsdotter, "The Tiffany Case," 24.

45. Ulfsdotter, "The Tiffany Case," 24.

46. *Diamonds Are Forever* (1971).

47. *Diamonds Are Forever* (1971).

48. Caplan, *Shaken & Stirred*, 273.

49. Mulvey, *Visual*, 26.

50. *Diamonds Are Forever* (1971).

51. *Diamonds Are Forever* (1971).

52. *Diamonds Are Forever* (1971).

53. *Diamonds Are Forever* (1971).

54. *Diamonds Are Forever* (1971).

55. Chapman, *Licence*, 135.

56. Andrew Sarris. "Films in Focus," *Village Voice*, December 16, 1971, 79.

57. Sarris. "Films in Focus," 79.

58. Hovey, "Lesbian Bondage," 52.

BIBLIOGRAPHY

Allen, Dennis W. "'Alimentary, Dr. Leiter': Anal Anxiety in *Diamonds Are Forever*." In *Ian Fleming & James Bond: The Cultural Politics of 007*, edited by Edward P. Comentale, Stephen Watt, and Skip Willman, 24–41. Bloomington: Indiana University Press, 2005.

Amis, Kingsley. *The James Bond Dossier*. New York: The New American Library, 1965.

Bennett, Tony, and Janet Woollacott. *Bond and Beyond: The Political Career of a Popular Hero.* New York: Methuen, Inc., 1987.

Black, Jeremy. *The Politics of James Bond: From Fleming's Novels to the Big Screen.* Lincoln: University of Nebraska Press, 2005.

Bold, Christine. "'Under the Very Skirts of Britannia': Re-reading Women in the James Bond Novels." In *The James Bond Phenomenon: A Critical Reader,* edited by Christoph Linder, 2nd ed., 205–19. Manchester: Manchester University Press, 2009.

Caplan, Robert A. *Shaken & Stirred: The Feminism of James Bond.* Bloomington, IN: Xlibris Corporation, 2010.

Chapman, James. *Licence to Thrill: A Cultural History of the James Bond Films.* 2nd ed. London: I.B. Tauris, 2007.

———. "'Women Were for Recreation': The Gender Politics of Ian Fleming's James Bond." In *For His Eyes Only: The Women of James Bond,* edited by Lisa Funnell, 9–17. London: Wallflower Press, 2015.

Denning, Michael, *Cover Stories: Narrative and Ideology in the British Spy Thriller.* London: Routledge & Kegan Paul, 1987.

Diamonds Are Forever. Directed by Guy Hamilton, performances by Sean Connery, Jill St. John, and Charles Gray. 1971. Beverly Hills and Los Angeles: MGM and Twentieth Century Fox, 2006, DVD, Ultimate Edition.

Eco, Umberto. "Narrative Structures in Fleming." In *The James Bond Phenomenon: A Critical Reader,* edited by Christoph Linder, 2nd ed., 34–55. Manchester: Manchester University Press, 2009.

Fleming, Ian. *Casino Royale.* 1953. New York: Penguin Books, 2002.

———. *Diamonds Are Forever.* 1956. Las Vegas: Thomas & Mercer, 2012.

———. *Doctor No.* 1958. New York: Penguin Books, 2002.

———. *From Russia with Love.* 1957. New York: Penguin Books, 2003.

Hovey, James. "Lesbian Bondage, or Why Dykes Like 007." In *Ian Fleming & James Bond: The Cultural Politics of 007,* edited by Edward P. Comentale, Stephen Watt, and Skip Willman, 42–54. Bloomington: Indiana University Press, 2005.

Macintyre, Ben. *For Your Eyes Only: Ian Fleming + James Bond.* London: Bloomsbury, 2008.

Mulvey, Laura. *Visual and Other Pleasures.* 2nd ed. London: Palgrave Macmillan, 2009.

Sarris, Andrew. "Films in Focus." *Village Voice,* December 16, 1971, 79.

Ulfsdotter, Boel. "The Bond Girl Who Is Not There: The Tiffany Case." In *For His Eyes Only: The Women of James Bond,* edited by Lisa Funnell, 18–27. London: Wallflower Press, 2015.

Woollacott, Janet. "The James Bond Films: Conditions of Production." In *The James Bond Phenomenon: A Critical Reader,* edited by Christoph Linder, 2nd ed., 117–35. Manchester: Manchester University Press, 2009.

SEVEN

The Eyes of Tiffany Case—And What They Tell about Ian Fleming's First Successful Female Character

Ihsan Amanatullah

BUILDING A BETTER HEROINE

Tiffany Case is Ian Fleming's first female character with a genuine personality; the female protagonists of his previous books are like cardboard next to her. *Casino Royale*'s Vesper Lynd was found "rather insipid" by Fleming's most prominent critical champion, Kingsley Amis.[1] Solitaire from *Live and Let Die* was little more than Bond's "personal prize"[2] or to be more specific, "the prize at his feet."[3] *Moonraker*'s Gala Brand held more promise in her initial disapproval of Bond but displayed little else in characterization.

This chapter argues that Tiffany Case's comparatively high level of characterization stems from three factors: (i) her emotional volatility, derived from a formative sexual trauma that causes an avoidance of relationships that Bond must overcome by proving his commitment; (ii) her origins in the American hard-boiled tradition, and how she inherits its worldliness and wisecracking humor; (iii) her increased agency, shown through the primacy of her gaze, which disrupts the character's objectification by drawing attention to her emotional needs and desires. After exploring these factors—and their implications and critical reception—this chapter will attempt to explain why Fleming's improved female protagonist, despite embarking on the road to marriage at the end of *Diamonds Are Forever*, disappears before the start of Bond's next adventure.

Understanding Case's characterization requires understanding her history of victimization and innocence. Felix Leiter insists to Bond that Case is an inherently good woman whose chances of staying away from the mob were slim from the cradle onward.[4] And as *she* tells Bond, even her name stems from an act of parental deprivation and patriarchal misconduct. Case's father was so disappointed she wasn't a boy that he left the family, giving her mother a thousand dollars and a powder case from Tiffany's. As if to re-affirm his masculinity, he joined the Marines to fight in World War II.[5] The absence of a father proves disastrous for the Cases: Tiffany's mother provides for them by running a successful brothel in San Francisco, but when she fails to pay protection money the local mob wrecks the establishment and gang rapes the sixteen-year-old Case, who runs away the next day. But after a round of transitory jobs, depression, and alcoholism, Case returns to live with her retired mother. Fleeing again, she ends up in Reno and attracts the attention of Seraffimo Spang, who initiates her into the Spangled Mob. Despite her membership, she remains—in the eyes of Leiter, Bond, and Fleming—the innocent victim of over-determined circumstance. Leiter insists she had no chance after her experience with the gang in San Francisco.[6]

Leiter adds that since her trauma Case has unsurprisingly vowed to have nothing to do with men.[7] She is attracted to Bond but fears that letting down her defenses (her sense of humor and instinctive avoidance of romance) will result in further trauma, so she displays a pattern of attraction and repulsion toward Bond, most memorably shown after Bond and Case's dinner at 21 in New York. In his attempt to find out more about the Spangled Mob, Bond asks too many questions and upsets his date, who is sick of working for crooks. He escorts Case back to her hotel room; at her door she switches from the start of an angry speech to a half-embrace, telling Bond to look after himself, because she doesn't want to lose him. She kisses him with a tenderness that is "almost without sex" but then breaks away and slams the door, after fiercely telling him to get away from her.[8] To enjoy closer relations of any kind with Case, Bond must show her that he can return the almost sex-free tenderness in her kiss.

Case's past and her present emotional dilemma make her the first character to fulfill the "general scheme" that Umberto Eco detects in Fleming's female protagonists: "the girl is beautiful and good" but "has been made frigid and unhappy by severe trials suffered in adolescence." These trials have "conditioned her to the service of the Villain," but "through meeting Bond she appreciates her positive human chances." In Eco's scheme, Bond goes on to possess but ultimately lose her.[9]

Tony Bennett and Janet Woollacott's incisive and influential study *Bond and Beyond* proceeds further by arguing that the standard female protagonist of a Bond novel furnishes "a source of narrative tension" in the form of "a troubling enigma which Bond must resolve," a "disturbing 'out-of-placeness.'"[10] In *Diamonds Are Forever* Case's out-of-placeness is her neurosis, which takes the form of mood swings between attraction and repulsion. This neurosis, caused by her sexual trauma, has left her with an insufficient or "faultily positioned" sexuality. Case is out of the place she would occupy "in a patriarchal order; defined, socially and sexually, in relation to men."[11]

For Bennett and Woollacott, "The absence of men" in the life of Fleming's typical female protagonist—whether through "the lack of a father" or "the overburdening presence of men of the wrong sort (in the form of rape)"—is responsible for "her skewed positioning in relation to traditional, patriarchal orderings of sexual difference." This accounts for her similarly "skewed positioning in the ideological divide between good and evil"—her employment by the villain. "Lacking a clear anchorage in the ideological ordering of the relationships between men and women," leaves her "insufficiently attuned to the distinction between right and wrong."[12] Therefore Bond must use his prowess to sexually readjust the heroine, since her sexuality is "basically 'on the right lines'" but "significantly awry," since it has yet to be fully formed.[13] His efforts will realign her "within the patriarchal sexual order," thereby "putting her back into place beneath him (both literally and metaphorically)."[14]

There is much to be said for how effectively this theoretical framework fits Tiffany Case, especially in light of Fleming's profound sexism. Yet *Diamonds Are Forever* fails to conform to critical generalizations regarding Fleming's fictional treatment of women, since Case significantly deviates enough from a generalized profile to become a genuine individual. Re-reading the text makes it possible to argue that, before meeting Bond, Case already had a place in a patriarchal order defined in relation to men and was already attuned to the distinction between right and wrong. When Bond enters her life he affords her an opportunity to exercise her agency by planning and enacting an escape from the Spangled Mob, whose wrongness Case has abhorred from the start. To flesh out these assertions, a detour through Fleming's conception of America is in order, since it ultimately accounts for the second factor in Case's heightened level of characterization.

GOOD AMERICANS, BAD AMERICANS, REAL AMERICANS, FAKE AMERICANS

In Fleming's Anglo-supremacist world, Case's Anglo-Saxon name and ethnicity makes her a "genuine" American—unlike her gangster bosses, who Bond does not consider American. With racist contempt, he describes them as lazy Italians in monogrammed shirts who spend their time eating spaghetti.[15] Fortunately, Case works for gangsters but remains a "genuine" civilized American, despite having roots in the

American hard-boiled tradition and its notorious femme fatales. There is no doubt of this tradition's influence on Fleming—asked by an interviewer to name his influences, he offered the names of "two splendid American writers, the great masters of the modern thriller, Dashiell Hammett and Raymond Chandler. I was influenced by these writers, by their extremely good style and the breadth and ingeniousness of their stories."[16]

Diamonds Are Forever repeatedly tips its hat to the Hammett/Chandler tradition. Felix Leiter moves from the CIA to Pinkerton's and refers to himself as a private detective.[17] A more prominent hat-tip is Tiffany Case's wisecracking, hard-boiled dialogue, to which can be applied the phrase Elizabeth Ladenson uses to categorize the speech of *Goldfinger's* Pussy Galore: the "American criminal-class idiom of the 'hardboiled' variety, a type associated with the North East, Chicago, or California, as in gangster films and the novels of Raymond Chandler or Dashiell Hammett."[18] In an essay recalling his friendship with Chandler, Fleming praised this idiomatic style of character speech above all else in Chandler's novels: "What holds the books together," he proclaimed, "is the dialogue. There is a throw-away, down-beat quality about Chandler's dialogue, whether wisecracking or not, that takes one happily through chapter after chapter in which there is no more action than Philip Marlowe driving his car or talking to his girl."[19]

Diamonds Are Forever emulates this quality through Case's dialogue, which takes one through chapters in which there is no more action than Bond and Case talking, most notably during dinner at 21 and onboard the *Queen Elizabeth*. Furthermore, the lion's share of wisecracking dialogue belongs to Case. Her assertive wisecracks have the slangy and aggressively impudent characteristics of the hard-boiled/Chandlerian idiom. When Bond asks if he can smoke, she tells him to go ahead if he wants to die that way.[20] After Bond reveals his real name, she mockingly asks why he didn't pick Joe Doe.[21] Drinking cocktails during their first date, Case asks if Bond intends to order dinner or hopes she'll pass out beforehand. So far, she adds, their date has been life with a lower-case l.[22] But despite her dialogue Case significantly departs from the hard-boiled tradition by inverting the stereotype of the femme fatale so memorably used by Chandler in *The Big Sleep, Farewell, My Lovely,* and *The Little Sister,* and by Hammett in *The Maltese Falcon.* The conventional femme fatale is a physically attractive ally who is ultimately revealed as evil and sexually threatening; Case is a physically attractive criminal who is ultimately revealed as good and sexually inexperienced. She has been turned toward crime by a personal trauma caused by American lawlessness and gangs—she is a product of American corruption but not truly corrupt.

Fleming's anti-Americanism is dealt with elsewhere in this volume, but it's necessary to briefly show how thoroughly corrupt Fleming's America is. As Leiter (one of the few good Americans) says, its gangsters have outlasted Al Capone and evolved. Instead of running liquor they run state governments, as in Nevada.[23] The gangsters inherit a deep legacy of American lawlessness. Taxi driver Ernie Cureo tells Bond the Las Vegas casinos were built with mob money, and he affirms the continuity between the mobsters and the Wild West, the heart of mythic America. The Last Frontier casino has a fake Western town, while the Tiara is decked out with staff in Western costumes. Cureo says Serrafimo Spang, the Tiara's owner, is crazily obsessed with the Old West, and has even bought himself a ghost town.[24]

That town is Spectreville, an old silver camp adorned with Western clichés ranging from a Wells Fargo bank to a saloon called The Pink Garter. A visiting Bond compares the setting to that of a lavishly made Western.[25] Spang even dresses in full Western costume, with leather chaps and revolvers in thigh holsters. He impresses even Bond, who thinks Spang should have looked silly and yet does not.[26] Bond had earlier dismissed Spang's kind as Italians pretending to be Americans, but in this moment Spang is fully American. He has become an avatar of the old and new West, inheritor of its ghost towns and casino boss of its boomtowns. He controls a crime network stretching from Vegas to Saratoga to New York (and London). So the Wild West lives on in American gangs; the American heritage of lawlessness continues as corruption.

In Fleming's eyes, organized crime is inseparable from America and perhaps its metonym. He presents Case's trauma as a direct result of America's corruption: though her mother paid protection money to the police, they failed to lift a finger against the mob, which enforced its own patriarchal order by raping Case. Her subordination to this sexually exploitive order results from her employment within it. The Spangled Mob outdoes the San Francisco one by directly running an organized prostitution ring.[27] Case even owes her job to the sexual interest of the Spangled Mob's boss—Spang was so aroused by her refusal to sleep with him that he decided to employ her.[28] That he did so to gradually overcome her resistance is indicated by the champagne and supper for two onboard his private train. Spang also makes Case wear costumes that objectify her as a Western pinup girl. In Spectreville Case appears in a white and gold Western dress that makes her look like Annie Oakley in the musical *Annie Get Your Gun*.[29] At the Tiara casino Case is one of the blackjack dealers, all of whom are female and dressed in a gray and black Western outfit (short skirt, sombrero, and half-Wellingtons over flesh-colored tights).[30] Thus objectified in a Western uniform designed to cause excitement, Case raises the libidos of several male players who find her as attractive as Bond does; with jealousy he watches eight men seat themselves at her table while others stand nearby to watch her.[31]

Case later reveals to Bond that the all-female dealers are another exploitative device wielded by the Spangled Mob: men like the female dealers and female players gain confidence from them, believing them to be sisters of a kind.[32] Female exploitation continues elsewhere in the casino: elderly, dead-behind-the-eyes housewives gather around the slot machines, playing with the near-mechanical compulsion of Pavlov's dogs.[33] How the mob abuses the women it employs is vividly demonstrated by Spang during his manicure at the Tiara. Made nervous by Bond, his jittery hands cause those of the female manicurist to slip and cut him. He springs out of his chair and slaps her to the ground. Turning to the barber he snarls "Fire that bitch" and stalks out of the room.[34] His language is no better toward Case, who he calls a "silly bitch."[35]

Fleming's depiction of a mobbed-up America and its mistreatment of women is hardly free from an ulterior motive, since it contributes to his Imperialist project of asserting British dominance. Christine Bold explains that in the Bond novels "the representatives of lesser nations are not just sexually impotent but sexually 'deviant,'" since "Fleming mounts a regulatory scheme that aligns good and bad nations with 'normal' and 'abnormal' sexual preferences." This scheme is clinched by the attitude of foreign agents toward women.[36] Bold's examples of this attitude include disinterest in women, sexual interest in ugly women, or extreme fetishism. But they do not include heterosexual interest in conventionally attractive women, i.e., the attitude considered "normal" by 1950s mainstream standards. "Deviant" sexuality among non-British villains certainly flourishes in *Diamonds Are Forever*, most obviously with the homosexual assassins Wint and Kidd but also with the members of the Detroit Purple Mob, described by Cureo as lavender pansies who carry golf clubs but can only handle the irons in their pockets.[37] Nevertheless, the main villain, Spang, demonstrates conventional, heteronormative sexual preferences in his attraction to Case, though dressing her in Western costumes suggests a degree of fetishism. Spang's attitudes toward women, encapsulated in his behavior toward his manicurist, express male privilege. His organization's practices toward women follow suit in being exploitative and objectifying, from prostitution on downward. The Spangled Mob, and by extension organized crime and the corrupt nation it's inextricable from (gambling is America's biggest industry, according to the British Secret Service[38]), represents the face of an extreme patriarchal order.

Case recoils from an order that can provide monetary protection but not personal fulfillment. She has done well with the Spangs and has always known where her next meal would come from, but as she tells Bond, a woman in their employ cannot have friends within such an organization. She has to proclaim her sexual unavailability or else end up with a heel for a partner.[39] If Case's "out-of-placeness" is created by a patriarchal order, her refusal to become sexually involved with any member of the Spangled Mob is a departure from conventional femininity *and* a protest against a brutal patriarchal order. Case's trauma-induced out-of-placeness does not translate into an insufficient distinction between right and wrong; as the next section of this essay attempts to demonstrate, Case's disgust with the mob is evident even in her introduction to the narrative, and her defection from the Spangled Mob is her own decision, planned to a degree that shows the extent of her agency. The order of her desires is self-directed and culminates in her decision to escape with Bond from the patriarchal order of the mob and America. That she escapes to a *British* patriarchal order, represented by the idealized figure of Bond, demonstrates Fleming's frequently deplored ideological limitations.

THE EYES HAVE IT

Building on Bennett and Woollacott, Michael Denning's essay "Licensed to Look" argues that the out-of-place heroine is repositioned by Bond (and Fleming) into "a new ordering of the sex/gender system, through the narrative code of pornography,"[40] which Denning defines as "a version of voyeurism" situated within a "narrative structured around the look, the voyeuristic eye, coding woman as its object." The "pornographic imagination" of Bond is thus built around voyeurism, rather than specific sexual acts.[41] Taking a somewhat similar approach to the visualization of female characters in the Bond novels, Christine Bold argues that the agency of Fleming's female protagonists is "denied by their manifest objectification in the fictional narrative"[42] and only recovered by their services to Bond, which allow him to establish British potency in victory over other nations.[43]

An explicitly objectifying form of voyeurism occurs during Case's appearances in Western costume, dealing blackjack at the Tiara and dressing like Annie Oakley in Spang's Spectreville. Boel Ulfsdotter's article on Tiffany Case draws upon Laura Mulvey's renowned essay "Visual Pleasure and Narrative Cinema" to observe that "Case has been commanded to wear a certain costume in order for her 'to-be-looked-at-ness' to please the villain above all else."[44] In the casino other men are also pleased: hence Bond's jealousy at his fellow players watching Case. But the most prominent objectification of Tiffany Case occurs in her introduction. Paradoxically this specific objectification also emphasizes Case's gaze, and despite being mediated from Bond's perspective, this gaze disrupts Case's objectification by stressing her emotional needs. It allows Bond and the reader a greater perception of Case's agency in the narrative, and its metaphorical embodiment.

Case is the heroine of a novel about diamonds—she is named after a jewelry store, wears a diamond ring, and is also *likened* to a diamond. The narrator observes that her eyes have a "rare quality of chatoyance." When subjected to light and movement, a chatoyant jewel changes the luster of its colors. Like chatoyant jewels, Case's eyes shift between a deep gray-blue and light gray.[45] The colors are akin to the blue-white fire Bond finds at the start of the narrative when he gazes into the center of a diamond and finds his eyes stung by its refracting and reflecting colors.[46] Over the course of the story, Bond learns to understand the centuries-long and quasi-sexual passion for diamonds. As a result, he falls in love with a diamond smuggler. Case becomes a diamond for him to possess and smuggle away from the mob. He does so by reversing the direction of the mob's diamond traffic and smuggling Case from America to London.

So far, so objectified, but as Case demonstrates, jewels do not have emotions or needs and she certainly does. Nor do they gaze back at their admirers, unlike Case, whose multi-faceted eyes reflect not only light but the state of her mind. Their chatoyance expresses her neurotic "out-of-placeness" and signals her mood swings between melancholy and passion and attraction and repulsion. *Diamonds Are Forever* pays careful attention to Case's eyes and their gaze, which call attention to her needs by fluctuating with her moods; they allow Bond to interpret the emotions of a human jewel.

Before meeting Case, Bond assumes his female co-smuggler will be a hardened female crook with "dead eyes." Finding himself mistaken, he gazes at Case's sinfully shaped mouth and decides it has not often sinned, judging from the levelness of her eyes and the hint behind them of tension and authority.[47] Inner and outer control are inscribed in her glance. Before entering Case's room Bond hears "Feuilles Mortes" ("Dead Leaves") emanating from her record player—a preview of the melancholy that will prove inseparable from her appearance and trouble her objectification. Bond enters to find Case sitting half-naked astride a chair, looking in the mirror with her back to him. He immediately and pleasurably senses arrogance in the posture of her shoulder and head, and when she transfers her self-directed gaze outward, she does so with authority, inspecting Bond in the mirror with brief coolness. She orders Bond to sit down and enjoy her melancholy record, George Feyer's *Echoes of Paris*. The obedient Bond does so and finds the music fitting; all the songs seem to be her own, since the record captures her tough manner, outright sexiness, and the poignancy Bond found in her eyes when they moodily surveyed him in the mirror.[48] Case's gaze—its authority inseparable from a poignancy accentuated by the music—complicates an otherwise sensual scene and prevents her from becoming no more than an erotic object or pinup. As Kingsley Amis observes, "a pinup can't have difficulties or fears or suspicions or hopes, personal or emotional baggage of any kind," whereas the female protagonist of a Bond novel "always has these."[49] Case is very far from being an exception.

Without the complications of her gaze, Case's introduction would indeed be the sort of pornographic voyeurism—Bond gazing at a pinup—that Denning perceives. Boel Uflsdotter argues that "Fleming's use of [a] pornographic stereotype to introduce Case can either be understood as completely unwarranted and therefore an expression of mere voyeurism" or as an attempt to show the readers that "Case is a woman who is in complete control of her own integrity and therefore unwavering even if seen semi-naked by a complete stranger."[50] Or as the narrator puts it, Case keeps her looks for only herself and doesn't mind what men think of them.[51] The negative counterpart to Case's introduction is her ordeal at the hands of Wint and Kidd in chapter 24. Bond finds Case naked aside from her pants, with her knees gripped between Kidd's thighs in a grotesque parody of rape, since Kidd has no sexual interest in women. There is no eroticism in the prose or in Bond's reaction—instead he notices the red marks on Case's face and her wild eyes, like those of a trapped animal.[52] Wint and Kidd's sole intention is to pornographically humiliate and degrade Case before executing her; they do so by removing control of her body. Her gaze becomes dehumanized in response.

Returning to Case's first meeting with Bond, we find her gaze also expressing self-assertion. When he looks appraisingly at her and hopes she won't get into trouble, she tells him to quit treating her like a little girl—she's on a job and can take care of herself. Her eyes flash and grow dark and impatient as she speaks. Bond smiles into her eyes and says he'll be a credit to her. When Bond asks if Case will have dinner with him in America, the answer first appears in her eyes; they lose their darkness as looks at him thoughtfully. She shows Bond to the door with a dismissive movement, but her confident eyes are almost warm.[53]

Bond's readings of Case's gaze grow more nuanced from here onward. In their first meeting he interpreted her gaze as a straightforward sexual challenge: her scornful and wide gray eyes seem to urge him to make a move, but only if he's top-quality.[54] But after Bond learns from Leiter about Case's traumatic past, he remembers her eyes gazing upon him, but this time their gaze is sullen.[55] The next time he meets her, at dinner in New York, he finds her melancholy gaze has gained further meaning. Case looks up at Bond through the smoke of her cigarette and her eyes deliver a new message: she likes Bond and everything is possible between them, but he must be patient and kind, because she doesn't "want to be hurt any more."[56] As mediated through Bond's interpretation (now influenced by knowledge of Case's backstory), her gaze asks that a victim of sexual assault be treated with sensitivity. This requirement is reinforced after dinner, when Bond accompanies Case back to her hotel room. Bond has upset her by asking too many questions about the mob, and at the door she confronts him with a gaze mingling assertion and vulnerability. She looks straight into his eyes, and Bond sees that her eyelashes are wet. Case kisses him, but when Bond starts to return the favor, she frees herself and deploys her gaze: looking at him with a sultry glow, she orders Bond to get away from her and slams the door.[57] Her assertive behavior enforces what her gaze had told Bond at dinner—be patient—and reestablishes her control.

Bond and Case's next meetings are in enemy territory, where Bond interprets her gaze as a covert sign of partnership. Watching with admiration as she deals crooked blackjack in Las Vegas, he looks into her gray eyes and finds a possible hint of amusement or complicity in the rigged game she's playing with him.[58] After Bond's cover is blown Case defends him (and herself) from the wrath of Spang. Her demeanor is calm aside from one giveaway: her eyes sweep over Bond and show fear for him.[59] Something much different replaces fear when Case rescues Bond by arranging their escape from Spectreville. Bond compliments her planning, puts his arm around her shoulders, and receives a literal reversal of his gaze—she smiles into his eyes.[60] When Bond says she'll be in trouble if Spang catches her, she tells him not to worry about her and assumes a joyful gaze: her eyes are happy and shining.[61] Her eyes shine yet again near the end of the novel, when Bond frees her from Wint and Kidd, thereby reciprocating her rescue of him.[62]

The accumulative effect of Case's gaze confirms Bond's emotional commitment to her. He wonders if she will come out of her shell, hardened by years of being alone, and receives an answer by remembering the moments when Case happily looked out from behind the masks of the roles she played for the mob.[63] Supplied an answer by a gaze no mask can hide, he finds himself falling in love. Onboard the *Queen Elizabeth*, Case says she can't get over her happiness and tells Bond not to mind her jokes. Bond's response is delayed so the narrator can describe the sunlight shining deep within her chatoyant gray eyes. After gazing at her, Bond says he doesn't mind, because everything about her is fine. Case gazes back: after looking into his eyes she is satisfied.[64] The reminder of the gem-like quality of Case's eyes is also a reminder that unlike gems they can gaze back at the beholder; in this case they radiate approval of affirmation.

OCCUPATION: SINGLE WOMAN

So says Case's passport description.[65] It undersells her skills and agency as a smuggler for (and later fugitive from) the Spangled Mob. As a guard in the Spangled Mob's smuggling operation, Case makes good on the authority in her eyes and gives smugglers their orders.[66] After questioning Bond she figures out the best way to smuggle the diamonds (inside golf balls), and makes Bond look amateurish by dismissing his suggestion to use suitcase handles. She directs the ensuing stages of the smuggling operation by providing Bond with precise instructions, telling him what documents to obtain, giving him hotel money, and making every major decision.[67] In her other job, as a cardsharp blackjack dealer, she is equally adept and earns Bond's wholehearted admiration: he wonders how she became so skilled, calls her card-handling brilliant, and says she could do anything with such talent. [68]

Case is also skilled at standing up to men and successfully defends herself when Spang lambastes her for letting Bond into the mob. She angrily tells him not to think he can push her around, reminding him that she had faithfully followed the mob's instructions, having trusted its competence in choosing carriers. [69] Case's break from the mob is even more impressive, since without this exercise of agency Bond would be dead. It is Case who wakes Bond from post-torture unconsciousness — when his willpower had evaporated and left him unwilling to move — and directs him through Spang's railroad station to a waiting handcar pre-filled with gas. She orders Bond onboard, after reassuring him she can drive the handcar, having already switched the necessary points. A much-impressed Bond whispers, "My God, you're a girl." [70] Her astute planning extends to retrieving Bond's Beretta, which he uses to put four bullets into Spang. Contrary to Bennett and Woollacott's assertion that the Bond heroine "threatens to divert the phallic power Bond needs in his contest with the villain," [71] Case directly gives Bond the phallic power he uses to kill the villain.

Case praises the escape she has masterminded by comparing it to a scene from a Buster Keaton film. [72] She thereby associates herself with Keaton's ingenious mastery of railroads, which he most famously demonstrated in *The General* (1927), whose handcar chase may have inspired *Diamonds Are Forever*'s. Examining the handcar, Case says getting more power out of it would be impossible even if her name were Casey Jones rather than Case, [73] which re-emphasizes her affinity with the railroad. By aligning herself with masculine masters of the railroad like Keaton and Jones, she breaks from the artifice of the *Annie Got Your Gun* image inflicted on her by Spang, which had more to do with objectification than with emulating Annie Oakley. Case displays further ingenuity by devising the idea of manipulating the rail points and branch line to wrong-foot Spang, which contributes to the demise of the villain and his train.

After Spang's defeat, Case *again* saves an exhausted and delirious Bond by guiding him from the desert to the highway. Without her Bond would not have kept "a straight course" — instead he would have stumbled around the desert until the sun finished him off. [74] In a metaphorical sense, Case has already kept Bond on a straight course throughout the novel by facilitating his infiltration of the Spangled Mob. He returns the favor by setting her onto a "straight" course of sexual awakening.

Case's decision to take Bond's side is prompted by inner direction, since from her very first appearance she shows disgust toward her employers and their world. *Diamonds Are Forever* is narrated from Bond's perspective (apart from the opening chapter and a section of the final chapter) but on one occasion the narration allows a glimpse into Case's thoughts, after her first meeting with Bond. Case's eyes brood as she walks toward her record player and plays "Je n'en connais pas la fin." ("I Don't Know the End"—a prophetic title). She wonders about the man who has so suddenly walked into her life. "Another damn crook" she thinks to herself in anger and despair: "Couldn't she ever get away from them?"[75] Curiously, in the closing section of the book aboard the *Queen Elizabeth*, Case tells Bond that during their first meeting she thought he was a crook, but right afterward she knew he wasn't.[76] This contradiction is perhaps explained by returning to the aftermath of the first meeting. After Case calls Bond another crook, "Je n'en connais pas la fin" ends, and the narration reveals that Case's face is now happy.[77] Subconsciously Case seems to have realized Bond was not a crook, or perhaps her subconscious had never thought that at all. In any case, her desire to escape the mob is already clear.

Though Case's negative first impression of Bond quickly gives way to a positive second, the conflict between these impressions lingers. Meeting Bond for dinner in New York, she tests his reactions by stressing his compatibility with the Spangled Mob. Her gaze precedes her voice: she looks at him with hardened eyes and says Bond will certainly get to know the mob, since he's just their type.[78] She treats him like another crook, as if to provoke him into proving otherwise or to protect herself by undermining her positive impression of Bond.

Protecting herself means protecting her traumatized mind and body from further hurt. She is upfront in doing so: at the start of dinner she tells Bond she will not sleep with him, so he shouldn't waste money on getting her tipsy. She will happily have a few drinks but refuses to drink his vodka martinis under any false pretense. Bond jokes she might change her mind after dinner; she says it would take more than fancy seafood to make her sleep with a man.[79] She's right, since Bond does *not* sleep with her after dinner. She demands he do more than buy dinner to prove himself a reliable partner.

Bond finally seems to have proven himself by the time the couple dine onboard the *Queen Elizabeth*, until he makes the mistake of wondering aloud if Case slept with Seraffimo Spang. This makes an insensitive mockery of her self-control, her traumatic past, her genuine loathing of the mob, and her self-respect. Her eyes blaze with anger[80] and she walks out of the Grill, forcing Bond to pursue her. She berates him for unkindness and forces him to clarify that he spoke out of jealousy, which would demonstrate commitment rather than spiteful disbelief in her character. Having made Bond apologetically declare his feelings, she grants approval through her gaze: her final response is not verbal, but instead conveyed through her laughing eyes.[81]

After Case has firmly tested Bond's commitment, she initiates sexual relations. First she tells Bond she has "never what you'd call 'slept with a man'" in her entire life.[82] Her choice of words interprets and classifies her sexual trauma. Case regards herself as essentially a virgin because she does not equate rape at the hands of men as having slept with them. She rejects the idea of sexual assault and rape preventing her from identifying as a virgin. She rejects a tenet of traditional patriarchal culture: In her view, to have slept with a man is an experience that can happen only on her own terms. Neither Bond nor the narration dispute Case's self-definition.

Case also decides where and when to initiate sexual relations with Bond. Perhaps mindful of the lingering memory of being assaulted in her mother's home, Case asks to make love in Bond's cabin, which she refers to as his house. Her word of command determines when Bond starts and what he will do: she demands everything Bond has ever done with a woman and demands it immediately.[83] Bennett and Woollacott characterize the Fleming heroine as "a free and equal partner" who "none the less, when it comes to the crunch (in bed) knows her place,"[84] but in this case Case determines the time, place, and circumstances of going to bed with Bond. She almost commands him to perform for her benefit.

After having endured years of emotional deprivation, Case also wants more than sexual relations. She believes every woman wishes to come home (she doesn't specify from where) and find a man's hat on the table in the hall. The problem, she tells Bond, is never finding the right man beneath the hat.[85] Believing she now has, Case pursues him by exploring the subject of marriage with Bond, who is also in love but wary of a formal commitment. She tells him no one can be complete or fully human when alone[86] and asks what sort of woman Bond would marry. His flippant answer (someone who can make love and Sauce Béarnaise) earns her derision (she wonders if Bond would really want anyone who fulfilled those conditions, regardless of intelligence, or lack of it). After Bond teasingly admits such a woman would need to have Case's card sense, personality, and looks, she unsuccessfully tries cornering him by asking if he would marry this ideal woman after finding her.[87] After they part for the night, she again takes the initiative, cooking Sauce Béarnaise and sending it to Bond's cabin, much to their shared amusement. The novel closes with the genuine possibility of marriage. As shown in the next section, even Bond's single doubt about life with Case gets cleared away to allow her the novel's last word.

DIAMONDS ARE FOREVER, BUT IS LOVE?

Another character's gaze will haunt Bond before Case gets the last word. After killing Wint and Kidd, Bond disposes of the bodies, encouraging himself with the prospect of enjoying a night of sleep with Case, enfolding her in his arms forever. "Forever?" Bond wonders. He looks into Kidd's face and the eyes of the dead man speak to Bond, saying only death is forever. Only what Bond did to Kidd is permanent.[88] The dead man's gaze states a truth that puts a question mark on Bond's future with Case. Kidd's gaze, though unearthly, harks back to what Tony Davies defines as the traditional role of the male gaze in the thriller, its service as the "true medium of exchange and authentic instrument of male combat, rivalry, and conquest." Masculinity is grounded "in the power of the gaze."[89] Kidd's posthumous gaze threatens to push aside Case's in Bond's mind.

In the final chapter, Bond recalls Kidd's gaze after having disposed of Jack Spang, the final villain, whose diamonds have outlived him. Bond decides the eyes of Kidd's corpse were wrong: death *and* diamonds are forever. Bond derides his train of thought as too solemn; he has simply experienced the end of one more adventure, and one of Tiffany Case's wry phrases could serve as its epitaph. He visualizes her ironic, impassioned mouth saying, "It reads better than it lives."[90] The male gaze, exemplified by Mr. Kidd, with its power to call into question Case's status, is ultimately overpowered by Case's words, the last words of the text. The adjectives Bond uses to describe her mouth combine the opposing sides of her personality, the ironic side he first encountered and the passionate side he helped coax out. Furthermore, the affinity between her chatoyant gaze and that of the eternal diamond gives further resonance to her triumph over Kidd's gaze. Case's phrase was originally employed to sum up her education in card dealing. When applied to Bond's adventures it levels the gap between her life and his.

Diamonds Are Forever ends with Bond and Case's lives set to merge, for though Bond has dodged her questions on marriage, he finally resolves to live with her. Just as Case wished to come home and find a hat on the hall table, Bond looks forward to coming back to his flat in the evening and finding Case there.[91] But in the following novel, *From Russia with Love*, Bond is single again: "Tiffany Case, his love for so many happy months, had left him" and sailed for America. Having withdrawn to a hotel during the "final painful weeks" of their relationship, she left behind a bereft Bond whose "mind still sheered away from the thought of her."[92] Bond tells his side of the story to M, admitting there was "some idea" of marriage, "but then she met some chap in the American Embassy," a Marine Corps major working for the Military Attaché. "I gather she's going to marry him," says Bond, since Case has returned with this man to the United States. "Probably better that way. Mixed marriages aren't often a success," claims Bond, and Case will enjoy America more than London. "She couldn't really settle down here," Bond concludes. "Fine girl, but she's a bit neurotic. We had too many rows. Probably my fault."[93]

Perhaps the breakup was foreseen in *Diamonds Are Forever*, when Bond jokingly told Case that wedlock to his ideal woman would devolve into the petty rows that seem to accompany many marriages, and he would probably grow claustrophobic and run out.[94] In *From Russia with Love* we learn plenty of rows did occur during Bond and Case's near-marriage, but it was Case who ran out. Bond blames himself for the rows, though not before he finds another cause in Case's neuroticism, the "out-of-place" part of her personality. In *Diamonds Are Forever* Bond had wondered if she would emerge from her neurotic shell and then acknowledged that taking Case "by the hand" would mean never letting go if she remained mentally troubled. He would have to assume "the role of the healer" or analyst for Case, who would transfer her trust and love to Bond as she progressed from illness to health.[95] As it turned out, Case *did* emerge from her shell after years of withdrawal and isolation, but her final step involved re-transferring her love to another man and dropping Bond's hand. Case's neuroticism may not have been miraculously cured by Bond, but he did successfully reactivate her sexuality. After experiencing her sexual reawakening and her first experience of couplehood, Case went her own way with a partner she found better suited to her. Case's future husband is a Marine, like her father, but he is also a diplomat and an improvement over her deadbeat Dad.

Bond's pessimism regarding mixed marriages seems to reinforce Umberto Eco's observation that Bond's erotic relationships "always end with a form of death, real or symbolic," leaving Bond to resume "willy-nilly his purity as an Anglo-Saxon bachelor" since "the race remains uncontaminated."[96] However, there is no indication that Tiffany Case is not Anglo-Saxon, and Bond's reasons for breaking up with her are unconvincing. In *Diamonds Are Forever* Case seemed comfortable in London and Bond showed no apprehension about mixed marriages, not even when parrying Case's advocacy of marriage.

Bond finally regards marriage as "the ultimate taboo for the professional spy," as Oliver Buckton puts it, and there are extra-textual and genre-related reasons for his avoidance of martrimony and its failure to occur in *From Russia with Love*. Marriage would lessen Bond's effectiveness as an identifiable fantasy-figure who "offers escapism both from the drudgery of daily labour and the stresses of domestic/family life for the readers."[97]

Raymond Chandler made a second genre-related point about Bond's relationships when reviewing *Diamonds Are Forever* for the *Sunday Times*: "Sadly enough his beautiful girls have no future, because it is the curse of the 'series character' that he always has to go back to where he began."[98] Nevertheless, *From Russia with Love* shows that Tiffany Case *does* have a future, but not with James Bond.

NOTES

1. Kingsley Amis, "Reference Guide," *The James Bond Dossier* (New York: New American Library, 1965), n.p.

2. Ian Fleming. *Live and Let Die* (London: Jonathan Cape, 1954; reprint, New York: Penguin Books, 2003), 178.

3. Fleming. *Live and Let Die*, 229.

4. Ian Fleming, *Diamonds Are Forever* (London: Jonathan Cape, 1956; reprint, Las Vegas: Thomas & Mercer, 2012), 69.

5. Fleming, *Diamonds Are Forever*, 198.

6. Fleming, *Diamonds Are Forever*, 70.

7. Fleming, *Diamonds Are Forever*, 69.

8. Fleming, *Diamonds Are Forever*, 78.

9. Umberto Eco, "Narrative Structures in Fleming," in *The Role of the Reader: Explorations in the Semiotics of Texts* (Bloomington: Indiana University Press, 1979), 154.

10. Tony Bennett and Janet Woollacott, *Bond and Beyond: The Political Career of a Popular Hero* (London: Macmillan, 1987), 115.

11. Bennett and Woollacott, *Bond and Beyond*, 115.

12. Bennett and Woollacott, *Bond and Beyond*, 115–16.

13. Bennett and Woollacott, *Bond and Beyond*, 118.

14. Bennett and Woollacott, *Bond and Beyond*, 116.

15. Fleming, *Diamonds Are Forever*, 19.

16. Roy Newquist, "Ian Fleming," in *Counterpoint* (Chicago: Rand McNally, 1964), 211.

17. Fleming, *Diamonds Are Forever*, 66.

18. Elizabeth Ladenson, "Pussy Galore," in *The James Bond Phenomenon: A Critical Reader*, ed. Christoph Linder, 2nd ed. (Manchester: Manchester University Press, 2009), 231.

19. Ian Fleming, "Raymond Chandler," *London Magazine* 6, no. 12 (December 1959): 50.

20. Fleming, *Diamonds Are Forever*, 33.

21. Fleming, *Diamonds Are Forever*, 37.

22. Fleming, *Diamonds Are Forever*, 72–73.

23. Fleming, *Diamonds Are Forever*, 129.

24. Fleming, *Diamonds Are Forever*, 152.

25. Fleming, *Diamonds Are Forever*, 165.

26. Fleming, *Diamonds Are Forever*, 167.

27. Fleming, *Diamonds Are Forever*, 44.

28. Fleming, *Diamonds Are Forever*, 70.

29. Fleming, *Diamonds Are Forever*, 168.

30. Fleming, *Diamonds Are Forever*, 144.

31. Fleming, *Diamonds Are Forever*, 147.

32. Fleming, *Diamonds Are Forever*, 199.

33. Fleming, *Diamonds Are Forever*, 139–40.

34. Fleming, *Diamonds Are Forever*, 155.

35. Fleming, *Diamonds Are Forever*, 172.

36. Christine Bold, "'Under the Very Skirts of Britannia': Re-Reading Women in the James Bond Novels," in *The James Bond Phenomenon: A Critical Reader*, ed. Christoph Linder, 2nd ed. (Manchester: Manchester University Press, 2009), 209–10.

37. Fleming, *Diamonds Are Forever*, 155.

38. Fleming, *Diamonds Are Forever*, 19–20.

39. Fleming, *Diamonds Are Forever*, 200.

40. Michael Denning, "Licensed to Look," in *Cover Stories: Narrative and Ideology in the British Spy Thriller* (London: Routledge and Kegan Paul, 1987), 102.

41. Denning, "Licensed to Look," 109.

42. Bold, "Under the Very Skirts," 216.

43. Bold, "Under the Very Skirts," 209–10.

44. Boel Ulfsdotter, "The Bond Girl Who Is Not There: The Tiffany Case," in *For His Eyes Only: The Women of James Bond*, ed. Lisa Funnell (New York: Wallflower Press, 2015), 22.

45. Fleming, *Diamonds Are Forever*, 34–35.

46. Fleming, *Diamonds Are Forever*, 11.

47. Fleming, *Diamonds Are Forever*, 34–35.

48. Fleming, *Diamonds Are Forever*, 34–35.

49. Amis, *James Bond Dossier*, 48.

50. Ulfsdotter, "Bond Girl," 21.

51. Fleming, *Diamonds Are Forever*, 34–35.

52. Fleming, *Diamonds Are Forever*, 218.

53. Fleming, *Diamonds Are Forever*, 38–39.

54. Fleming, *Diamonds Are Forever*, 34–35.

55. Fleming, *Diamonds Are Forever*, 70.

56. Fleming, *Diamonds Are Forever*, 73.

57. Fleming, *Diamonds Are Forever*, 78.

58. Fleming, *Diamonds Are Forever*, 146.

59. Fleming, *Diamonds Are Forever*, 174.

60. Fleming, *Diamonds Are Forever*, 177.

61. Fleming, *Diamonds Are Forever*, 178.

62. Fleming, *Diamonds Are Forever*, 222.

63. Fleming, *Diamonds Are Forever*, 190.

64. Fleming, *Diamonds Are Forever*, 196–97.

65. Fleming, *Diamonds Are Forever*, 23.

66. Fleming, *Diamonds Are Forever*, 21.

67. Fleming, *Diamonds Are Forever*, 36–37.

68. Fleming, *Diamonds Are Forever*, 198.

69. Fleming, *Diamonds Are Forever*, 172.

70. Fleming, *Diamonds Are Forever*, 176.

71. Bennett and Woollacott, *Bond and Beyond*, 137.

72. Fleming, *Diamonds Are Forever*, 177.

73. Fleming, *Diamonds Are Forever*, 179.

74. Fleming, *Diamonds Are Forever*, 184.

75. Fleming, *Diamonds Are Forever*, 40.

76. Fleming, *Diamonds Are Forever*, 197.

77. Fleming, *Diamonds Are Forever*, 40.

78. Fleming, *Diamonds Are Forever*, 75.

79. Fleming, *Diamonds Are Forever*, 71.

80. Fleming, *Diamonds Are Forever*, 200.

81. Fleming, *Diamonds Are Forever*, 201.

82. Fleming, *Diamonds Are Forever*, 202.

83. Fleming, *Diamonds Are Forever*, 211.

84. Bennett and Woollacott, *Bond and Beyond*, 123.

85. Fleming, *Diamonds Are Forever*, 200.

86. Fleming, *Diamonds Are Forever*, 198.

87. Fleming, *Diamonds Are Forever*, 199.

88. Fleming, *Diamonds Are Forever*, 223–24.

89. Tony Davies, "The Divided Gaze: Reflections on the Political Thriller," in *Gender, Genre, and Narrative Pleasure*, ed. Derek Longhurst (London: Unwin Hayman, 1989), 118.

90. Fleming, *Diamonds Are Forever*, 235.

91. Fleming, *Diamonds Are Forever*, 191.

92. Ian Fleming. *From Russia with Love*, (London: Jonathan Cape, 1957; reprint, New York: Penguin Books, 2003), 98–99.

93. Fleming. *From Russia with Love*, 105.

94. Fleming, *Diamonds Are Forever*, 199–200.
95. Fleming, *Diamonds Are Forever*, 190.
96. Eco, "Narrative Structures," 155.
97. Oliver S. Buckton, "Licensing the Professional Spy," in *Espionage in British Fiction and Film since 1900: The Changing Enemy* (Lanham, MD: Lexington Books, 2015), 135–36.
98. Raymond Chandler, "Bonded Goods," *Sunday Times*, March 25, 1956, p.7.

BIBLIOGRAPHY

Amis, Kingsley. *The James Bond Dossier*. New York: New American Library, 1965.
Bennett, Tony, and Janet Woollacott. *Bond and Beyond: The Political Career of a Popular Hero*. London: Macmillan, 1987.
Bold, Christine. "'Under the Very Skirts of Britannia': Re-Reading Women in the James Bond Novels." In *The James Bond Phenomenon: A Critical Reader*, edited by Christoph Linder, 205–19. 2nd ed. Manchester: Manchester University Press, 2009.
Buckton, Oliver S. "Licensing the Professional Spy." Ch. 4 in *Espionage in British Fiction and Film since 1900: The Changing Enemy*. Lanham, MD: Lexington Books, 2015.
Chandler, Raymond. "Bonded Goods." *Sunday Times*, March 25, 1956, p.7.
Davies, Tony. "The Divided Gaze: Reflections on the Political Thriller." In *Gender, Genre, and Narrative Pleasure*, edited by Derek Longhurst, 118–35. London: Unwin Hayman, 1989.
Denning, Michael. "Licensed to Look." Ch. 4 in *Cover Stories: Narrative and Ideology in the British Spy Thriller*. London: Routledge and Kegan Paul, 1987.
Eco, Umberto. "Narrative Structures in Fleming." Ch. 6 in *The Role of the Reader: Explorations in the Semiotics of Texts*. Bloomington: Indiana University Press, 1979.
Fleming, Ian. *Diamonds Are Forever*. London: Jonathan Cape, 1956; reprint, Las Vegas: Thomas & Mercer, 2012.
Fleming, Ian. *From Russia with Love*. London: Jonathan Cape, 1957; reprint, New York: Penguin Books, 2003.
Fleming, Ian. *Live and Let Die*. London: Jonathan Cape, 1954; reprint, New York: Penguin Books, 2003.
Fleming, Ian. "Raymond Chandler." *London Magazine* 6, no. 12 (December 1959): 43–54.
Ladenson, Elizabeth. "Pussy Galore." In *The James Bond Phenomenon: A Critical Reader*, edited by Christoph Linder, 220–37. 2nd ed. Manchester: Manchester University Press, 2009.
Newquist, Roy. "Ian Fleming." Ch. 20 in *Counterpoint*. Chicago: Rand McNally, 1964.
Ulfsdotter, Boel. "The Bond Girl Who Is Not There: The Tiffany Case." In *For His Eyes Only: The Women of James Bond*, edited by Lisa Funnell, 18–27. New York: Wallflower Press, 2015.

Culture, Consumption, and America
in *Diamonds Are Forever*

EIGHT

Attitudes Are Forever

America Disdained

Matthew B. Sherman

A subtext of Ian Fleming's *Diamonds Are Forever* and his other James Bond stories, despite his protagonist being a firm ally of the United States, Fleming mocks America as a dystopia, rich in underworld crime and other evils prompted by rampant consumerism. A closer look may shed insight on Anglo-American relations in the latter half of the twentieth century and on Fleming's snobbery, albeit subtle snobbery couched in sumptuous language. Thriller author Raymond Chandler wrote in his review of *Diamonds Are Forever*, "The remarkable thing about this book . . . is that is written by an Englishman. The scene is almost entirely American and it rings true to an American. I am unaware of any other writer who has accomplished this."[1]

Arguably, Chandler was correct, if Americans admit to loathing their own nation. By contrast, author and essayist Christopher Hitchens hit the mark regarding Fleming's xenophobia, observing that "[t]he central paradox of the classic Bond stories is that, although superficially devoted to the Anglo-American war against communism, they are full of contempt and resentment for America and Americans."[2] Fleming's resentment may have stemmed from his combative, restless nature, as he sought lifelong to hold in check internal tensions caused by his diametrically opposed ideas. Accordingly, Umberto Eco, an early James Bond essayist, analyzed Fleming's works from a structuralist point of view, marking pervasive Manichean and Hegelian conflicts in James Bond and Ian Fleming. Though Eco later challenged "oversimplistic applications of structuralist ideas,"[3] the Fleming Bond titles indeed evince these conflicts, including the personal luxuries of Bond's faddish tastes versus his willingness to be deprived and tortured, Anglo-Saxon moderation and Puritan restraint versus the excesses of foreign villains, chance and Bond's intuition versus enemy calculation, and idealism versus greed. These are Fleming's lifelong uncertainties as projected onto Bond, including his own love of immense luxury despite self-deprivation, and the tension between his rampant xenophobia and his burning love for travel far outside Britain.

Fleming's personal lows included being "the world's worst stockbroker,"[4] pressed into the trade by his wealthy family, and being a scandalous man who could neither commit to the love of one woman nor ever satisfy his demanding mother. If great stories are built in part as mythic retellings of the lives of authors, then Bond is heroism personified, if propelled by agonies of despair.[5] Yet Fleming's personal shortcomings, like James Bond's, were balanced in the extreme by his many successes: as a top journalist and columnist for both the Reuters News Agency and *The London Times*, as a successful manager of foreign correspondents and also wartime commandos, as a highly popular children's author with *Chitty Chitty Bang Bang*, as a prestigious and groundbreaking collector of modern first editions, as an accomplished travel writer, and as the premier thriller writer of his century. Taken together, Fleming's writing, its mastery of pace and setting fused to his variously repressed and expressed inner conflicts, help make his James Bond stories soar as travelogues and social commentary, and not just as spy thrillers.

Further, as early as the first Bond text, *Casino Royale*, Fleming renounced all psychology as the motive of narrative and passed to a formalistic method.[6] If Bond is a blunt instrument, it is because his sensitivity is dull from the pain of various personal and professional betrayals and from committing murder for his country. Like his *Casino Royale* opposite, Le Chiffre (aka The Number), 007 is a cipher, a man in shadow who stands against evils without and within, ranging from SMERSH, SPECTRE and mobsters to his own inner lassitude and accidie. Fleming, through his alter ego Bond, is St. George against dragons, despite definite unsaintly habits.

Eco therefore sees Bond as Fleming's psychological conflict resolver, an archetypal folktale hero following a formulaic path through each of his adventures. Using modern equivalents of magical folktale help, including Q Branch gadgets and the people Bond wins to his cause, 007 journeys on epic quests, defeats malevolent beings, and gains significant rewards.[7] Consequent to Fleming's angst, however, it is often an inept United States and not just women in peril that needs rescuing. An American crisis is averted by Bond in no less than 10 of the 14 Fleming Bond titles and 18 of the 26 Bond films to date, totaling 70 percent of the James Bond novels and films! James Bond rescues America continually.

Fleming titles in this vein include *Casino Royale* (where Bond gambles recklessly at baccarat, essentially a 50:50 game of chance, using American funds to defeat a Communist villain), *Live and Let Die* (Bond halts American gold smuggling and gangster rackets), *Diamonds Are Forever* (diamond smuggling, mobster crime), *Dr. No* (Cape Canaveral's space program launches are destroyed), *Goldfinger* (the theft of Fort Knox's extensive gold deposits), "For Your Eyes Only" (Cuban murderers at ease in Vermont are assassinated by Bond), "The Hildebrand Rarity" (007 alibis the murderer of an American spouse-beater), *Thunderball* (Miami is threatened with a nuclear weapon), *The Spy Who Loved Me* (mafia insurance fraud, rape, and murder), *The Man with the Golden Gun* (drug smuggling and an induced stock market collapse), and "007 in New York" (Bond has to step in where New York City lacks a vital rendezvous point).

"America rescue films" include *Dr. No* (Cape Canaveral launches are disrupted), *Goldfinger* (the irradiation of Fort Knox gold), *Thunderball* (Miami is threatened with a nuclear weapon so Bond leads an undersea team off Biscayne Bay against the villain and his henchmen), *Casino Royale '67* (world leaders are to be replaced by doubles and billions are to be killed), *You Only Live Twice* (stopping America from being pushed into a nuclear war with the USSR), *On Her Majesty's Secret Service* (the world's food supply threatened), *Diamonds Are Forever* (American diamond smuggling, kidnapping, industrial and corporate espionage), *Live and Let Die* (heroin smuggling throughout America), *The Spy Who Loved Me* (forestalling an American/Soviet nuclear war), *Moonraker* (the U.S. space shuttle program is hijacked to be used toward world annihilation), *Octopussy* (an American military base will be destroyed to force U.S. unilateral disarmament), *Never Say Never Again* (American nuclear warheads are stolen to extort the NATO powers), *A View to a Kill* (San Francisco fishermen are disrupted and Silicon Valley is to be destroyed), *The Living Daylights* (Bond helps the CIA by taking out their field target), *Licence to Kill* (Bond destroys American fugitives and drug smugglers), *Casino Royale '06* (Bond thwarts a disguised terrorist attack on a U.S. airline designed for the shorting of airline stock), *Quantum of Solace* (007 intervenes in a bad CIA deal), and *Spectre* (America's intelligence agencies are utterly compromised and the British services are soon to follow).

The novel *Diamonds Are Forever* is no exception to the "save America today rule" as Bond has to stop a distinctly American diamond smuggling cartel, one with only the barest branches in the United Kingdom itself. Fleming packs much disdain for America in *Diamonds*, a fast-moving, 70,000-word thriller. Even America's first mention in the novel is as a haven for mobsters, a complicit beneficiary of their diamond smuggling. Bond's Secret Service head, M, informs his agent that diamond smuggling money, stolen from British legal trade, is bound for America, and American leaders couldn't care less. M describes the American gangs as prevalent and powerful, and the U.S. Federal Bureau of Investigation as detached, even callous, since diamond smuggling is only a fraction of gangland activity. Indeed, not only is the cartel using America's generous tax laws to benefit further from their activities, but America itself is profiting from the surfeit of cheap, black market diamonds.

After this briefing, Bond, who now has a bad taste of America in his mouth, interrogates M's Chief of Staff, Bill Tanner, asking what M is concerned about, jibing, "America's a civilized country. More or less." After all, American diamond brokering isn't some type of SMERSH operation in totalitarian Russia. Tanner, frustrated, replies that their mutual boss deeply respects American gangsters, as big movers and shakers who cause him anxiety. Bond persists, saying these people are mere pasta-slurping derelicts who wear far too much cologne. Tanner blasts Bond for his shortsighted view, providing a litany of anti-American invective, then rails against the gangs, describing them as responsible for millions of American drug addicts, millions of dollars squandered on gambling, and over 7,000 murders committed annually in the States. He damns Bond and suggests 007 gets hold of the right MI6 reports on the prevalent illegal activities among Britain's most powerful ally. Although Bond persists in underestimating American gangsters, M and Tanner have at least therefore disclosed how it is that Americans seem to crave stolen diamonds at a discount, and piles of drugs, gambling, and murders.

Much of the American decay that Fleming disapproved of is urban in setting. In *Diamonds* Bond returns to New York, a city he found to be in *Live and Let Die* a great atom bomb target, a city that has lost its soul. The atom bomb quip is just part of the critical vein that bleeds throughout *Live and Let Die*. Bond scholar and filmmaker John Cork comments that the verdict on what Fleming called a tough place ruled by dollars is sheer repulsion at the dross of America's middle class.[8] The faces of ugly Americans are captured in Fleming's prose as bored, begrudging, and scarred. And the *Live and Let Die* narrative starts to unfold not in some grand vista or fruited plain but in St. Petersburg, Florida, where an aged middle class sits inert, pressed together, wretches who can't see or hear or even chew with real teeth, drooling, mumbling, and seeking the secrets of advanced longevity in a sunny clime.

On Bond's New York flight in *Diamonds Are Forever* he is treated to further (awful) American sights as he gazes upon sprawling Boston and the "lovely" New Jersey Turnpike before he descends toward the hazy mess that is the New York suburbs.[9] Then upon deplaning, Bond judges his customs officer paunchy, and sweaty, as it is nearly 100° Fahrenheit in the simmering city that also suffered a heat wave during Bond's previous visit.

Later, 007 will be forced to take up to four showers per day, stuck without air conditioning in the city, but soon enough in the detestable heat, a mobster arrives to chauffer Bond to Manhattan and away from the desolate prairie of Idlewild [Kennedy] Airport. The heavy sent to drive Bond has a mean look and a face like an axe; worse, he is an obvious heavy, since he allows his gun to print through the pocket of his slacks.[10] This man chauffeurs Bond to meet yet another American oddity of ugliness, a red-haired, hunchbacked gangster, Shady Tree (Fleming's ever-present wordplay is evident here, as the man is bent over like the branch of a shade tree), who also suffers from incessant ulcers.

Ian Fleming had a writer's gift to make common occurrences, such as stepping through a New York airport and customs to be driven through a city, ring with rich prose, creating an exciting travelogue for readers. But Fleming's snobbery made his American travelogues the stories of a people who'd lost their way pursuing a consumerist utopia, a deadly sin to the author. For example, Fleming would write a nonfiction travel memoir while visiting fourteen cities, called *Thrilling Cities*, but his publishers feared releasing an American edition as his New York essay was scathing. Its opening sentence describes Fleming disliking his New York adventures more than in the other 13 cities. Fleming had further included blameworthy details from a biting essay titled *City without a Soul*. Additionally, he cited New Yorkers for rude behavior ranging from amateur bribery to loving scandals. But rather than editing his work to soften his publishers, Fleming added a new James Bond short story of some 2,000 words to please them, called "007 in New York."

True to form, however, he was able to couch further anti-American snobbery within, this time as Bond's snobbery rather than Fleming's directly, using pithy, patronizing remarks hidden inside Fleming's opulent language. Over half the text of "007 in New York" mocks America's greed and manias. For example, as Bond muses about cuisine, he damns everything to perdition with the possible exception of steak and seafood. Bond opines that American food is flavorless inside a nation peppered with jejune restaurateurs who praise their frozen food. Only Italian American food has distinct flavor. Finally, Bond wonders (albeit only rhetorically, annoyed) whether New York has any market like Paris's Les Halles or London's Smithfields, with tempting fresh food proudly shown, figuring American rubes would think food left out on display was a health risk.[11]

Fleming (as Bond) goes on to say New York does have everything, even pornographic films and a sadomasochistic bar as recommended for people watching by Bond's closest American friend, CIA agent Felix Leiter. The hook of this short story, in case the inserted knife was yet to be fully twisted within this Anglo-American wound, is how the poor little zoo in Manhattan's Central Park lacks a reptile house, foiling Bond's choice of rendezvous point and nearly compromising his mission! Bond's contact even threatens suicide when she seeks this nonexistent reptile house to meet him. Fleming concludes the whole balls-up is the fault of New York City, rather than an assumptive Bond.[12]

Even Bond's ever-ready (sycophantic) help, Felix Leiter, is called a good American rather than just an American.[13] Leiter provides frequent plot exposition and also potshots at American follies. Kingsley Amis wrote that Leiter is "[s]uch a nonentity as a piece of characterization . . . he, the American, takes orders from Bond, the Britisher . . . Bond is constantly doing better than he."[14] And in *Diamonds Are Forever*, Leiter represents a disabled America, bearing a hook for a hand and a prosthetic leg, injuries from a prior mission where Bond had to save his life then also solve his American crime problem for him.

Arguably, the United States isn't all bad in *Diamonds Are Forever*. For example, Bond and Leiter praise Leiter's "Studillac" car. This triumph of American engineering, a hybrid of a Studebaker with a Cadillac engine placed inside, was crafted just outside New York City. Yet Leiter also disdains America's Corvettes and Thunderbirds as he reminds Bond that the Studebaker's American designer was actually the French-born engineer, Raymond Lowey.[15]

As Leiter drives Bond upstate to Saratoga in his Studillac, they pause for a working lunch at "The Chicken in the Basket." This restaurant described by Fleming doesn't serve the sort of foie gras and caviar familiar from the Bond novels and films, but is rather a crummy roadside dump without exotic equipment, whose specials of fried chicken and local mountain trout had spent months in a freezer, and are served by an uncaring wait staff.[16] Historic Saratoga isn't much better when Bond and Leiter arrive. The small city proves to be a pit of vile gamblers and gangsters, despite Bond liking the woodsy town and its horse racing atmosphere. Bond considers the gambling overlords of Saratoga to be only second-rate villains. Sifting through his memories, Bond almost fondly recalls, by contrast, the icy, chess-playing Soviets (who will array against him in the next novel, *From Russia with Love*) the talented if obsessive Germans, the MI6 staff including the agents willing to throw their lives away for small salaries with a bit of adventure added . . . even the hated Slavs, whom Bond usually excoriates otherwise, he now regards as dangerous compared to the Americans, whom he considers fantasy, cardboard characters.[17]

More of these rude American gamblers and gangsters intrude as Bond journeys on to Las Vegas, where chapter 15's title, "Rue de la Pay," becomes a sample of Fleming's sterling wordplay: here a quadruple wordplay on 1) Rue de la Paix, the Parisian street name, 2) the diamond jewelers who line this Paris street, 3) the fabulous Las Vegas Strip, built from mob money laundering and American gambling losses, and 4) Bond's receipt of payment for diamond smuggling.

Fleming was a master of wordplay and of tight prose, having been honed as a journalist and editor of high standing, beginning with writing terse but colorful dispatches while stationed in Moscow to cover a Stalinist show trial. Fleming also bore a razor-sharp wit, enough to trade barbs at will with his close friend, the brilliant satirist Noël Coward. Thus, he was able to pack more into wordplay or a short bon mot than most authors. Memorably for one example, as he has Bond trudging through the Vermont woods toward an assassination mission in "For Your Eyes Only," Bond's mind wanders in a stream of consciousness and he sums the Fleming pantheon of American wonders, and not for the good, thinking that the very best two American offerings are oyster stew (which Fleming praised as served by New York's Oyster Bar, which remains a mainstay today inside Grand Central Station), and chipmunks![18] Need one say more about a disdaining attitude that rates America far below Britain as civilization's last bastion? How about chipmunk meat served in oyster stew to serve on an overseas flight to America?

Later in *Diamonds Are Forever*, Fleming's left-handed travelogue continues, as Bond flies to Las Vegas by way of Los Angeles. Readers see otherwise magnificent sights through rather jaundiced eyes as Bond passes not exotic Death Valley but its graveyard waste, only to fly above red mountains, "like gums bleeding over rotten teeth" and a bit of green "in the midst of the blasted, Martian landscape."[19] Sightseeing looks still worse to Bond close-up, on the ground. He enters the Vegas casino run by his enemies and takes note of this lair meant to catch not spies but degenerate, greedy Americans, thinking Las Vegas a true hoods' paradise. Vegas is a deadly trap for the unwary, especially if the unwary include the uncouth, vulgar Americans. The whole town, to Bond, is filled with dirty, ugly machines, themselves eroding even as they churn, stealing hard-earned money. The women glued to these one-armed bandits are Pavlovian dogs to Bond, drooling, craving, their mouths slavering, their hands (or is it paws?) discolored from long hours working the slots.[20]

This is hardly the glamorous atmosphere of gaming in an elegant setting that Bond craves in *Casino Royale*. Further, even the American games themselves are déclassé to Fleming. Bond challenges Leiter that America uses an extra zero on their roulette wheels and can keep their neon lights to themselves, Europe offering better percentages to players. Leiter takes the defensive position, responding that America's national game, craps, offers a scant one percent house advantage, but Bond decries the game, saying Leiter can keep America's kiddie games and that the kind of people Bond gambles against have nerves of steel, even when thousands of pounds are on the line and the cards look bad.[21]

Then again, the oft-present snobbery of Bond may be simply a part of Fleming's substantial bag of writer's tricks, for Fleming gave every indication elsewhere that he thoroughly *adored* Las Vegas. In his tour de force *Thrilling Cities*, Fleming clearly marked Vegas as a favorite among the 14 international cities he visited, calling the city "a fantastic caravanserai"[22] with "every fabulous sight"[23] and remarking that, viewed from on high by night, Vegas is a "great gambling resort" that "looks like a twinkling golden river" in the desert.[24] This is, of course, in stark contrast to having the city nestled among the "rotten teeth mountains" Bond had abhorred by day in *Diamonds Are Forever*.

It may be, therefore, that whether by turns praising America or burying it, Fleming is merely ensuring that his stories remain fascinating. He succeeded, and this has kept American purchases of the Fleming books brisk for 65 years to date. Simon Raven put it well in his review *of Dr. No*, as he responded to Bernard Bergonzi's snooty complaint that Fleming's work was finding a keen audience "at what one can only call Establishment level":

> What I do suggest is that Commander Fleming, by reason of his cool and analytical intelligence, his informed use of technical facts, his plausibility, sense of pace, brilliant descriptive powers and superb imagination, proves sheer entertainment such as I, who must read many novels, am seldom lucky enough to find. It may well be, as Mr. Bergonzi suggests, that Fleming's conscious reaction to the dowdiness of the Welfare State has induced him to create fictitious pleasure-domes so splendiferous as to be merely vulgar: the menus in *Dr. No* are a joy to read for all that.[25]

There is much still to chew on from menus, however, as Bond's standby refuge on mission, food, is often a letdown in the United States. In *Live and Let Die*, James Bond experiences such U.S. culinary wonders as the worst coffee imaginable, because American coffee is bad, but bad American coffee is the most horrible served on Earth. Such a "fine" beverage to accompany scrambled eggs that are as horrible as Bond had predicted they would be, offerings on a greasy menu in a greasier diner, where the sad wait staff sit near restrooms that contain filthy secrets within. At least, Bond supposes, the horrible Florida diner he has chosen for him and Solitaire to wait for a train can't kill orange juice, due to the state's proximity to fresh fruit, although he remains depressed to have to even sit in the dirty, tired space.[26]

Likewise in *Diamonds Are Forever*, when a hungry Bond tries to eat promptly in a Las Vegas casino's restaurant, a substandard hostess bends to arrange his place setting and displays a large chest, if a fake one. Ten long minutes then pass before Bond finally receives a roll with butter and crudités, along with a waitress's promise to serve Bond promptly, yet ten further minutes pass before he can even place his order, although the restaurant is only half-full with diners. "Long on courtesy and short on service," is Bond's sardonic response.[27] Food jibes are all the more telling in *Diamonds* and throughout the Fleming canon, as secret agent 007 is an action hero but also an epicure of the highest order. Like his creator, Ian Fleming, Bond relishes exotic cuisine, is fastidious in his choices, and takes real comfort in comfort food.

James Bond also eats a lot. Enough to fill a book. Bond's world is filled to the uttermost with food, glorious food, with an astonishing amount of meals piled high within. Each of the Fleming books and also those of the Bond continuation novelists describe the savory details of a dozen to three dozen delicious meals or more, and someone drinks or has food onscreen about every five minutes across the 26 Bond films.[28] Indeed, Fleming's Bond fantasizes about food and drink far more often than about women.[29] This propensity to ruminate over cuisine makes the incessant assaults on American food particularly glaring in Fleming's canon and not just "007 in New York," although that short story remains a scathing indictment, stating that all American food tastes alike, equally tasteless, never fresh, featuring watery coffee and eggs the wrong color. Bond, you see, had formerly needed to keep a New York flat, and in his spare time he roamed local grocers to secure his cherished brown eggs. Finally he was told by an honest grocer that Americans assume brown eggs are dirty eggs. And the toast the eggs would sit upon! Bond finds soggy bread only, even in cosmopolitan New York. Bond feels the wet toast is the fault of errant British sailors seeking to bring proper British toast racks to their American cousins before their boat sinks offshore in ignominy!

Interestingly, even America's Bond fans adhere to Fleming's food snobbery and anti-American sentiment when it comes to their hero. For example, continuation author Raymond Benson, whose books are full of the sort of rich details on food and vehicles that pepper the Fleming stories, once had the temerity to have Bond dine inside a "gaudy" Tex-Mex restaurant in Austin, Texas, under the direction of Felix Leiter, in *The Facts of Death*. Fans were alarmed, and vocal in their staunch disapproval. No matter that Benson's wry comments are on par with Fleming's left-handed compliments, so that the famed Texas restaurant Bond enters is filled with "the youth of America in all their glory, and in all shapes, sizes," including "shabby pseudohippies with long hair and tie-dyed T-shirts" or that Bond finds the décor within "overly festive and much too colorful," and is "put off by the atmosphere" at an eatery that "wasn't his kind of place" and therefore, he tells Leiter precisely so.[30]

No matter that the restaurant they patronize, the original Austin Chuy's, was good enough to have spawned a chain now grown to 100 locations in 19 states. Fans were incensed that Bond would dare eat Tex-Mex cuisine at all, with most of the more strident critics being American Bond fans. No matter that Bond has an assignation while undercover as a donor inside a sperm bank in the same novel. The food cries were louder! Bond can certainly visit America, say American fans, but surely he wouldn't deign to actually *eat* indigenous cuisine while on a mission there.

Unfortunately, the women don't fare much better than the food in *Diamonds Are Forever*, other than the extraordinary Tiffany Case, a triumphant hustler who saves Bond's life, having overcome the teenage trauma of a gang rape by mobsters. Much like the cruel Spang brothers who now employ Case's services, the women parading through America are wholly unremarkable. Bond is decided, for example, regarding the patrons lining the giant swimming pool outside the lush Tiara hotel owned by the Spang brothers, that perhaps one in one hundred patrons is fit enough to show off at the pool,[31] an especially scathing remark for 1955, when the average American was also a svelte American.

For author Benjamin Pratt, who has examined the work of Fleming from the perspective of the frontal assaults on what Fleming had in print called the modern seven deadly sins, including greed and accidie, *Diamonds Are Forever* is an epic tale admonishing against hypocrisy. The Spang brothers, the lead hypocrites of the novel, lead respectable public lives as resort owners and Hatton Garden merchants, but dole out rough mob justice to those who cross them. This is certainly because great criminals like Goldfinger and Dr. No are foreign but brilliant, but the Americans gangsters, not so much—even the word hypocrisy is telling, with its Greek root providing the etymology of "acting, faking." (These American chaps aren't even supervillains, they're fakes.)

Jack and Seraffimo Spang represent a cog, if a powerful one, inside the greater hypocrisy of an America whose back is firmly turned, as described above, on their diamond smuggling stranglehold on the British economy. Why? To provide Americans with cheaper glittery baubles, with which the Spang boys bedeck themselves in at their Neverland Ranch near Death Valley. The Spangled Mob's name is therefore Fleming's wordplay on the American Spang brothers, as in "The Star-Spangled Banner," and also the Spangs' sparkly smuggled diamonds and the spangled western gear they flaunt at their private hideout. The flag waves, the diamonds glitter, but all is merely hypocrites' gold.

In Fleming, even Bond killing the Spang boys cannot stop the inevitable grind of the dread American Spangled Mob. Jack Strap, one of the hoods assembled years after the *Diamonds* caper, when joining Auric Goldfinger's congress to heist Fort Knox, has all the seeming panache of a Las Vegas casino leader, but Bond susses out the man, guessing he had merely coldly killed all his rivals in the Spang gang to ascend, sometime after Bond himself had disposed of the Spang brothers.[32]

The Spangled Mob itself remains the least fleshed out of all of Fleming's villainous organizations. Seraffimo Spang doesn't even care to know what Bond's name is, figuring he's some type of British cop come calling. Thus he taunts Bond with torture anonymously, meaning to give Bond pause by calling him only, "Mister Whosis."[33] His one spoken sentence describing the torture Bond will face is as pithy as anything Fleming wrote elsewhere, but hardly the typical multi-page pre-torture soliloquy of the more defined (non-American) Fleming villains!

The name "Seraffimo" comes from "seraph," and the man is an angel of death to Bond, but as he's also just an American hood, not replete with the psychological complexity and keen cunning of the rest of Fleming's oeuvre. Serrafimo Spang is a bullying goon, more of a Hell's Angel than a truly evil angel. And his brother, Jack Spang, is solely that, a literal jack or tool for his mobster brother, a publicly undistinguished front man for the Spang diamond concern in London. Jack Spang is in fact just a big foot soldier, an underling of sorts, as were the literal jacks of the playing cards Fleming loved. This Spang is all angles and wired dark hair, with giant, hairy hands at the end of very long arms. Bond feels he's competent but hard and still looking to prove himself.[34] In other words, he's an American ape of a man, a cold killer and one without much personal, villainous style.

Indeed, Bond, while deep into his undercover mission against the Spangs yet still disdainful of the American villains, fiercely rues the day he ever went undercover against them. And then, Bond realizes in an epiphany that he feels dirty and sick simply because he's spent too long amongst the over-perfumed if powerful and violent gang members. His diamond smuggling cover is stupid, since poor Bond has to confront only a grimy American mob in *Diamonds* and not supervillains. But over a cup of (surely watery) American coffee, Bond figures he simply misses being James Bond instead of an alias, Peter Franks. Homesick, therefore, he curses the Spangs and the entire city of Las Vegas.[35] So it is that the Nevada of *Diamonds Are Forever* is a hellish place, filled with goons, over-weight people, bad food, and gambling traps for the naïve.

The sole reprieve comes for the Spangs when it is revealed near the end of the novel that Jack Spang is actually the enigmatic "A B C," who has been running the diamond smuggling operation. He continues to kill people in the pipeline, and is therefore the beginning and the end of the pipeline and the mission, the very ABC's of diamond smuggling. But as much as Bond will respect the immense calculation of Auric Goldfinger, Bond disrespects the Spangs. As Bond shoots Jack's helicopter down us-ing spangled tracer bullets, rather than reflect in awe upon the man's devious power, he thinks instead of Spang as the golfing nut who made regular business trips to France, and of M's words that the man was ostensibly an upstanding society man.[36]

Yevgenya Strakovsky has commented on the arc of the Fleming canon as reflecting the post–World War II period, with its growing acceptance in the West of the banality of evil, starting with the detached testimony of the Nuremburg trials defendants and their ilk.[37] The Spang brothers, likewise, do like to play dress up in their fake Western town, but are otherwise rather banal. Jack Spang hides in British society as a dull, up-standing American, and his brother plays in public at being a successful casino operator but is uncouth. So while a part of the hypocrisy Pratt cites is for Jack Spang to act a model citizen, while being sleazy behind closed doors, Bond merely has to casually sit astride a Bofors 40 mm cannon to blast the man's helicopter from the sky, dismissing him with phallic power. Whether a good enough American, like Felix Leiter or a bad enough American, like a Spang protagonist, most Americans are truly mere footnotes in Bond's dashing life.

Finally, even Ian Fleming's racism is projected to become a distinctly American problem in *Diamonds Are Forever*. Bond is led to consider that merry olde England is fortunate, while America has never quite solved its race problems. Leiter himself wryly concurs, having corrected Bond's use of foul language while in America, saying that those in the United States are so sensitive about race that a jigger of liquor must be called by its politically correct name, "jegro."[38]

Ian Fleming and James Bond were certainly products of their times, Fleming first placing Bond's birth circa 1919. Their misogyny and narrow worldview dates them from a bygone era. And in 1950s England with its rapidly shrinking empire, it must have been refreshing for British readers to enjoy not only a masculine, opinionated spy, but Ian Fleming's gentle and also not-so-gentle fun poked at America's dystopian greed and consumerism.

The film version of *Diamonds Are Forever* fares no better for the United States, for Sean Connery's record-breaking 1971 return to the screen as 007 is riddled with attacks on Americans throughout the sendup script written by Tom Mankiewicz. Screenwriter Mankiewicz, Hollywood royalty himself (his father Joseph L. Mankiewicz won Academy Awards for Best Director and Best Screenplay Writing and lensed the epic *Cleopatra* with Burton and Taylor, his uncle Herman J. Mankiewicz wrote *Citizen Kane*, and a dozen Mankiewicz cousins are notable screenwriters and producers) crafted some of the peppiest and most scintillating dialogue of the Bond series, but also treated *Diamonds* like a spoof of all things American.

Examples abound, literally every few minutes on screen. The CIA agents are grossly incompetent and lose track of villain Ernst Stavro Blofeld and Tiffany Case, despite there being not less than 30 CIA agents on the floor of the Circus Circus casino, with still more watching Case from above with cameras and binoculars! They ultimately lose their quarry when screaming children exit one of the circus shows—as they do on a clockwork basis every time the show runs—as somehow these thirty-plus agents missed this show's regular exodus of children, when they surveilled the entire casino floor to prepare to follow Case.

Tiffany Case herself comes on strong as played by Jill St. John, supremely confident and verbally sparring with Bond as she first appears on screen. Yet she quickly degenerates into a dumb American bimbo, who ultimately undoes Bond's success in disabling the villain's death satellite, before she knocks herself into the ocean with the recoil from her ineptly fired gun. Her descent into a pawn moved lazily about the board by James Bond may fulfill Ian Fleming's concept that "men want a woman whom they can turn on and off like a light switch,"[39] but most of the non-American femme fatales fare more competently in the series.

The American police in *Diamonds* are, to a person, Keystone Cops who cannot stop or even slow Bond, crashing a dozen cars as they bumble through the Las Vegas streets. Shady Tree is still a connected smuggler and savvy, as in the novel. Indeed, he is savvy enough to star in a one-man Vegas comedy show, but his act hasn't bothered to add fresh material in 40 years. Tree is killed by American assassins, in a death stupidly timed before the last diamonds are smuggled up the gangster pipeline. Tree was supposed to live a bit longer before his fellow foolish Americans do him in.

Tree's grossly ignorant, uncouth henchmen are dismissed as a "brain trust" by Felix Leiter. Yet Felix Leiter is such a fool, he is not even smart enough to deduce where Bond might possibly have hidden 22 pounds of diamonds *inside* a cadaver (one guess would solve the mystery for most viewers). Scientist Klaus Hergersheimer destroys Bond's hasty cover story by doing what he shouldn't do, disturbing Dr. Metz's secret laboratory. Wint and Kidd remain the vicious American murderers they were in the novel as Winter and Kidd, but give away the game with their poor knowledge of wine and Mr. Wint's smelly cologne (after all, according to Fleming, American gangsters wear too much cologne). They die shrieking, destroyed by 007 with their own flaming shashlik and exploding bombe surprise, in the ultimate American food fight.

There are indeed many more foolish Americans parading through *Diamonds Are Forever*. Hapless gambler "Maxie" is a silly boob who loses all his money over sexy house shill and hustler Plenty O'Toole, but can't even land her for a date afterward. And O'Toole is not merely a Bond ingénue but dumb as a board. After being thrown from a high window and surviving due to sheer luck (when she plunges into an Olympic pool that her idiot killers didn't know lies beneath Bond's hotel room) O'Toole pursues Bond and Case unto her death, in another stupid hit, since O'Toole is taken for Case by the ever-dumb American assassins. Bambi and Thumper are the Bond girls who show far more promise initially, animalistically assaulting Bond and getting the best of him, but only for a few tense moments, before he shuts them down quickly, simply, by holding their silly American heads underwater in a swimming pool.

Even the hotel elevator Bond hitches a ride upon is boarded by ignorant tourists who have found the wrong car! And billionaire Willard Whyte, modeled (several steps down) after the reclusive genius engineer and groundbreaking filmmaker Howard Hughes, can't do much better. His distinctly American aide-de-camp, Bert Saxby (named in the script's wordplay as "Albert R. Saxby" after Bond producer Albert R. Broccoli) ineptly fails to kill Whyte, but during the attempt, Whyte can't seem to comprehend that Saxby, sliding down the scree beneath his home, riddled with bullets, is stone dead. So Whyte insists that Saxby's cadaver, be told that Whyte has chosen to fire him from his employ.

Whyte's security staff are no better, letting Bond unveil their hoaxed moon landing while escaping their motorbikes by using a stolen Moon buggy. Whyte's key satellite technicians are just as poor in IQ, and appear absolutely astonished that they have lost control of a rocket launch, despite having granted full security clearance to Blofeld—the same villain who has previously hijacked nuclear missiles to threaten the world with near-impunity!

Blofeld himself revels in his triumphs over all the dumb Americans and Bond, stating that "as La Rochefoucauld observed, 'Humility is the worst form of conceit.'"[40] This grand villain wants to prod the West into meeting his demands and threatens to use his killer satellite, telling his nemesis his thoughts even as he demeans America: "As you see, Mr. Bond, the satellite is at present over Kansas. If we destroy Kansas, the world may not hear about it for years. Perhaps New York. All that smut and traffic. It would give them a chance for a fresh start."[41] Shades of Fleming's "beloved" New York in the novel.

Diamonds Are Forever is an underrated Bond film, and a very funny Bond film, with more canny laughs and inside jokes for its audience than any of the Bonds except perhaps 1967's spoof, *Casino Royale*. Yet most of the laughs come at the expense of Americans, a curious choice for Bond's American film producers to have upheld. Of course, for James Bond himself, as Fleming put it, the end of *Diamonds Are Forever* was not just an American adventure but merely the end of one of many adventures, for which Tiffany's dry remark could serve as the headstone, "It reads better than it lives."[42]

NOTES

1. Raymond Chandler, "Review of Diamonds Are Forever," *The Sunday Times*, April 1, 1956, 9.

2. Christopher Hitchens, "Bottoms Up," *The Atlantic Monthly*, April 2006, 101.

3. David Walton, *Doing Cultural Theory* (Thousand Oaks: SAGE Publications Ltd, 2012), 42.

4. Andrew Lycett, *Fleming: The Man behind James Bond* (New York, St. Martin's Press. 2013), 64.

5. Kristen Brennan, "Star Wars Origins: Dune," Moongadget.com, moongadget.com/origins/dune.html Accessed (August 18, 2017).

6. Umberto Eco, "The Narrative Structure in Fleming," in *Il Caso Bond aka The Bond Affair*, ed. by Oreste Del Bueno and Umberto Eco (New York: Macdonald & Co., 1966), 218.

7. David Walton, *Doing Cultural Theory* (Thousand Oaks: SAGE Publications Ltd, 2012), 45.

8. John Cork, "Introduction," in *Live and Let Die* (London: Vintage, 2017), xv.

9. Ian Fleming, *Diamonds Are Forever* (Seattle: Thomas & Mercer, 2012), 52.

10. Fleming, *Diamonds Are Forever*, 54.

11. Ian Fleming, "007 in New York," in *Octopussy and The Living Daylights* (Seattle: Thomas & Mercer, 2012), 89.

12. Fleming, "007 in New York," 91.

13. Ian Fleming, *Casino Royale* (Seattle: Thomas & Mercer, 2012), 36.

14. Kingsley Amis, *The James Bond Dossier* (London: Jonathan Cape, 1965), 153.

15. Amis, *The James Bond Dossier*, 44.

16. Fleming, *Diamonds Are Forever*, 82.

17. Fleming, *Diamonds Are Forever*, 99.

18. Ian Fleming, "For Your Eyes Only," in *For Your Eyes Only* (Seattle: Thomas & Mercer, 2012), 65.

19. Fleming, "For Your Eyes Only," 131.

20. Fleming, "For Your Eyes Only," 140.

21. Fleming, "For Your Eyes Only," 66.

22. Ian Fleming, *Thrilling Cities* (London: Jonathan Cape, 1963), 102.

23. Fleming, *Thrilling Cities*, 98.

24. Fleming, *Thrilling Cities*, 95.

25. Simon Raven, "Gilt-Edged Bond," *The Spectator*, April 4, 1958, 22.

26. Ian Fleming, *Live and Let Die* (Seattle: Thomas & Mercer, 2012), 74–75.

27. Fleming, *Live and Let Die*, 75.

28. Matt Sherman, *James Bond's Cuisine: 007's Every Last Meal* (Seattle: CreateSpace, 2014), 6.

29. Sherman, *James Bond's Cuisine*, 23.

30. Raymond Benson, *The Facts of Death* (London: Hodder & Stoughton, 1998), 92.

31. Fleming, *Diamonds Are Forever*, 137.

32. Ian Fleming, *Goldfinger* (Seattle: Thomas & Mercer, 2012), 212.

33. Fleming, *Diamonds Are Forever*, 172.

34. Fleming, *Diamonds Are Forever*, 30.

35. Fleming, *Diamonds Are Forever*, 142–43.

36. Fleming, *Diamonds Are Forever*, 233.

37. Yevgenya Strakovsky, "Behind Enemy Lines: The Conscience of Russian Spies in *From Russia with Love* and *The Americans*," South Atlantic Modern Language Association '89, November 3, 2017.

38. Strakovsky, "Behind Enemy Lines," 58.

39. Robert A. Caplen, *Shaken & Stirred: The Feminism of James Bond* (Bloomington, IN: Xlibris, 2010), 34.

40. *Diamonds Are Forever*, DVD. (1971; Los Angeles, CA: MGM, 2013)

41. *Diamonds Are Forever* (1971).

42. Fleming, *Diamonds Are Forever*, 235.

BIBLIOGRAPHY

Amis, Kingsley. *The James Bond Dossier* London: Jonathan Cape, 1965.

Benson, Raymond. *The Facts of Death*. London: Hodder & Stoughton, 1998.

Brennan, Kristen. "Star Wars Origins: Dune." Moongadget.com. moongadget.com/origins/dune.html Accessed (August 18, 2017).

Caplen, Robert A. *Shaken & Stirred: The Feminism of James Bond*. Bloomington, IN: Xlibris, 2010.

Chandler, Raymond. "Review of Diamonds Are Forever." *The Sunday Times*, April 1, 1956, 9.

Diamonds Are Forever. 1971. DVD. Los Angeles, CA: MGM, 2013.

Eco, Umberto. "The Narrative Structure in Fleming." In *Il Caso Bond aka The Bond Affair*, edited by Oreste Del Bueno and Umberto Eco, 203–65. 1st ed. New York: Macdonald & Co., 1966.

Fleming, Ian. *Casino Royale*. Seattle, Thomas & Mercer, 2012.

———. *Diamonds Are Forever*. Seattle, Thomas & Mercer, 2012.

————. *For Your Eyes Only*. Seattle, Thomas & Mercer, 2012.

————. *Goldfinger*. Seattle, Thomas & Mercer, 2012.

————. *Live and Let Die*. Seattle, Thomas & Mercer, 2012.

————. *Live and Let Die*. London, Vintage, 2017.

————. *Thrilling Cities*. Jonathan Cape, 1963.

————. "007 in New York." In *Octopussy and The Living Daylights*. Seattle, Thomas & Mercer, 2012.

Fleming, Ian. "Ian Fleming Quote." izQuotes. http://izquotes.com/quote/62939 (accessed December 8, 2017).

Hitchens, Christopher. "Bottoms Up." *The Atlantic Monthly*, April 2006.

Lycett, Andrew. *Ian Fleming: The Man behind James Bond*. New York, St. Martin's Press. 2013.

Pratt, Benjamin. *Ian Fleming's Seven Deadlier Sins and 007's Moral Compass*. Canton, Front Edge Publishing, 2008.

Raven, Simon. "Gilt-Edged Bond." *The Spectator*, April 4, 1958.

Sherman, Matt. *James Bond's Cuisine: 007's Every Last Meal*. Seattle, CreateSpace, 2014.

Strakovsky, Yevgenya. "Behind Enemy Lines: The Conscience of Russian Spies in *From Russia with Love* and *The Americans*." South Atlantic Modern Language Association '89, November 3, 2017.

Walton, David. *Doing Cultural Theory*. Thousand Oaks: SAGE Publications Ltd, 2012.

NINE

The Desert of the Real

Diamonds Are Forever *as a Hollywood Novel*

Mark David Kaufman

In the HBO science-fiction series *Westworld*, a Wild West theme park offers the ultimate getaway, a simulated environment where the cares and responsibilities of the real world are traded for cowboy hats and six-shooters.[1] This is the American West, not as it was, but as Hollywood imagined it, complete with player pianos, congenial prostitutes, and charismatic outlaws. However, people don't flock here for the pony rides and poker games; this isolated resort caters to the basest aspects of human nature. In the park, wealthy "guests"—corporate CEOs and philanthropists—feel free to rape, rob, and murder in cold blood. Their victims are android "hosts" whose memories are mercifully wiped at the end of each day—that is, until they become sentient. Based on the 1973 film written and directed by Michael Crichton, *Westworld* is essentially *Jurassic Park* in spurs, a cautionary tale about the dangers of cultural reification. This is Frontierland gone mad.

Over sixty years ago, Ian Fleming conjured his own version of an adult theme park—a simulated Old West town built as a playground for psychopaths—in his fourth James Bond novel, *Diamonds Are Forever* (1956).[2] The parallel is not as odd as it seems; as early as 1965, Kingsley Amis had already pointed out the close relationship between spy fiction and science fiction, both of which "[combine] nightmare with plausibility" by "technologizing" fantasy and mythology.[3] In Fleming's novel, the American myth-made-real is Spectreville, a John Fordian mirage in the Nevada desert, a closed set with clapboard shops, a saloon, and a work-

157

ing locomotive. This is the lair of the Spangled Mob, American gangsters whose Las Vegas-based operation is the business end of an international diamond-smuggling pipeline that 007 has been sent to investigate. Like Westworld, Spectreville is a dystopian parody of Western capitalism, the confluence of too much money, too much imagination, and too little accountability.

In this essay, I will argue that Spectreville is one element of the novel's larger concern with Hollywood culture and the violence that underlies its myth-making: the violence to the real, the erosion of both the ability and the desire to maintain a distinct separation between reality and representation. In spite of the fact that James Bond has become a cinematic icon, surprisingly little critical attention has been paid to the influence of Hollywood on Fleming's original novels. That is to say, commentators have overlooked the way the novelist's vision both reflects and reflects upon the movie industry and its cultural ramifications. Granted, to characterize *Diamonds Are Forever* as a "Hollywood novel" is problematic, considering that, aside from two brief scenes, the narrative's primary North American settings are Las Vegas and Saratoga. Nor does it seem, at first glance, to have the same thematic foci as other novels representative of the genre, such as the conflict between art and mass entertainment, which Chip Rhodes[4] argues is central to texts like Nathanael West's *The Day of the Locust* (1939), Evelyn Waugh's *The Loved One* (1948), and Raymond Chandler's *The Little Sister* (1949).[5] But *Diamonds Are Forever* does share with these novels a preoccupation with America as a land of simulacra, defined by the postmodern philosopher, Jean Baudrillard, as images with no basis in actuality, but which masquerade as representations of real life[6]—or what Rhodes, following Baudrillard, describes as "a self-enclosed world of simulations that has erased and replaced 'reality,' leaving only performances that are always already signifiers, fictions, illusions that become real when (and if) they convince someone of their 'reality.'"[7] In the course of his investigation, Bond, having assumed the identity of a diamond smuggler, infiltrates a world where illusions become flesh: he eats an "English breakfast" that isn't really an English breakfast; he bets on a horse race with fixed results; he renews his friendship with Felix Leiter, now aping the speech and mannerisms of a film noir private eye; and he thwarts a group of stage-gangsters who pretend to be cowboys in their own private, tumbleweed town. Ultimately, *Diamonds Are Forever*, like other Hollywood novels, leaves its readers questioning whether there is any difference between identity and performance. In doing so, the novel reveals a parallel between filmmaking and espionage, two spheres of modernity invested in the manufacturing of illusions.

THE DREAM FACTORY

What exactly constitutes a Hollywood novel? In *Politics, Desire, and the Hollywood Novel* (2008), Chip Rhodes argues that the term does not simply signify fiction set in the locale but rather fiction that "[defamiliarizes] the main ideologies that undergird Hollywood."[8] Often, these novels are penned by disillusioned screenwriters and others who have experienced the life firsthand. Not surprisingly, Rhodes writes, "the 'stars' of Hollywood novels are artists who have an ambivalent relation to the film industry. Their ambivalence figures both their contempt for the convention-driven films that are generally produced and their investment in the same formulas."[9] In short, they are sellouts, and, worst of all, they know it. For Rhodes, however, the unifying theme of the genre is not, ultimately, the conflict between art and commercialism but the relationship between art and sexual desire. Adopting a simultaneously psychoanalytic and Marxist perspective, Rhodes reveals the influence of Freudian thought on Hollywood novels of the studio era (roughly the 1920s to the 1960s), especially the theory of sublimation, the process of finding "socially acceptable outlets for socially unacceptable longings," which nullifies any distinction between so-called "high" art and popular entertainment.[10] This formation is always haunted by the specter of thwarted desire, for the sublimation is never truly satisfactory, and the excess of longing, the frustration over failure, erupts as violence. Therein also lies the political dimension of the genre. "Since the early years of the film industry, there has been a tendency to equate Hollywood with some form of democracy," Rhodes observes, and Hollywood itself "has been the most persistent purveyor of this view of the film industry, happily exploiting the American myth of reinvention by which an individual can break out of a static, inegalitarian class structure and create an autonomous identity."[11] Of course, this Horatio Alger fantasy is belied by the real-life pecking order imposed by the studio system. Accordingly, Hollywood novels evince "disdain for the discourse of democracy,"[12] representing the film industry—and, by extension, American culture—as a dubious "dream factory."[13]

Nathanael West's 1939 novel, *The Day of the Locust*, is paradigmatic of the studio-era novels. After a stint working as a B-movie scriptwriter for Columbia Pictures, during which he lived in a hotel on Hollywood Boulevard, West understood the motivations and desperations of the people who, as he puts it in the book, "come to California to die."[14] Written and set during the Great Depression, the novel focuses on the individuals who have travelled to the West Coast seeking a new life, only to find a two-dimensional promised land. The main protagonist, Tod Hackett, is a Yale-educated artist who has secured a job in scenic design, painting sets and backdrops for movies. During the day, Hackett inhabits of world of jumbled fantasies, a backlot where a paper mâché sphinx rubs shoulders with the Trojan horse in the shadow of a Mayan temple. At one point, Hackett kicks back in a rocking chair in front of a faux Western saloon and observes "an Arab [charge] by on a white stallion" followed by "a truck with a load of snow and several malamute dogs."[15] In the after hours, when he isn't fashioning fake castles and sunsets, he works obsessively on a giant painting titled *The Burning of Los Angeles*, an apocalyptic vision of hellfire and mayhem, a pretentious commentary on consumerism. However, Hackett's desire to produce an authentic work of art falls flat; just as his surname hints that his art is ultimately a "hack" job, his sensationalist painting is no different from the B-movies and exploitation pictures that feed the masses, the people whose disillusionment with California reaches its boiling point:

> Their boredom becomes more and more terrible. They realize that they've been tricked and burn with resentment. Every day of their lives they read the newspapers and went to the movies. Both fed them on lynchings, murder, sex crimes, explosions, wrecks, love nests, fires, miracles, revolutions, wars. This daily diet made sophisticates of them. The sun is a joke. Oranges can't titillate their jaded palates. Nothing can ever be violent enough to make taut their slack minds and bodies.[16]

The novel ends when a street altercation triggers a bloody riot on Hollywood Boulevard. Ironically but inevitably, Hackett's expressionistic nightmare comes to life, revealing the violence that bubbles beneath the surface of the American dream of reinvention, the desire to "be somebody" in a world that cares about no one.

In the course of his cultural vivisection, West reflects on the manner in which various modes of representation—performance, fakery, forgery, and so on—paradoxically achieve a measure of authenticity. At one point in the novel, Hackett visits a nightclub and watches a transvestite stage show. The cross-dresser's performance is so convincing that after a while his identity is eclipsed by his feminine persona:

> He had a soft, throbbing voice and his gestures were matronly, tender and aborted, a series of unconscious caresses. What he was doing was in no sense parody; it was too simple and too restrained. It wasn't even theatrical. This dark young man with his thin, hairless arms and soft, rounded shoulders, who rocked an imaginary cradle as he crooned, was really a woman.[17]

When the song ends and the dream is broken, it is the young man's clumsy return to his male self that suddenly strikes Hackett as counterfeit: "He tripped on his train, as though he weren't used to it, lifted his skirts to show he was wearing Paris garters, then strode off swinging his shoulders. His imitation of a man was awkward and obscene."[18] The actual and the virtual are reversed. Here and elsewhere, West's novel anticipates Baudrillard's *Simulacra and Simulation* (1981) and becomes, as Rhodes puts it, "one of the most insightful literary meditations on the substitution of simulations of reality for reality itself in an entertainment age."[19] Simulation, for Baudrillard, constitutes "the generation by models of a real without origin or reality: a hyperreal."[20] Like a "map that precedes the territory," the hyperreal is a fiction that achieves the force of truth.[21] As a result, the real is obscured, abandoned, like a wasteland, or what Baudrillard terms the *"desert of the real."*[22] In *The Day of the Locust*, the backlot of Hackett's studio contains a set for an Orientalist epic, a "desert that was continually being made larger by a fleet of trucks dumping white sand."[23] But this is not the desert of the real in the Baudrillardian sense; the desert of the real is the nightmarish realization that there is not even a "real desert" beneath the "fake desert" — indeed, that there is no longer a real at all beyond the simulation.

For Baudrillard — and, I will suggest, for Fleming — Disneyland is the "perfect model of all the entangled orders of simulacra."[24] Ultimately, the Magic Kingdom's relation to hyperreality is not that its "illusions and phantasms" contrast a more authentic world beyond its walls, though Baudrillard does make a striking comparison between the theme park and its parking lot, "a veritable concentration camp."[25] Rather, "Disneyland is presented as imaginary in order to make us believe that the rest is real, whereas all of Los Angeles and the America that surrounds it are no longer real, but belong to the hyperreal order and to the order of simulation."[26] To put it another way, the promises of capitalism, the myth of reinvention, are, in a sense, the "real" magic spells obscured by the sorcery of the Disney villain. The only transformation that takes place, magical or otherwise, is the substitution of hyperreality for reality. Essentially, it is this realization at the end of West's novel that triggers the eruption of violence and collapse of social order.

Whether or not Fleming was aware of West's dystopian vision of Los Angeles, he was undoubtedly familiar with another Hollywood novel that likewise explores the implications of hyperreality *avant la letter*, Evelyn Waugh's *The Loved One* (1948). Inspired by the author's short stay in southern California, where he had (reluctantly) come to discuss the possibility of adapting *Brideshead Revisited*, Waugh's black comedy offers a Brit's-eye-view of Hollywood and the film industry. Subtitled "An Anglo-American Tragedy," the novel focuses on a young English poet and expatriate named Dennis Barlow who has lost his job as a writer for Megalopolitan Pictures and taken up work at a pet crematorium called the Happier Hunting Ground. After the suicide of his fellow "exile," Sir Francis Hinsley, Barlow finds himself making funeral arrangements at Whispering Glades, an ostentatious cemetery based on the real-life Forest Lawn in Los Angeles, which Fleming refers to in *Thrilling Cities* as "America's Waugh Memorial."[27] Like its nonfictional counterpart, Whispering Glades is a Disneyland for the dead. Here, Waiting Ones (the bereaved) can choose to have their Loved Ones (the deceased) interred in any number of themed park zones, such as Poet's Corner, for writers, or

Shadowland, for filmmakers. There is a mock-Oxford church and a Lake Isle of Innisfree based on the poem by W. B. Yeats. The gravestones and statuary are masterpieces of kitsch: "Here a bearded magician sought the future in the obscure depths of what seemed to be a plaster football. There a toddler clutched to its stony bosom a marble Mickey Mouse."[28] A mishmash of fantasies, the park recalls the film studio backlot of *The Day of the Locust*, its gaudy spectacles a testament to its founder, Wilbur Kenworthy—known as "THE DREAMER"[29]—a Walt Disney of the underworld. Appropriately, after spending time in this land of simulacra, Dennis the ex-screenwriter turns from poetry to plagiarism, sending Shakespearean sonnets under his own name to Aimée Thanatogenos, a crematorium cosmetician who once worked at the Beverly-Waldorf but now prefers the company of corpses. Whispering Glades emerges as a macabre parody of a film studio, the final destination of a soulless entertainment industry that subsists on clichéd storylines and hackneyed themes. In Waugh's Hollywood, there is no such thing as originality, only lifeless copies of copies. Beautiful corpses.

Like many Hollywood novels, *The Loved One* associates movie-making with death. Another novel with a similar theme, a novel most likely familiar to the creator of James Bond, is Raymond Chandler's *The Little Sister*, published in 1949. A writer whom Fleming admired and would later come to know, Chandler spent a number of years working as a screenwriter in Hollywood, where he developed a keen antipathy toward the film industry despite achieving a great deal of success (and money). Two of his screenplays were nominated for an Academy Award: *Double Indemnity* (1944), co-written with Billy Wilder, and *The Blue Dahlia* (1946). Working with demanding directors like Wilder made him bitter and defensive; he felt that writers in Hollywood were largely unappreciated. In a now-infamous 1945 article in *The Atlantic Monthly*, Chandler lambasts the industry as a whole. "The making of a picture," he observes, "is an endless contention of tawdry egos, some of them powerful, almost all of them vociferous, and almost none of them capable of anything much more creative than credit-stealing and self-promotion."[30] From the writer's perspective, the movie industry shares something in common with the world of espionage: "The superficial friendliness of Hollywood is pleasant—until you find out that nearly every sleeve conceals a knife."[31]

The Little Sister is, in essence, the fictional counterpart to Chandler's takedown of Tinseltown. The fifth Philip Marlowe novel finds the hardboiled detective investigating a missing person, a search that takes him deep into the seedy underworld of Los Angeles, a collage of movie stars, drugs, and blackmail—and a fair number of icepicks sticking out of people's necks. In the course of his misadventures, Marlowe experiences his share of Hollywood and its hypocrisies. Cruising Ventura Boulevard, the detective takes note of the glitzy surfaces that barely conceal a rotten interior: "I drove on past the gaudy neons and the false fronts behind them, the sleazy hamburger joints that look like palaces under the colors, the circular drive-ins as gay as circuses with the chipper hard-eyed car-hops, the brilliant counters, and the sweaty greasy kitchens that would have poisoned a toad."[32] Rhodes, however, does not read *The Little Sister* as "a wholesale dismissal of a Hollywood-dominated American culture. . . . Rather, Hollywood is the institution that gives faithful expression to an intractable, if regrettable, human nature."[33] More specifically, Rhodes contends, Chandler's novel works to subvert the American myth of reinvention.[34] "Wonderful what Hollywood will do to a nobody," Marlowe muses at one point.

> It will make a radiant glamour queen out of a drab little wench who ought to be ironing a truck driver's shirts, a he-man hero with shining eyes and brilliant smile reeking of sexual charm out of some over-grown kid who was meant to go to work with a lunchbox. Out of a Texas car hop with the literacy of a character in a comic strip it will make an international courtesan, married six times to six millionaires and so blasé and decadent at the end of it that her idea of a thrill is to seduce a furniture mover in a sweaty undershirt.[35]

As Rhodes points out, Chandler evinces "contempt for the working class and rural America,"[36] the people for whom Hollywood is simply the enabler, a kind of drug dealer. The final line of the novel arguably sums up Chandler's antidemocratic disillusionment, an ironic remark dropped by an ambulance worker preparing to wrap up the last of the book's many corpses: "I guess somebody lost a dream."[37]

When Fleming met Chandler at a luncheon party at the poet Stephen Spender's house in 1955, the latter was in his middle sixties, depressed and suicidal after the recent death of his wife (and cat), and, by his own admission, "drinking two bottles of Scotch a day."[38] Meanwhile, Fleming had just published his third James Bond novel, *Moonraker*. He relished the opportunity to meet the famous detective writer, and he wasted little time securing Chandler's official endorsement of his work. Chandler admired the Englishman's grasp of American culture and dialogue, as evidenced in *Live and Let Die*. Though American, Chandler had grown up in and around London, and "[he] was interested in the way English public-school boys (like himself) tackled writing about American gangsters."[39] Fleming, however, worried whether Chandler would like his next book, which, while also set in the United States, had far "more fantasy" than the previous novels.[40] Even so, Fleming's fourth novel shares not only with *The Little Sister* but also with *The Day of the Locust* and *The Loved One* a critical reflection on the American "dream factory." Fleming was not, like the authors of so many Hollywood novels, a disgruntled screenwriter—not, as Rhodes puts it, one of those "embittered artists who left Hollywood with their literary egos badly bruised"[41]—but he was a bestselling novelist torn between derision and desire for Hollywood recognition.

This ambivalence comes through in *Diamonds Are Forever*, a book that critiques the culture of simulation and yet ends with 007 sitting in the Beverly Hills Hotel looking like he has "just finished work at the studios"[42]—in effect, already a movie star six years before Sean Connery won his first hand at Baccarat.

SIMULACRA ARE A GIRL'S BEST FRIEND

It's fair to say that Ian Fleming had mixed feelings about the United States. After reading the manuscript of *Live and Let Die*, William Plomer, Fleming's friend and literary editor at Jonathan Cape, shared his impressions with the novelist in a letter dated May 15, 1953: "What I particularly like is the Bond's-eye-view of America. . . . The whole thing is done with great dash & one believes in it most of the time as one believes in a highly disturbing dream."[43] Plomer's contradictory language—Fleming's America is as believable as a nightmare—is a testament to the author's characterization of the United States as both a land of plenty and a land of living death. Solitaire's description of St. Petersburg, Florida, is a case in point. "It's the Great American Graveyard," she tells Bond. "It's a terrifying sight, all these old people with their spectacles and hearing-aids and clicking false-teeth."[44] For his part, Bond is less horrified by American retirees than by American cuisine. In Fleming, food is always an indication of a culture's worth. Although Bond and Leiter do enjoy one ostentatious American meal "at its rare best,"[45] the British agent is generally put off by the local fare. Sitting in the "unwashed, dog-eared atmosphere" of a Florida diner, Bond orders scrambled eggs because he considers it the safest thing on the menu.[46] Bond's dislike of American cooking is matched only by his disdain for American automobiles, which, with the exception of Leiter's "Studillac" in *Diamonds Are Forever*, "[lack] personality and the patina of individual craftsmanship that European cars have."[47] These criticisms have a political, even traitorous, undertone. As Christopher Hitchens observes, "the central paradox of the classic Bond stories is that, although superficially devoted to the Anglo-American war against communism, they are full of contempt and resentment for America and Americans."[48]

At the same time, Fleming understood the importance of the American marketplace, especially the glamor of the silver screen. "Fleming was angling for Hollywood," Hitchens writes, "however much he may have despised it."[49] In fact, Fleming imagined 007 as a movie star from the beginning. In *Casino Royale* (1953), Vesper Lynd tells Mathis that Bond reminds her of Hoagy Carmichael,[50] the American singer and actor who had appeared in a number of films, including Howard Hughes's *The Las Vegas Story* (1952). Fleming likewise considered *Moonraker* a film treatment posing as a novel. After the British director and producer Sir

Alexander Korda read a proof of *Live and Let Die* and wrote Fleming a letter of praise, the novelist responded that his next book would make for even better movie material.[51] More specifically, in a letter to Korda on January 6, 1954, Fleming claims that during the war he first conceived what would become *Moonraker* as "a film story."[52] The author even seems to have taken an interest in filmmaking itself. In a Letter to W. Somerset Maugham the following April, Fleming records that he recently sat behind Orson Welles at an airport buffet and "eavesdropped on his views on the wide screen cinema which, for your information, he says is a hopeless shape for an intelligent producer."[53] There is a certain amount of intrigue in the thought of the famous spy novelist spying on the famous director, making a mental note of the latest technical developments in the industry he hoped to infiltrate.

Fleming had the opportunity to see Hollywood for himself later that year, on a whirlwind American tour to carry out research for *Diamonds Are Forever*. In September 1954, Fleming contacted his American friend, Ernest Cuneo, a lawyer and former OSS liaison whom he had met during the war while working for the British Security Co-ordination in New York. He hoped Cuneo would not only help him plan the trip but also join him as a traveling companion and guide to Las Vegas and "the Hollywood world."[54] Cuneo agreed, and Fleming crossed the Atlantic on the *Queen Elizabeth*, arriving in New York in early November. From there, the two traveled by rail, first taking the *Twentieth Century* to Chicago and then the *Super Chief* to Los Angeles. Although unimpressed by American cars, Fleming was fascinated with trains, especially the classic American lines. According to John Pearson, "[he] loved their size, their smell, their power, their comfort, as well as the sense that once you had embarked on a long journey in one you were in a private world and in a way immune from the laws of the states and cities through which you passed."[55] After experiencing what Bond, in *Live and Let Die*, calls "the romance of the American railroads,"[56] Fleming courted a different sort of outlaw romance in Chicago, where he annoyed Cuneo by preferring to visit sites associated with Al Capone instead of the Chicago Institute of Fine Arts.[57] Even before setting foot in Hollywood, Fleming was seeking a Hollywood version of America, an America of famous railroads and infamous gangsters.

After Chicago, Fleming's short stay in Los Angeles gave him a taste of Hollywood life and provided him with additional material for *Diamonds Are Forever*. But it was also a business trip. By 1954, he was "angling" (to borrow Hitchens's term) not only for big-screen adaptations but also for a television series featuring Bond. This was a sign of the times. By the mid-1950s, the studio system was in decline. According to Rhodes, this was the result of complicated factors, including antitrust laws and changing viewing habits, but it was likewise due to the growing importance of television, which the studios were then trying to get a piece of themselves.[58] Fleming had already broken ground on the small screen. In October, CBS had broadcast a live, hour-long adaptation of *Casino Royale*, starring American actor Barry Nelson as "Jimmy" Bond and Peter Lorre as Le Chiffre. Although the special took considerable liberties and was marred by technical issues, it gave Fleming enough cachet to pursue additional opportunities while in Hollywood. Through his West Coast agent, "Swanee" Swanson, Fleming discussed selling film rights for *Live and Let Die* and *Moonraker* with Stanley Meyer, the producer of *Dragnet* at Warner Bros., but Fleming ultimately rejected Meyer's offer of $500 for the option. Swanson concluded that Fleming was "a very nice guy" but likewise "a very vague man."[59] "Clearly," Andrew Lycett writes, "the pace of the movie world was unfamiliar."[60] Fleming's account of his later trip to Hollywood in 1959 may shed some light on the writer's initial experience with the film industry. After revisiting "America's Waugh Memorial"—that is to say, Forest Lawn cemetery—Fleming had an uncomfortable business lunch with an unnamed producer, which he records in a vein worthy of Chandler:

> As all foreign authors know, Hollywood likes to have first bite at anyone who is 'new' and even moderately successful, and at twelve-thirty I was having lunch in the Brown Derby with a producer who wanted to make a fortune out of me in exchange for a glass of water and a crust of bread. I was treated to the whole smart rag-bag of show-biz pressure-talk in between Eggs-Benedict and those eighty per cent proof dry martinis that anaesthetize the uvula.[61]

The novelist had better luck with the research side of his 1954 trip. Before moving on to Las Vegas, where he and Cuneo engaged in an all-night, champagne-soaked casino crawl, Fleming had the opportunity to discuss the American mafia with Captain James Hamilton of the LAPD, who was Chandler's source as well.[62] For Fleming, organized crime was itself a genre of performance art, an extension of Hollywood posturing, wheeling, and dealing, and its public stage was the Strip. "The casino," according to Pearson, "was the only theatre Ian Fleming ever enjoyed."[63]

Fleming's 1954 tour reinforced his image of America as a land of specious spectacles. The structure of *Diamonds Are Forever*, I contend, parallels the Englishman's trip to the United States in that the Los Angeles sections provide a conceptual frame for understanding the novel's depiction of Las Vegas and environs as an oasis of simulacra in the midst of an indifferent desert. Fleming, like the other Hollywood novelists previously discussed, anticipates the Baudrillardian idea of the hyperreal, in which the model supplants (or becomes) the original. The Hollywood fantasy of America—the America of Old West shootouts, roaring trains, and melodramatic gangsters—is made material in Fleming's novel by characters who copy the conventions of the silver screen. In Baudrillard's terms, they "attempt to make the real, all of the real, coincide with their models of simulation."[64] The result is not only physical violence but violence to the very notion of authenticity.

Diamonds Are Forever is a cinematic novel, both formally and thematically. Even before Bond sets foot in the United States, the book is preoccupied with simulacra, with the inability—and, in some ways, inconsequentiality—of differentiating between the authentic and the fake. After its famous opening scene of a scorpion in its final moments, which Umberto Eco judges to be a narratologically "purposeless" sequence akin to the opening titles of a film,[65] the novel quickly establishes diamonds themselves as a metaphor for the dissolution of the real. When we first see 007, he has been tasked by M with differentiating between genuine diamonds and worthless but attractive fakes. He fails completely. The rock he has been scrutinizing, a dazzling stone with rainbow-flashes, is actually, M reveals, just a common piece of quartz.[66] From this scene onward, the British agent is beset by forgeries of various kinds. At the House of Diamonds, Rufus B. Saye strikes Bond as a human "chunk of quartz."[67] This description, coming so close on the heels of Bond's lapidary lesson, hints at the American businessman's spurious persona. Indeed, we later learn that this stony visage belongs to Jack Spang, the co-boss (with his brother, Seraffimo) of the Spangled Mob. From the start, Bond dismisses the gang as a collection of stage-gangsters who have learned their mannerisms from popular media. Once in New York, his impression is confirmed. Observing the outline of a gun in a thug's pocket, Bond concludes that American gangsters have watched "too many films."[68] In comparison with the professional killers he encounters as a secret agent, the mafia are little more than "teenage pillow-fantasies."[69] Hollywood-inspired poseurs or not, however, the Spangled Mob are real criminals capable of real violence. Moreover, in Fleming's novel, the heroes are just as likely as the villains to copy actors (who are themselves copies without originals); Felix Leiter, Bond discovers, has now assumed the role of a wisecracking private eye.[70] In the Las Vegas casinos, the sheriffs, like the dealers, are dressed as Hollywood cowboys.[71]

The novel's gangsters and lawmen are not the only indications of hyperreality; tourist trinkets and food also remind Fleming's readers that the modern world is, for the most part, counterfeit. In *Simulacra and Simulation*, Baudrillard asserts that "the era of simulation is inaugurated by a liquidation of all referentials."[72] That is to say, representations are no longer modelled on authentic sources; the representation *is* the source. During his layover in Ireland, Bond wanders Shannon airport and marvels at the tacky assortment of souvenirs standing in for an Ireland that never was.[73] Later, on the plane to New York, he suffers through a faux English breakfast.[74] As in *Live and Let Die*, Fleming reserves his most damning criticism for the American diner; Bond and Leiter visit a tacky, Western-themed restaurant that looks more like "something out of science fiction."[75] Fleming's descriptions of American highway "culture" (to use the author's own scare-quotes) are amplified in his later novels. In *The Spy Who Loved Me* (1962), Vivienne Michel characterizes Lake George in the Adirondacks as a kind of roadside Disneyland knockoff, "a gim-crack nightmare of concrete gnomes, Bambi deer and toadstools, shoddy foodstalls selling 'Big Chief Hamburgers' and 'Minnehaha Candy Floss,' and 'Attractions' such as 'Animal Land' ('Visitors may hold and photo-graph costumed chimps'), 'Gaslight Village' ('Genuine 1890 gas-light-ing'), and 'Storytown USA,' a terrifying babyland nightmare which I need not describe."[76]

Disneyland and its bizarro imitators offer a concentrated version of what happens in American culture in general: the substitution of specta-cle for authenticity. Baudrillard notes that the theme park's "values are exalted by the miniature and the comic strip. Embalmed and pacified."[77] Similarly, in Waugh's *The Loved One*, the effigy of the toddler clinging to his "marble Mickey Mouse"[78] has the effect of sanitizing death, trans-forming the afterlife into a Saturday morning cartoon, a reward for faith-ful consumerism. For Fleming, Las Vegas is essentially another theme park, "a fantastic caravanserai."[79] Like Disneyland, which herds its visi-tors down predetermined pathways under the illusion of free choice, the casino's gaudy excesses are a cover for what Bond labels "The Gilded Mousetrap School" of architecture.[80] The empty-eyed slot players are conditioned, the agent imagines, not unlike drooling, Pavlovian dogs.[81] In *The Loved One*, the British expatriate Sir Francis makes a similar obser-vation concerning Hollywood and its hangers-on:

> Did you see the photograph some time ago in one of the magazines of a dog's head severed from its body, which the Russians are keeping alive for some obscene Muscovite purpose by pumping blood into it from a bottle? It dribbles at the tongue when it smells a cat. That's what all of us are, you know, out here. The studios keep us going with a pump. We are still just capable of a few crude reactions—nothing more. If we ever got disconnected from our bottle, we should simply crumble.[82]

Likewise dehumanized, the denizens of the Strip, zombie-like in their dogged persistence, reveal the dark side of capitalism. Las Vegas and its delights have a way of changing human beings, as Fleming writes in *Thrilling Cities*, into "caricatures of humanity."[83]

If Las Vegas represents an extension of Hollywood hyperreality, its fullest expression in *Diamonds Are Forever* is Spectreville, an immersive Western world that is effectively an adult version of Disney's Frontier-land, which, incidentally, had its grand opening in July 1955 while Flem-ing was preparing his novel for publication. Like *The Day of the Locust*, with its backlot "Last Chance Saloon" and a down-at-heel Indian wan-dering around town with a sandwich board touting "GENUINE RELICS OF THE OLD WEST,"[84] Fleming's novel features an Old West simulation drawn from movies and other forms of popular culture. Upon arrival at the Spangled Mob's desert playground, Bond sees a clapboard town with the usual nineteenth-century amenities. Naturally, there is a saloon, complete with swing-doors and a honkey-tonk player-piano. For Bond, the scene recalls "something out of an exceptionally well-mounted 'Western.'"[85] Appropriately, the agent soon gets into an extended bar fight with two goons, a Hollywood action sequence that is suddenly halted by the command to "Cut."[86] In the doorway, Bond sees Seraffimo Spang in elaborate cowboy getup, accompanied by a similarly attired Tiffany Case.[87] Fleming's parody of a movie set is both humorous and unsettling. For all its contrivances, Spectreville is, paradoxically, a real fake, a dream that draws blood. According to Baudrillard, "[the] impossibility of rediscovering an absolute level of the real is of the same order as the impossibility of staging illusion. Illusion is no longer possible, because the real is no longer possible."[88] In Fleming's novel, Bond finds the juxtaposition of comical, make-believe surroundings with the threat of actual violence to be strangely unnerving. Shortly after Spang's cinematic entrance, the threat is realized. Bond is kicked senseless by Wint and Kidd, two goons with names that sound more like Western outlaws than gangsters. This beating is simultaneously an ironic compounding and subversion of hypermasculine tropes; homosexual hitmen wearing football boots give 007 a "Brooklyn stomping" in the middle of an iconic cowboy setting— and all of it offstage, leaving the reader to imagine Bond's humiliation at the feet of his foes.[89]

Unlike the sterilized pleasures of Frontierland, Spectreville offers a more sinister sort of wish fulfillment. The appeal of the "Wild West" is its lawlessness, its ability to give free rein to (male) fantasies of sadism and sexual domination. In the mobster's playland, the British agent discovers "The Cannonball," a luxuriously refurbished 1870 locomotive and Pullman coach. Like the train in *Westworld* that transports the "guests" from the staging area to the park itself, the Spang line, Bond learns, is a moveable orgy of booze and call girls.[90] The train also becomes the vehicle for another Hollywood set piece, a chase scene worthy of the golden age of cinema. After Bond and Case escape on a petrol-powered handcar, they leave a massive explosion in their wake, which Case likens to a stunt from "an old Buster Keaton film."[91] During the ensuing chase, with Spang and his locomotive bearing down on them, Bond manages to shift the speeding train to a branch line, sending it straight into the side of a mountain—another Keatonesque stunt reminiscent of the famous train crash in *The General* (1926). This cartoonish death is appropriate for a man who was, in life, little more than a caricature, "a stage-gangster, surrounded with stage properties."[92] And yet 007 has his cinematic side as well. If the literary Bond draws upon the myth of the British hero of adventure fiction, from Sherlock Holmes to Bulldog Drummond, he is likewise the spiritual successor of the classical Hollywood action star, whose over-the-top devices come in handy in sticky situations. Just as

Chandler's Philip Marlowe (more cynically) recognizes his own "techni-color dialogue"[93] and even imagines himself as a Hollywood cowboy—"Two-gun Marlowe, the kid from Cyanide Gulch"[94]—Bond, during the chase scene, assumes the role of a big-screen daredevil. Similarly, in *You Only Live Twice* (1964), the agent escapes from Blofeld's diabolical castle, a veritable "Disneyland of Death,"[95] by clinging to a balloon, an idea inspired by "a flashback to one of the old Douglas Fairbanks films when the hero had swung across a wide hall by taking a flying leap at the chandelier."[96] Clearly, watching movies can save your life.

The novel's ambiguous relationship to Hollywood, its simultaneous denigration and celebration of artificiality, manifests itself structurally in the two California scenes that frame Bond's adventure in the West. In his study of Fleming, Umberto Eco evidently considered these sections not important enough to include in his outline of the novel's "fundamental moves" and "side issues."[97] However, the two Hollywood interludes reinforce the book's preoccupation with simulation. The first is an aerial panorama of Los Angeles as Bond is flying to Las Vegas. Under Bond's gaze, swank neighborhoods and industrial complexes merge inconspicuously with the fantasy world of the film studios. All are bound by an endless and indifferent desert that throws into relief the mirage of civilization.[98] Fleming's catalog of "gimcrack sets," which would sound at home in *The Day of the Locust*, includes "Western ranches" that anticipate the equally spurious Spectreville.[99] This initial view of Hollywood, re-layed at an ironic distance, is eventually replaced by a more naturalized depiction as Bond becomes increasingly associated with movie tropes. After the Nevada section, during which 007 and Ernie Cureo (whose name is a nod to Ernie Cuneo) hide from thugs in a drive-in theater,[100] Bond, Case, and Felix drive back to Los Angeles and find themselves cruising Sunset Boulevard on their way to the Beverly Hills Hotel. The hotel, which Fleming would later call "the friendliest hotel in Hollywood,"[101] serves as the backdrop for a prophetic metamorphosis: James Bond becomes a movie star—at least notionally. In this city of illusions, his "battle-scarred face" seems little more than a clever makeup job.[102] The image is appropriate, considering the agent escapes from the clutches of the Spangled Mob by way of a Hollywood stunt, but this scene also manifests Fleming's desire to see his creation on the big screen, larger than life, like the gigantic actors Bond and Cureo watch at the drive-in. Fittingly, 007 then embarks on an amorous journey with Case, herself a former "studio extra"[103] now dressed to the nines in an ironic salute to "the best those Hollywood pansies can dream up."[104]

Ironically, the 1971 film version of *Diamonds Are Forever* does away with these Hollywood references altogether, except perhaps for one curious scene.[105] Bond learns that the entrepreneur Willard Whyte is being held captive at his summer house outside of Las Vegas. When he arrives, he is met by Whyte's two female bodyguards, acrobatic assassins who identify themselves as "Bambi" and "Thumper." Bond's tussle with these scantily clad beauties, who seem in retrospect to anticipate the "fembots" of Austin Powers fame, is a tongue-in-cheek episode in what is surely one of the campiest Bond films. Nevertheless, their Disney-inspired names, coupled with their cold but violent demeanor, reinforce the thematic association of Hollywood with death that we find not only in Fleming but in Hollywood fiction in general. Fleming's innovation, which he develops in his subsequent work, is to establish a correspondence between the world of cinematic invention and the world of international intrigue, both of which trade in images, shadows, and myths.

In his fifth novel, *From Russia with Love* (1957), Fleming emphasizes that spies are essentially professional actors and that espionage itself shares much in common with movie-making. "Has it ever occurred to you," Darko Kerim asks Bond at one point, "that our kind of work is rather like shooting a film?"[106] The world of intrigue, Kerim suggests, is all about setting a scene, getting the players into place, and hoping for a bit of chemistry. SMERSH, the counterintelligence arm of the KGB, understands this as well. In order to frame and assassinate the legendary British agent, the Russians devise a plan in which a low-level officer, Tatiana Romanova, pretends to defect because she has fallen in love with 007 based on his dossier. Though skeptical, M accepts the possibility that Bond may have achieved the rather paradoxical status of a secret celebrity. "Suppose you happened to be a film star instead of being in this particular trade" M tells Bond. "You'd get daft letters from girls all over the world stuffed with Heaven knows what sort of rot about not being able to live without you and so on."[107] In Istanbul, where Bond is instructed to help the girl escape in exchange for a Russian decoding machine, Kerim advises the agent to imitate the cruel but handsome persona his dossier photo suggests: "Behave like that image. Act the part."[108] After meeting in person, the "Garbo-esque" Romanova[109]—who is, of course, playing a part herself—tells Bond that he looks "like an American film star," much to the British agent's chagrin.[110] The identification of the lovers as actors is further reinforced by their being surreptitiously filmed in the act of love by two sweaty SMERSH agents. They are now, quite literally, movie stars.

Or porn stars. Fleming's associations of his characters with Hollywood and its culture are never wholly glamourous. In *From Russia with Love*, voyeurism hints at an underlying violence that emerges elsewhere in the novel. Perhaps the most startling and surreal image in the book is the gigantic Marilyn Monroe billboard that serves as a backdrop for bloodshed. Made even more monstrous by Bond's rifle scope, the nightmarish vision reveals the ugly substratum—the wasteland of the real—obscured by the Hollywood fantasy. When the doomed Krilencu emerges from a door in her mouth, the beauty icon completes her transformation into a goddess of death: from her lips, the assassin hangs "like a worm from the mouth of a corpse."[111] This scene, which eerily anticipates Monroe's suicide five years later, reinforces the notion that cinematic myth-making constitutes the death of the real. This idea also haunts Kerim's untimely murder on the Orient Express. Bond discovers the bodies of his friend and the assassin "frozen in a ghastly-death struggle that might have been posed for a film."[112] In the age of simulacra, actual death appears unreal, like something staged for the pleasure of theater audiences.

Both *Diamonds Are Forever* and *From Russia with Love* share with the Hollywood novel genre the idea that the supposedly "real world" is itself a kind of production, a projection of shadows. This hyperreal reversal dramatizes what Slavoj Žižek, building on Baudrillard, sees as the condition of contemporary culture in general. "[It] is not . . . that Hollywood stages a semblance of real life deprived of the weight and inertia of materiality," Žižek writes; rather, "the ultimate truth of the capitalist utilitarian despiritualized universe is the dematerialization of the 'real life' itself, its reversal into a spectral show."[113] Indeed, this "spectral show" has the effect of reifying Fleming's own mythos. Is not Osama bin Laden, Žižek asks, "the real-life counterpart of Ernst Stavro Blofeld, the master-criminal in most of the James Bond films, who was involved in the acts of global destruction?"[114] What Žižek is getting at here is that Fleming's fiction—potentially, all fiction—constitutes, in Baudrillard's terms, a "precession," a model that generates its own hyperreality.[115] But we need not look to such sensationalized examples to see the simulacrum at work. Just as the literary 007 is always already a movie star, Fleming's novels are cinematic prior to their big-screen adaptations. The effect is often uncanny. In *Moonraker*, the writer seems to invent the iconic cold opening of every James Bond movie: "It was like being inside the polished barrel of a huge gun."[116]

Yet, for all his desire to see his hero's name on the marquee (or at least the TV), Bond's cinematic success proved to have a bitter side. In his final days, Fleming lamented that the movie tie-in edition of *Goldfinger* looked like an advertisement for the film. "And," he wrote to his publisher, "on the back I see that Sean Connery gets at least twice the size type as the author."[117] Fleming never lived to see the film premiere, but Bond's apotheosis was already complete. As Pearson puts it, once the books became movies, "the public image" of 007 was no longer in Fleming's hands. "The professional myth makers had taken over."[118]

NOTES

1. Jonathan Nolan and Lisa Joy (creators), *Westworld*, based on *Westworld* by Michael Crichton (Burbank, CA: Warner Bros., 2016).

2. Ian Fleming, *Diamonds Are Forever* (1956; Las Vegas: Thomas and Mercer, 2012).

3. Kingsley Amis, *The James Bond Dossier* (New York: American Library, 1965), 135.

4. Chip Rhodes, *Politics, Desire, and the Hollywood Novel* (Iowa City: University of Iowa Press, 2008).

5. Nathanael West, *The Day of the Locust* (1939; New York: Signet Classic, 1983); Evelyn Waugh, *The Loved One* (1948; Boston: Back Bay, 1977); Raymond Chandler, *The Little Sister* (1949; New York: Vintage, 1988).

6. Jean Baudrillard, *Simulacra and Simulation*, trans. Sheila Faria Glaser (Ann Arbor: University of Michigan Press, 1994), 6.

7. Rhodes, *Politics*, 127.

8. Rhodes, *Politics*, 2.

9. Rhodes, *Politics*, 6.

10. Rhodes, *Politics*, 4.

11. Rhodes, *Politics*, 1.

12. Rhodes, *Politics*, 2.

13. Rhodes, *Politics*, 41.

14. West, *Day*, 23.

15. West, *Day*, 126.

16. West, *Day*, 192–93.

17. West, *Day*, 147.

18. West, *Day*, 147.

19. Chip Rhodes, "Hollywood Fictions," in *The Cambridge Companion to the Literature of Los Angeles*, ed. Kevin R. McNamara (Cambridge: Cambridge University Press, 2010), 136.

20. Baudrillard, *Simulacra*, 1.

21. Baudrillard, *Simulacra*, 1.

22. Baudrillard, *Simulacra*, 1. Italics in original.

23. West, *Day*, 126.

24. Baudrillard, *Simulacra*, 12.

25. Baudrillard, *Simulacra*, 12.

26. Baudrillard, *Simulacra*, 12.

27. Ian Fleming, *Thrilling Cities* (London: Jonathan Cape, 1963), 82. Fleming indicates that he revisited the cemetery during his second trip to Los Angeles in 1959. This would suggest that he was already familiar with Waugh's Hollywood novel on his first visit to the city in late 1954 to carry out research for *Diamonds Are Forever*.

28. Waugh, *Loved*, 80.

29. Waugh, *Loved*, 39.

30. Raymond Chandler, "Writers in Hollywood," *Atlantic Monthly*, November 1945, accessed August 2, 2017, https://www.theatlantic.com/magazine/archive/1945/11/writers-in-hollywood/306454/.

31. Chandler, "Writers in Hollywood."

32. Chandler, *Little*, 79.

33. Rhodes, *Politics*, 88.

34. Rhodes, *Politics*, 89.

35. Chandler, *Little*, 158.

36. Rhodes, *Politics*, 89.

37. Chandler, *Little*, 250.

38. Raymond Chandler, *The Raymond Chandler Papers: Selected Letters and Non-Fiction, 1909–1959*, ed. Tom Hiney and Frank MacShane (New York: Atlantic Monthly, 2000), 214.

39. Andrew Lycett, *Ian Fleming: The Man behind James Bond* (Atlanta: Turner, 1995), 270.

40. Fergus Fleming, ed., *The Man with the Golden Typewriter: Ian Fleming's James Bond Letters* (New York and London: Bloomsbury, 2015), 225.

41. Rhodes, *Politics*, 2.

42. Fleming, *Diamonds Are Forever*, 187.

43. Fleming, ed., *Man with the Golden Typewriter*, 37–38.

44. Ian Fleming, *Live and Let Die* (1954; New York: Penguin, 2003), 111.

45. Fleming, *Live and Let Die*, 9.
46. Fleming, *Live and Let Die*, 110.
47. Fleming, *Live and Let Die*, 124.
48. Christopher Hitchens, "Bottoms Up," *Atlantic Monthly*, April 2006, 101.
49. Hitchens, "Bottoms Up," 104.
50. Ian Fleming, *Casino Royale* (1953; New York: Penguin, 2002), 34.
51. Lycett, *Ian Fleming*, 250.
52. Fleming, ed., *Man with the Golden Typewriter*, 54.
53. Fleming, ed., *Man with the Golden Typewriter*, 57.
54. Fleming, ed., *Man with the Golden Typewriter*, 82
55. John Pearson, *The Life of Ian Fleming* (New York: McGraw-Hill, 1966), 197.
56. Fleming, *Live and Let Die*, 93.
57. Lycett, *Ian Fleming*, 263.
58. Rhodes, *Politics*, 13.
59. Quoted in Lycett, *Ian Fleming*, 265.
60. Quoted in Lycett, *Ian Fleming*, 265.
61. Fleming, *Thrilling*, 82.
62. Lycett, *Ian Fleming*, 265.
63. Pearson, *Life*, 171.
64. Baudrillard, *Simulacra*, 2.
65. Umberto Eco, *The Role of the Reader: Explorations in the Semiotics of Texts* (Bloomington and London: Indiana University Press, 1979), 166.
66. Fleming, *Diamonds Are Forever*, 10.
67. Fleming, *Diamonds Are Forever*, 30.
68. Fleming, *Diamonds Are Forever*, 54.
69. Fleming, *Diamonds Are Forever*, 99.
70. Fleming, *Diamonds Are Forever*, 66.
71. Fleming, *Diamonds Are Forever*, 141.
72. Baudrillard, *Simulacra*, 2.
73. Fleming, *Diamonds Are Forever*, 50–51.
74. Fleming, *Diamonds Are Forever*, 51.
75. Fleming, *Diamonds Are Forever*, 82.
76. Ian Fleming, *The Spy Who Loved Me* (1962; New York: Penguin, 2003), 63.
77. Baudrillard, *Simulacra*, 12.
78. Waugh, *Loved*, 80.
79. Fleming, *Thrilling*, 100.
80. Fleming, *Diamonds Are Forever*, 138.
81. Fleming, *Diamonds Are Forever*, 140.
82. Waugh, *Loved*, 14.
83. Fleming, *Thrilling*, 97.
84. West, *Day*, 184.
85. Fleming, *Diamonds Are Forever*, 165.
86. Fleming, *Diamonds Are Forever*, 167.
87. Fleming, *Diamonds Are Forever*, 168.
88. Baudrillard, *Simulacra*, 19.
89. Fleming, *Diamonds Are Forever*, 173
90. Fleming, *Diamonds Are Forever*, 153.
91. Fleming, *Diamonds Are Forever*, 177.
92. Fleming, *Diamonds Are Forever*, 183.
93. Chandler, *Little*, 196.
94. Chandler, *Little*, 192.
95. Ian Fleming, *You Only Live Twice* (1963; New York: Penguin, 2003), 171
96. Fleming, *You Only Live Twice*, 198.
97. Eco, *Role*, 157–59.
98. Fleming, *Diamonds Are Forever*, 130.
99. Fleming, *Diamonds Are Forever*, 130.

100. Fleming, *Diamonds Are Forever*, 158.
101. Fleming, *Thrilling*, 82.
102. Fleming, *Diamonds Are Forever*, 187.
103. Fleming, *Diamonds Are Forever*, 69.
104. Fleming, *Diamonds Are Forever*, 196.
105. Richard Maibaum and Tom Mankiewicz, *Diamonds Are Forever*, directed by Guy Hamilton and performed by Sean Connery (London: Eon, 1971).
106. Ian Fleming, *From Russia with Love* (1957; Thomas and Mercer, 2012), 131.
107. Fleming, *From Russia with Love*, 109.
108. Fleming, *From Russia with Love*, 156.
109. Fleming, *From Russia with Love*, 155.
110. Fleming, *From Russia with Love*, 185.
111. Fleming, *From Russia with Love*, 178.
112. Fleming, *From Russia with Love*, 219.
113. Slavoj Žižek, "Welcome to the Desert of the Real!," *South Atlantic Quarterly* 10, no. 2 (Spring 2002): 385–86.
114. Žižek, "Welcome to the Desert of the Real!," 387.
115. Baudrillard, *Simulacra*, 17.
116. Ian Fleming, *Moonraker* (1955; New York: Penguin, 2003), 109.
117. Fleming, ed., *Man with the Golden Typewriter*, 371.
118. Pearson, *Life*, 307.

BIBLIOGRAPHY

Amis, Kingsley. *The James Bond Dossier*. New York: American Library, 1965.
Baudrillard, Jean. *Simulacra and Simulation*. Translated by Sheila Faria Glaser. Ann Arbor: University of Michigan Press, 1994.
Chandler, Raymond. *The Little Sister*. New York: Vintage, [1949] 1988.
———. *The Raymond Chandler Papers: Selected Letters and Non-Fiction, 1909–1959*. Edited by Tom Hiney and Frank MacShane. New York: Atlantic Monthly, 2000.
———. "Writers in Hollywood." *Atlantic Monthly*, November 1945. Accessed August 2, 2017. https://www.theatlantic.com/magazine/archive/1945/11/writers-in-hollywood/306454/.
Eco, Umberto. *The Role of the Reader: Explorations in the Semiotics of Texts*. Bloomington and London: Indiana University Press, 1979.
Fleming, Fergus, ed. *The Man with the Golden Typewriter: Ian Fleming's James Bond Letters*. New York and London: Bloomsbury, 2015.
Fleming, Ian. *Casino Royale*. New York: Penguin, [1953] 2002.
———. *Diamonds Are Forever*. Las Vegas: Thomas and Mercer, [1956] 2012.
———. *From Russia with Love*. Las Vegas, Thomas and Mercer, [1957] 2012.
———. *Live and Let Die*. New York: Penguin, [1954] 2003.
———. *Moonraker*. New York: Penguin, [1955] 2003.
———. *The Spy Who Loved Me*. New York: Penguin, [1962] 2003.
———. *Thrilling Cities*. London: Jonathan Cape, 1963.
———. *You Only Live Twice*. New York: Penguin, [1964] 2003.
Hitchens, Christopher. "Bottoms Up." *Atlantic Monthly*, April 2006.
Lycett, Andrew. *Ian Fleming: The Man behind James Bond*. Atlanta: Turner, 1995.
Maibaum, Richard, and Tom Mankiewicz. *Diamonds Are Forever*. Directed by Guy Hamilton and performed by Sean Connery. London: Eon, 1971.
Nolan, Jonathan, and Lisa Joy. *Westworld*. Based on *Westworld* by Michael Crichton. Burbank, CA: Warner Bros., 2016.
Pearson, John. *The Life of Ian Fleming*. New York: McGraw-Hill, 1966.
Rhodes, Chip. "Hollywood Fictions." In *The Cambridge Companion to the Literature of Los Angeles*, edited by Kevin R. McNamara, 135–43. Cambridge: Cambridge University Press, 2010.

————. *Politics, Desire, and the Hollywood Novel*. Iowa City: University of Iowa Press, 2008.

Waugh, Evelyn. *The Loved One*. Boston: Back Bay, [1948] 1977.

West, Nathanael. *The Day of the Locust*. New York: Signet Classic, [1939] 1983.

Žižek, Slavoj. "Welcome to the Desert of the Real!" *South Atlantic Quarterly* 10, no. 2 (Spring 2002): 385–89.

TEN

A Happy Selection

The Representation of Food and Drink in the Book and Film of Diamonds Are Forever

Edward Biddulph

INTRODUCTION

Picture the following scene from the film of *Diamonds Are Forever*.[1] James Bond and Tiffany Case are on board a cruise ship on their way back to England, having thwarted Blofeld's evil plan. As Bond and Case relax in their suite, the villainous couple Wint and Kidd enter, disguised as waiter and chef respectively, with a trolley laden with dishes. "Compliments of Willard Whyte," Wint explains to a puzzled Bond, who had not been expecting room service. Wint proceeds to go through the menu: "Oysters *Andaluz*, shashlik, titbits, prime ribs *au jus*, *salade* Utopia, and the *pièce de résistance—la bombe surprise*." It is not too long, though, before James Bond smells a rat—or rather Wint's potent aftershave—and realises that it is Blofeld's hitmen, not the ship's staff, who are serving dinner. As Wint wraps a chain around Bond's neck, Kidd advances toward Bond with flaming skewers that hold the by now well-done shashlik. Bond hurls the contents of a brandy bottle at Kidd, whose jacket is quickly set alight. The flaming Kidd runs to the balcony and jumps overboard. Meanwhile, Caes throws the *bombe surprise* at Wint and misses, but as it crashes to the floor, the bomb hidden inside falls out. Bond then tosses Wint judo-style over his shoulder, chains the bomb to Wint's wrists, pulls Wint's arms between his (Wint's) legs, and tips him over the balcony just as the bomb explodes. Putting aside for the purpose of this essay the point, significant though it may be, that Bond's final actions are paradoxically both hyper-masculine (Bond having assaulted Wint's sexuality) and homoerotic (Wint's reaction appearing to express pleasure, rather than pain), in more ways than one, the villains have had their just desserts.

The scene is unusual, as food is rarely so prominent in the James Bond film series. Certainly, there are other films where the camera is allowed to linger on food. There is, for instance, Bond's dinner with Kamal Khan in *Octopussy*[2] at which he is served a soufflé and a stuffed sheep's head, Bond's meal with Kristatos in *For Your Eyes Only*,[3] and the mounds of chicken, potatoes, rice and bananas served to Blofeld's "Angels of Death" in *On Her Majesty's Secret Service*.[4] More often, though, food provides set dressing—a bowl of breakfast fruit at Bond's hotel in *Live and Let Die*,[5] a tray of oysters carried by Nick Nack in *The Man with the Golden Gun*,[6] a well-stocked kitchen in *The Living Daylights*,[7] for instance. Or else food is mentioned, but not seen. Thus, Bond orders figs and yogurt from his hotel room in *From Russia with Love*,[8] discusses conch chowder with Domino in *Thunderball*,[9] and comments on his skewered lamb in *Casino Royale*.[10] The food itself makes no screen appearance.[11]

Contrast this with the James Bond novels, where food is presented frequently, and readers are invited to savor the food that is placed before Bond. Through the course of the literary series, Bond consumes the best part of a hundred meals. The novels of *Goldfinger*[12] and *On Her Majesty's Secret Service*[13] represent the peaks of Bond's prandial adventures with an above-average meal count—I calculate a mean of seven meals per book, excluding the short stories and non-Fleming Bond books[14]—but *Diamonds Are Forever* is not far behind.[15] The books offer a diverse spread of food, but there are also the creature comforts, notably scrambled eggs, which appear almost in every book.

Ian Fleming admitted that in writing his thrillers, he wanted to stimulate "the reader all the way through, even to his taste buds," continuing that he had "never understood why people in books have to eat such sketchy and indifferent meals."[16] There is certainly an element of the exotic in the books, not least in *Diamonds Are Forever*. For readers of mid-1950s Britain, which had only just seen the end of post-war rationing, Ian Fleming's descriptions of avocados, beef Brizzola, caviar, and Cresta Blanca vermouth must have seemed sophisticated, luxurious, even mystifying, and utterly unattainable. Through Bond, the readers of his adventures became armchair food tourists. Readers' perceptions of the food today are likely to be very different. With many of Bond's food items commonplace and readily available on supermarket shelves, today's readers are likely to view the descriptions indifferently or even as quaint.

This essay will compare the literary and cinematic James Bond as portrayed in the book and film versions of *Diamonds Are Forever* through the character's attitude to food and drink. It will consider the extent to which the descriptions of food in the novel reflect Ian Fleming's own dining experiences and habits, and will discuss the notion of Bond as a culinary tourist. Finally, the essay will examine how changes in menus and dining habits since 1956 have shaped and altered readers' perceptions of, and engagement with, the food presented in the novel and film.

"ANYTHING YOU SAY": COMMENTARY ON THE FOOD AND DRINK IN THE NOVEL

The first chapter of *Diamonds Are Forever* contains an account of feasting that is every bit as descriptive as subsequent references to dining. In the scrub of French Guinea, a scorpion captures a beetle—itself searching for better pastures—and executes it with the lash of its deadly tipped tail: "Then for an hour, and with great extreme fastidiousness, the scorpion ate its victim."[17] The act of killing and the consumption of the victim could be metaphorical, alluding to the villain of the piece and his anticipated merciless pursuit of selfish gratification. Like any Bond villain, too, the scorpion is undone by its own greed. Drawn out of its lair by hunger, the scorpion feasts on its prey with its defences down and fails to heed the sound of a helicopter—a signal of its death—in the distance.[18] Ultimately, the scorpion is crushed underneath a rock wielded by a diamond smuggler waiting for the helicopter that heralded its death. A foretaste of events to come, the episode echoes through the novel. Food brings villains out into the open where they are observed and their destruction is plotted. Masters of their own little world (for instance Tingaling Bell) find that there is someone more powerful watching over them. The strong crush the weak, and the good crush the bad.

By chapter 3, we are treated to more appetising fare—James Bond's lunch of dressed crab washed down with a pint of black velvet at Scott's.[19] This is a treat for Bond. Lunch typically consists of more mundane meals, such as the grilled sole, a mixed salad, cheese, toast, wine, and coffee that Bond takes in the staff canteen in *Moonraker*.[20] For readers coming to the literary Bond after being introduced to the character through the film series, Bond's acknowledgment that lunch at Scott's is something out of the ordinary might challenge their perceptions. Unlike the cinematic Bond, the literary Bond cannot live by caviar alone. Bond's self-awarded treat evokes our empathy too. The Bond of the novels is just like the rest of us office workers, inventing weak excuses to escape the lunchtime monotony. Bond's lunch might appear to be "typical Bond," but the gesture is touching and humanizing.

Earlier in the chapter, food is used to paint an image of James Bond's prospective foes, the American gangsters controlling the diamond smuggling racket. Bond caricatures them as over-scented spaghetti- and meatball-loving Italian bums.[21] There is the hint of snobbery in Bond's comment, and even, it could be argued, hypocrisy when a similar dish in a later adventure brings the comment to mind. In *Thunderball*, he fantasizes while at the Shrublands health clinic about consuming a large dish of spaghetti Bolognese containing plenty of chopped garlic, accompanied by the rawest Chianti.[22] When Bond comes to fulfill his fantasy, at Lucien's in Brighton, Ian Fleming underlines the coarseness of the meal with the language of the boxing ring, as Bond scores "a left and right" of the dish and the wine.[23] The basis for the two dishes are, in terms of ingredients, largely identical, but there are contrasts. While spaghetti Bolognese originated in Italy, spaghetti and meatballs is Italian American. Both are, judging by Fleming's descriptions, coarse and unsophisticated, but the former has a purity and honesty that the latter lacks.

A BOAC flight from London to New York provides the novel's next description of food: a welcoming tray of cocktails and caviar and smoked salmon canapés, which would be brought to Bond's seat.[24] Bond does not seem overly enthused by the prospect, despite his fondness for smoked salmon, as admitted in *Moonraker*.[25] The Stratocruiser touches down at Shannon airport, where Bond consumes a dinner of steak, accompanied by champagne and an Irish coffee—coffee and whiskey, topped with cream, apparently an invention of Shannon airport's chef.[26] Then it is back on the plane for the overnight flight to New York. Breakfast is disparagingly described as an inappropriate assortment advertised as an English country house breakfast.[27] That the food descriptions in this chapter are so paltry is notable. The food is almost devoid of detail. We do not know how Bond orders his steak, what brand of champagne he drinks, and quite what constitutes an English country house breakfast. In his novels, Ian Fleming has described bad food in as much detail as the good; consider *Live and Let Die*, where, for instance, food judged to be eyewash by Bond is described in a short paragraph.[28] Here, though, the lack of explanation and opinion is telling. The detail is as bland as the food—neither good nor bad, merely sustenance for the job in hand.

Contrast this with the presentation of food in chapter 8 of *Diamonds Are Forever*, which is a case of famine to feast. Felix Leiter, private eye, former CIA agent, and one of Bond's best friends, bumps into Bond on the streets of New York. Leiter takes Bond to Sardi's, an upmarket restaurant in the heart of the city's theatre district, for lunch. Bond visits the washroom, then rejoins Leiter at the table. Leiter has ordered the drinks (medium dry martinis with Cresta Blanca, a Californian brand) as well as the food (smoked salmon and Brizzola, which Leiter describes as the best cut of the finest beef) in Bond's absence.

> "Suit you?"
> "Anything you say," said Bond. "We've eaten enough meals together to know each other's tastes."[29]

We learn later in the chapter that the salmon is from Nova Scotia, which Bond considers a poor substitute for the Scottish product, but that the

Brizzola is as Leiter had described.[30] To finish, Bond has half an avocado with French dressing and an espresso. As neither is mentioned by Leiter, the implication is that these items are ordered by Bond himself.

Like the meal itself, the food description and its subtext are rich and give us plenty to chew on. Let us first examine the exchanges between Bond and Leiter. From a superficial reading, the interplay reveals a domestic relationship. Indeed, to modern eyes, the scene has a distinct homoerotic subtext. Leiter is clearly in charge, ordering a drink for Bond in Bond's absence. Fortunately, he has made the right choice, remembering the martinis prepared in the same way that Bond and Leiter drank together in Harlem during their adventure against Mr. Big in *Live and Let Die*.[31] Leiter's dominance continues with the ordering of the food, which he does so again on Bond's behalf. Bond's response suggests a familiarity with each other that extends beyond that which might be expected between colleagues to one that might be expected between close friends or even a couple in a domestic relationship. This is not so much of leap. The 1950s in Britain was a time when women were expected to marry and surrender their ambitions in the workplace to become housewives, a role that demanded subservience toward their husband and the maintenance of the husband's approval. Men, meanwhile, were the providers and decision-makers.[32] In this light, and with Bond's words, "Anything you say," in mind, it is easy to cast Felix Leiter in the role of husband and provider, and Bond as the submissive wife.

Such an interpretation is, it must be admitted, irresistibly provocative, but it ignores the critical elements of contemporaneous social context and the conventions of hospitality. For Fleming and others within a similar social environment, it would not have been untypical for the host of a restaurant meal—that is, the person who invites another party to dinner, arranges the booking or the choice of table, takes care of the bill, and is generally responsible for the dining event—to select and order the food on behalf of his or her guests. Such practice is reflected in the literature of the time. For example, in *The Battle of Basinghall Street*, a 1935 novel by E. Phillips Oppenheim, we read that at Ciro's, Lord Sandbrook "sent for a *maitre d'hotel* and selected the dinner" before his dining companions had arrived. When one of his party does arrive, he tells them: "I've ordered dry martinis, unless you prefer something different." He has even specified the table: "Hope you'll like the table," he tells another of his party. "I have a weakness for a corner and I don't care to be too near the music." We are subsequently told that "the table was the best in the room, the dinner perfectly ordered and served."[33] In this light, we can identify Felix Leiter as the host, and James Bond as his guest. This much is confirmed in the text, when Bond tells Leiter that Leiter can buy him a drink and lunch, to which Leiter agrees and takes him to Sardi's.[34] The episode effectively repeats a dining event described in chapter 1 of *Live and Let Die*. Having been informed of Bond's arrival at the St. Regis hotel in New

York, Leiter orders lunch on Bond's behalf before seeing him. The meal, like that at Sardi's, is quintessentially American: soft-shell crabs, hamburgers, and French fries.[35] To modern readers, the homoerotic subtext of Bond and Leiter's relationship at Sardi's, and before that at the St. Regis, is very clear. Whether Fleming intended this to be the case is a moot point, but it remains reasonable to suggest that contemporaneous social convention with regard to hospitality, which is reflected in the dining descriptions, permitted such a relationship to develop by providing opportunities for gender conventions to be subtly subverted.

What of the food itself? We know from his dinner with M at Blades in *Moonraker* that James Bond is fond of salmon and considers Scottish salmon to be the finest.[36] The Brizzola appears to be a new taste for Bond, and perhaps also for many of Ian Fleming's readers. The dish is described as beef straight-cut across the bone, which is roasted, then broiled. This is not dissimilar from the description given to journalist Earl Wilson in December 1971 by Robert Kriendler, president of New York's famous 21 Club. He defined Brizzola as "charcoal-broiled prime rib of beef with bone intact."[37] Wilson also reported that President Richard Nixon regularly ordered Brizzola when he ate at the club during his visits to New York. Returning to Sardi's, James Bond's meal represents the second time, so far as readers are aware, that Bond eats avocado served with French dressing for dessert, the first occasion being during a meal with Vesper Lynd in *Casino Royale*.[38] The placement of the avocado at the end of the meal, though somewhat unusual now, is a nod to the tradition, particularly in Britain, of serving savory food at the end of the meal in order, it has been claimed, to cleanse the palate before drinking sweet or fortified wines.[39] Accordingly, M finishes his meal at Blades with a marrow bone before ordering a brandy,[40] and Bond continues with the savory choice in later adventures. In *Dr. No*, for example, Bond opts for angels on horseback (oysters wrapped in bacon) to finish a meal of caviar, grilled lamb cutlets, and salad.[41] The tradition survives today largely with the still regular appearance of the cheese board on restaurants' dessert menus.

Chapter 9 sees James Bond with Tiffany Case in the 21 Club itself on 21 West 52nd Street. Bond offers a gambit with his suggestion for dinner, shellfish and Hock, but Case is not impressed, stating that it would take more than Crabmeat Ravigotte to get her into bed with a man. Instead, she tells Bond that she'll have the "caviar . . . 'cutlets,' and some pink champagne."[42]

Bond has the same. We learn that the champagne is Clicquot Rosé and that the cutlets are served with asparagus with mousseline sauce. All this is preceded by vodka martinis, shaken, not stirred, along with slivers of lemon peel in a wine glass, which Bond twists and sinks into his cocktail. The meal concludes with coffee and, courtesy of "Mac" Kriendler, a

Stinger made with white crème de menthe, which Bond decides to have after Case orders one for herself.[43]

If Bond's meal at Sardi's follows convention, his meal at the 21 Club defies it. Here Bond could be identified as the host—it is he, after all, who suggests the dinner date[44]—but the interplay points to a more ambiguous relationship between him and Case, and conventions quickly break down as roles are reversed. Bond's choice for dinner is rejected by Case, who makes her own choice, and then he decides to have the same as her. Bond orders the meal for them both, but he is reminded by Case to do so. Bond pays the check, but after Case tells Bond that dinner is on her. On the other hand, how serious was the shellfish suggestion? Bond is uncharacteristically unspecific in the type of shellfish, and his line could more generously be regarded as flirtatious banter, much like his reference to conch chowder as an aphrodisiac in his conversation with Domino in *Thunderball*.[45] He would in any case be tempted by the lamb cutlets and asparagus, having eaten almost the same meal at Blades in *Moonraker*.[46] In that meal, the sauce on his asparagus is Béarnaise, not mousseline. Ian Fleming was "corrected" by a reader of *Moonraker*, who insisted that asparagus is served with mousseline, not Béarnaise sauce.[47]

Caviar, along with martinis, has come to be synonymous with James Bond, and with good reason. By the fourth adventure, only in *Live and Let Die* is there no caviar. While we would expect Bond to drink champagne (Clicquot, having appeared in *Casino Royale*, is a label with which he is familiar), the Stinger is something of a surprise choice, and, as Case suggested it, returns us to the idea of Bond emasculated. Bond would, however, come to have another Stinger during the Thunderball affair.[48]

Bond's dinner the day after his meal with Case is a comparatively simple supper by himself at Voisin's of vodka martinis, *oeufs* Benedict, and strawberries.[49] Bond is inordinately fond of eggs, but he only rarely has eggs in this form. This represents the first instance of eggs Benedict in the novels, the next occasion being in *The Man with the Golden Gun*.[50] There, the dish is described as "Eggs Benedict," the replacement of the French word for eggs reflecting, perhaps, that the dish by the mid-1960s seemed less sophisticated. Strawberries have appeared in previous adventures, but this is the first occasion of which we know that Bond has eaten strawberries himself; in *Casino Royale*, Vesper Lynd has strawberries,[51] while in *Moonraker*, they are M's choice.[52]

The following day, Bond accompanies Felix Leiter to Saratoga. They stop for lunch at a roadhouse called "The Chicken in the Basket." Fleming describes the establishment in pejorative terms, presumably conveying Bond's thoughts, although Bond seems to be impressed by the speed of the service of his scrambled eggs, sausages, hot buttered rye toast, Miller's High Life beer, and iced coffee.[53] It is not clear whether both Leiter and Bond or Bond alone ate this meal, but for Bond it represents a safe choice. Bond consumes scrambled eggs with almost obsessive regularity throughout his adventures, beginning with *Casino Royale*. In an early draft of *Live and Let Die*, Bond ate scrambled eggs so frequently that a reader suggested that Bond's habits would be a security risk.[54] Elizabeth Hale regards Bond's egg consumption as symbolizing his "identity as an individualist, as an ordinary but discerning consumer, and as an agent of life and death." Focusing on two Bond novels, *Thunderball* and *On Her Majesty's Secret Service*, Hale suggests that eggs are a source of Bond's power—he fortifies himself for the tasks ahead by eating scrambled eggs—and are symbolic of Bond's role as a man and killer.[55] This is compelling—after all, Fleming wrote in response to a critic of Bond's meals that "four fried eggs has [*sic*] the sound of a real man's meal"[56]—but it risks somewhat overegging the pudding and downplaying Fleming's own predilection for eggs, and the impact that this had on Bond's own food choices.

Of the other items in Bond's lunch, sausages are more unusual for Bond, but rye toast would feature in later stories (e.g., *Thunderball*),[57] as would the Miller High Life,[58] which gives lie to the view that Bond never drinks beer.

As with Bond's dinner at Shannon Airport, Bond's evening meal at a roadside diner close to his motel, the Sagamore, in Saratoga is perfunctorily described: a chicken dinner costing $2.80, washed down with two bourbon old-fashioneds.[59] Fleming's more detailed description of the restaurant itself (air-conditioned and, like the motel, typical of the American way of life) has the ring of verisimilitude, and Bond's meal, though not further explained, is also undoubtedly authentic. The "Chicken Dinner" was a common menu item in diners and low-price restaurants across America. According to a 1956 menu, the "Chicken Dinner" from the well-known restaurant at Knott's Berry Farm in California cost $2.25.[60] Bond has, of course, seen a chicken dinner before. In *Live and Let Die*, Bond considers the Special Fried Chicken Dinner at a cost of $3.75 on the menu of Sugar Ray's in New York.[61] The chicken at Knott's Berry Farm and Sugar Ray's is fried, and we can reasonably suggest that Bond's chicken at Saratoga is prepared in the same way. That the chicken dinner is not described in more detail either in *Live and Let Die* or *Diamonds Are Forever* suggests that Ian Fleming intended Bond to have prior knowledge about what the meal constituted.

In the morning, Felix Leiter and James Bond carry out some early morning surveillance at the stables, after which Leiter promises a hell of a breakfast.[62] It is curious that Fleming provides no details of the breakfast, except that we know that Bond ate it. Possibly Bond was too preoccupied by the job in hand to notice what he was eating. We may also note that Bond acts on Leiter's instruction. As appears to be the case with the ordering of dinner back in New York, Bond takes a subordinate role. Later in the day at a racetrack restaurant, Bond defers to Leiter's local knowledge and orders bourbon and branch water, which Leiter tells him is fashionable in racing circles, to accompany a steak (sadly judged to be adequate only).[63] Despite the natural-sounding name, Bond suspects the branch water to be from the tap behind the bar, a reflection that provides a moment of reassurance that he remains *au fait* with the local context.

James Bond's final dinner at Saratoga is in a relatively upmarket restaurant, the Pavilion. Bond dines with Leiter, but on Leiter's terms. Leiter tells Bond to return in an hour so that they can get a good dinner together.[64] While at the restaurant, Leiter chooses the dishes on Bond's behalf and orders the meal, Maine lobster with melted butter, and then observes to Bond that the meal would not taste as good if the Spang boys were eating spaghetti with Caruso sauce at an adjacent table.[65]

Felix Leiter's comment about the Spang boys echoes Bond's view of the eating habits of American gangsters that he expressed to Bill Tanner after M's briefing.[66] What food the Spang boys do eat, however, does not include pasta. Earlier, Bond observes gangsters taking a meal of soft-shell crabs, frankfurters, and sauerkraut. Pissaro, Shy Smile's owner, has his head down on his food, though glances from time to time toward his companion's plate "as if he might reach across and fork something off it for himself."[67] Fleming takes the unsophisticated and uncouth dining behavior of the gangster a step further, as he brings out the wild animal in Pissaro, whose sense of entitlement extends to his companion's food.

Leiter orders dry martinis made with Cresta Blanca vermouth, but at the end of the meal, he suggests that he and Bond have a final bourbon and branch water.[68] This appears to be an error; bourbon had not been mentioned in the context of the meal until then, and it is possible that Fleming had forgotten that Leiter and Bond had been drinking martinis.

James Bond travels to Las Vegas alone and arrives at the Tiara. There he has lunch (not described) and dinner comprising a complimentary tray of olives and celery lined with orange cheese, a bread roll and butter, a dozen cherrystone clams, and a steak, all accompanied by at least two vodka dry martinis.[69] Bond is not impressed by the service, but considers the dinner excellent. Fleming adds a suggestion of cannibalism to the meal: "Bond munched his steak as if it was Mr. Seraffimo Spang's fingers."[70] The gesture reflects a self-disgust brought about by Bond's association, in the guise of a diamond smuggler, with sordid gangsters, and briefly Bond displays the same animalistic behavior that Fleming attributed to Pissaro. Fortunately, Bond uses the incident to strengthen his resolve to force the pace and make something happen. The power of the Spangs is all consuming, and so Bond must in turn consume the enemy. The lone wolf in sheep's clothing must once again become the hunter.

Bond's next reported meal is another under-described breakfast (we know that it is huge) eaten on the way to California with Felix Leiter and Tiffany Case,[71] and the final meal that is described in any detail—four small slivers of steak on toast canapés, served with a small bowl of Béarnaise sauce prepared by Tiffany Case herself[72]—is taken in his cabin on board the ocean liner the *Queen Elizabeth* (Bond eats at the Veranda Grill subsequently, but no details are provided).

The food is unremarkable by Bond's standards, but the Béarnaise sauce has a hidden meaning. Earlier on the ship, Bond reveals to Case that the sort of woman he might marry is "[s]omebody who can make Sauce Béarnaise as well as love."[73] The sauce that Case makes is in effect the first part of a marriage proposal (another role-reversal for Bond), and a promise of the second part. Indeed, the lovemaking follows shortly afterward.

I'LL HAVE WHAT HE'S HAVING

While we cannot vouch for every item of food mentioned in *Diamonds Are Forever*, it is a truism that the meals encountered by James Bond in this novel and others reflect Ian Fleming's own tastes and gastronomic experiences. Fleming's fondness for scrambled eggs is well documented. The author himself admitted that scrambled eggs were his favorite food,[74] and declared that "scrambled eggs never let you down."[75] Dinners in Victoria Square, Fleming's London home, would often consist simply of six scrambled eggs eaten in front of the fire,[76] and at his Jamaican retreat, Goldeneye, Fleming enjoyed breakfasts of pawpaw, black coffee, scrambled eggs, and bacon.[77] Lamb cutlets and asparagus, consumed by Bond and Tiffany Case at the 21 Club, is a classic pairing. We know that the dish was prepared for Ian Fleming and the real James Bond, the American ornithologist whose name Fleming appropriated for his hero, at Goldeneye in 1964,[78] and it is likely that the dish was prepared on occasion before then. Fleming and his literary creation also visited the same restaurants.

Like James Bond, Fleming lunched at Scott's, albeit more frequently,[79] and annual visits to New York included dinner at the fashionable restaurants, Sardi's and the 21 Club among them.[80] A letter dated May 1957 from Fleming to his American friend, Ernest Cuneo, who provided much of the detail of the New York scenes in *Live and Let Die* and *Diamonds Are Forever*, includes the promise of caviar at the 21 Club during Fleming's next visit to the city.[81] Being a regular air traveller to the United States, Fleming often stopped at Shannon airport, saying as much in a letter to the commercial division manager of the airport on May 29, 1956,[82] and so he experienced Bond's meal there, including the Irish coffee, firsthand. As Jeremy Strong suggests, "Bond's tastes most assuredly classify Fleming."[83]

"MOUTON ROTHSCHILD IS A CLARET": COMMENTARY ON THE FOOD AND DRINK IN THE FILM

The James Bond of the novel appears to be a gastronomic tourist; he eats as the locals do (even if the locals tend to be the wealthier ones eating at the more exclusive establishments), and is open to new tastes and experiences, even if he is dependent on a friend with local knowledge to show him where and what to eat, to the point of undermining his own masculinity. The Bond of the film of *Diamonds Are Forever*[84] is altogether a different beast. It must of course be admitted that food and drink are very poorly represented in the film. Food is no more poorly represented than it is in most Bond films, but with regard to drink, Bond is almost abstemious. He is seen drinking just three times, although bottles and glasses are visible in the background of various other scenes. Nevertheless, food and drink are critical to the film, appearing in two scenes that bookend the film. Food and drink serve both to develop the plot and convey Bond's connoisseurship and general expertise in all things. At the start of the film, Bond's own expertise is acknowledged during a briefing at the Treasury:

Sir Donald Munger: Sherry?

M: Not for me, thanks. Doctor's orders.

Munger: Commander Bond?

Bond: Yes, thank you.

Munger: You've been on holiday, I understand. Relaxing, I hope.

Bond: Hardly relaxing but most satisfying. Cheers. Pity about your liver, sir. It's an unusually fine Solera. '51, I believe.

M: There is no year for sherry, 007.

Bond: I was referring to the original vintage on which the sherry is based, sir. Unmistakable.

Munger: Precisely. Tell me, Commander. How far does your expertise extend into the field of diamonds?

Bond: Hardest substance found in nature. They cut glass. Suggest marriage. They've replaced a dog as a girl's best friend. That's about it.

M: Refreshing to hear there's one subject you're not an expert on.[85]

Bond's obscure information on sherry notifies the viewer that Bond is a connoisseur and, more generally, is knowledgeable. But context is all. While Bond's expertise irritates M here, it can also impress him, as we see three films later in *The Spy Who Loved Me*[86] when M praises Bond for the facts he recalls at a briefing in a game of one-upmanship with rival Soviet agent, Triple X. We would expect, then, the cinematic Bond to know about, say, bourbon and branch water and Cresta Blanca vermouth. Not that we demand technical details. We leave such things to gadget-master Q. (Compare Bond's casual recalling of facts with Q's precise response to Case's amazement at his fruit-machine gadget: "An electromagnetic RPM controller. Been aching to give it a try. You see, pressure on the case when the desired symbols appear causes the rotation of the cylinders to stutter at the precise moment needed to . . . "[87]) Bond's delivery is self-assured and insouciant and allows Bond the luxury of expertise without obvious effort. But Bond does not know everything. The same expression of expertise is also used to paper over the gaps, for example about diamonds, and M sees through it.

Still, Bond has knowledge where it counts. In a variation of a trope introduced in *From Russia with Love*—("Red wine with fish. That should have told me something," Bond admits after Red Grant has revealed himself to be an enemy agent. "You may know the right wines," Grant replies, "but you're the one on your knees"[88])—Bond exposes Wint and Kidd, disguised as waiters delivering room service, as Blofeld's henchmen, not only from Wint's potent aftershave, but also his poor winemanship:

Wint: Wine, sir? Mouton Rothschild '55.

Kidd: May we begin?

Bond: Please do.

W: A happy selection, if I may say.

B: I'll be the judge of that. That's rather potent. Not the cork—your aftershave. Strong enough to bury anything. But the wine is quite excellent. Although, for such a grand meal, I had rather expected a claret.

W: Of course. Unfortunately, our cellar is rather poorly stocked with clarets.

B: Mouton Rothschild is a claret. And I've smelt that aftershave before. And both times I've smelt a rat.[89]

Knowledge of wine, again, separates the hero from the villain, the gentleman from the scoundrel. Though not permitted to demonstrate it in the book of *Diamonds Are Forever*, winemanship is an expertise that the Bond of the cinema shares with the literary Bond. That much is clear, for example, in *Casino Royale*—"[Blanc de Blanc Brut 1943] is not a well-known brand," Bond explained to his companion, "but it is probably the finest champagne in the world"[90]—or *On Her Majesty's Secret Service*, in which Bond reveals his knowledge of viniculture of the Moselle region.[91] By comparison, New York, Saratoga, and Las Vegas represent unfamiliar territory for Bond.

Returning to the food brought in by Wint and Kidd, the dishes sound appropriately mysterious, foreign, and sophisticated, and this is an aspect that is retained from the novels. We may note, too, that shashlik is skewered lamb, a dish that Bond would have in a later adventure, *Casino Royale*.[92]

FROM CHICKEN DINNERS TO KFC: HOW READERS' RESPONSES TO BOND'S MEALS HAVE CHANGED OVER TIME

British readers devouring *Diamonds Are Forever* in 1956 are likely to have responded to James Bond's meals in a very different way to readers today. For the readers of 1956, Bond's food must have seemed sophisticated, highly tempting, and somewhat puzzling, as is clear from just two of Bond's dishes: the chicken dinner that he consumes at a diner in Saratoga, and the avocado he eats at Sardi's. Chicken dinners in 1950s Britain meant not the fried chicken that Bond is likely to have eaten in the diner in Saratoga, but roast chicken with all the trimmings, often offered as prizes at village fetes and club raffles. The *Biggleswade Chronicle and Bedfordshire Gazette*, for example, reported on July 13, 1951 that a "chicken dinner," comprising "a large cooked chicken, the usual vegetables and a bottle of champagne" was won by a Miss Jean Newton at a Mid-Beds Young Conservative fete.[93] A "substantial chicken dinner" was offered to the winner of a skittles competition at the St. Andrew's Youth Fellowship annual fete in 1955.[94] Fried chicken found no regular place on the family dining table in the 1950s, and Kentucky Fried Chicken would not open its first restaurant in the UK until 1965.[95]

What about the avocado, which Bond consumes with a French dressing at Sardi's? Avocados—or avocado pears, as they were called (and before that "alligator pears")—were known before 1956, but were regarded as an exotic novelty. A report in the *Aberdeen Evening Express* published in 1956 noted the arrival from South Africa (from where many avocados were imported) of a Mr. Lionel Leon, chairman of an avocado growers' association, who was in the UK visiting London's West End restaurants to "study British reaction to the avocado pear": "They have the right idea," he is reported as saying. "They serve them as an *hors d'oeuvre*."[96] The restaurant district that Mr. Leon visited suggests that avocados were not yet available for mass consumption, and the impression is not dispelled by a feature in praise of the avocado (best served "simply with an oil-rich French dressing") in high-society magazine *The Tatler* in 1958.[97] Inevitably, then, when avocados did reach supermarket shelves, consumers remained confused. According to the retailer's records, when the fruit was introduced onto the shelves of the high-street store Marks and Spencer in 1959, shoppers routinely attempted to eat avocados as a dessert fruit, for instance by stewing them and serving with custard.[98]

While the later 1950s brought exciting changes to the household kitchen, memories of the wartime deprivations and rationing that only fully ended in 1954 would have been fresh in readers' minds. Eggs, Bond's totemic food, remained on the ration books along with most other dairy foods until 1953.[99] Bond's prodigious consumption of eggs would have been far from the norm in most British households. In 1957, the year after *Diamonds Are Forever* was published, the British Egg Marketing Board devised a marketing campaign with the slogan "Go to work on an egg" to promote egg sales after the many years of restricted supply.[100]

We can get a more objective sense of changing dietary and culinary patterns by examining the "shopping basket" of household goods, a list of representative items and services bought by UK households that forms the basis for the retail prices index (RPI) and, latterly, the consumer price inflation index (CPI). As the prices of those goods and services rise or fall, so too does the total cost of the shopping basket, which therefore serves as a useful means of tracking inflation. Deciding what constitutes representative items, or which goods should be removed from the list and which should come in to replace them, is necessarily subjective, but the list is reassessed annually to ensure that the index reflects typical household expenditure and consumer habits.[101] The result is a valuable measure of changing food consumption in Britain.

Looking at the "basket of goods" for 1956, shoppers reading *Diamonds Are Forever* in that year could in theory have prepared some of the meals consumed by Bond or otherwise described in the book. Eggs for Bond's scrambled eggs or eggs Benedict are in the basket, as is salmon for smoked salmon, sausages for lunch, and a beef joint for Brizzola. There are certain items we would not expect to see on the list, such as shellfish and caviar, but there are notable absences, among them chicken, spaghetti, minced beef (for meatballs), lamb cutlets, and steak.[102] Steak and chicken (in this case a roasting chicken) would not be considered typical of household expenditure until 1962, while spaghetti, minced beef, and lamb chops (not exactly cutlets, but close enough) were not introduced into the "shopping basket" until after 1980. Of the book's fruit, avocados and strawberries were included only after 1987.[103]

By 2017, the food presented in *Diamonds Are Forever* is more closely aligned with typical household expenditure. The "basket of goods" includes pasta (spaghetti is now one of the many types available), steak, beef mince, lamb chops, chicken breasts, whole chicken, and chicken takeaways ("chicken dinners" from KFC and similar outlets), chipped potatoes or french fries, sausages, salmon, shellfish in the form of prawns, eggs, avocados, and strawberries.[104] It has never been easier to eat like James Bond. Some items have not yet made it into the shopping basket. Asparagus, lobster, crab and caviar remain outside it, which is reflective of their continued status as sophisticated or luxury items.

The "basket of goods" for 1956 does not mean that items not on the list were not available at that time. Minced beef, for instance, would generally not have been available ready prepared and packaged, but produced by mincing a cut of beef at home or asking the butcher to do it. Other items not in the basket could have been purchased from specialty stores. If desired, and with a degree of determination, readers could have recreated the food described in *Diamonds Are Forever*. What the "basket of goods" reveals, however, is the food that was typically bought by British households, and the data are clear; the meals of the *Diamonds Are Forever*, or at least their ingredients, were not a routine part of the household kitchen until some 30 or so years after the book's publication.

We can look at consumer patterns another way. Cookbooks offer us an insight into the dishes that households eat or aspire to eat. Even if the dishes described are never cooked, they nevertheless fit into a cultural environment that reflects what people are eating; the recipes are, in other words, "of their time." If we compare two cookbooks, one (reasonably) contemporary with the first edition of *Diamonds Are Forever*, the other published more recently, we gain a good sense of how readers' attitude to the food of the novel changed over time. Marguerite Patten's *Family Cookbook* is a useful cookbook to examine. The first edition was published in 1964, eight years after *Diamonds Are Forever* was published, and there have been various editions and revisions up to 2007.

In her introduction to the 1964 edition, Marguerite Patten writes that the recipes were "chosen to be simple enough for family fare," but reveals that the book also contains "some of the special recipes that have become famous on the continent."[105] The presence of the exotic and out-of-the-ordinary means that there is much we recognize from *Diamonds Are Forever* in the 1964 edition. There is a recipe for lobster (lobster à la Catalane), crab (crab *au gratin*), spaghetti (with a Bolognese sauce), steak, lamb cutlets, poached and scrambled eggs, and a reference to smoked salmon as an ideal *hors d'oeuvre*.[106] Avocados and asparagus, however, are absent.

The 2007 edition is extensively revised, and much expanded at 192 pages, compared with 94 pages for the 1964 edition. Again, there is much in the 2007 edition that readers would recognize from *Diamonds Are Forever*. Recipes for canapés have now been introduced, with the advice that "crab and smoked salmon make excellent toppings."[107] Four avocado-based recipes are included; three are starters, the other a dessert, but none served with French dressing, though a recipe for French dressing is given elsewhere in the book. The cookbook includes recipes for asparagus (in a cream sauce), crab (devilled), lobster (*Americaine*), steak, spaghetti (served with various sauces), poached eggs with hollandaise sauce—the basis for eggs Benedict, and scrambled eggs.[108]

Compared with the 1964 edition, the range of food presented in the 2007 cookbook matches the food described in *Diamonds Are Forever* more closely. Nevertheless, the earlier edition suggests that much of the food in the novel would not have been considered too fantastic by British readers in the mid-1960s, even if the meals, or rough approximations of them, were not routinely prepared (as is suggested by the "basket of goods" of the period). The 2007 edition includes more elements of the novel's food, but its expansion, with several recipes associated with certain items, such as avocados and spaghetti, indicates that the items have become ordinary.

FOOD TOURIST OR CAUTIOUS DINER?

In his 2013 paper, Jeremy Strong suggests that James Bond expressed in his food choices the qualities both of neophobia and neophilia. The former represents Bond's "reluctance to consume unfamiliar foods," the latter "a willingness to try new taste sensations."[109] We see the expression of both attitudes in the novel of *Diamonds Are Forever*. Some of Bond's food choices repeat items recorded in earlier adventures—the avocado at Sardi's, the lamb cutlets and asparagus at the 21 Club, and the scrambled eggs in "The Chicken in the Basket" restaurant—and are reassuringly familiar to Bond. But then there are the new tastes—the Brizzola and martinis made with the domestic Cresta Blanca vermouth at Sardi's, the Stinger at the 21 Club, the Miller High Life beer at "The Chicken in the Basket," the branch water with his bourbon at the Saratoga racetrack, the Maine lobster with melted butter at the Pavilion. It is revealing that most of Bond's new tastes are drinks. In his alcohol consumption, Bond's attitude is strongly "when in Rome do as the Romans do"; in his food consumption, he has a tendency to play it safe. When Bond does eat new foods, it is done so in the company of the local expert, in this case Felix Leiter, who serves as host and guide. Leiter has an equivalent role in Bond's gastronomic education to Kerim Bey in *From Russia with Love* or Tiger Tanaka in *You Only Live Twice*. We could point to the chicken dinner that Bond consumes in a Saratoga diner as a rare case of Bond actively seeking a regional taste, but even here, Bond is familiar with the dish, having encountered it during his last visit to the United States in *Live and Let Die.*

James Bond's food choices, then, seem much too conservative for Bond to be regarded as a food tourist. There are other traits that could reasonably define the food tourist that Bond also lacks. Lucy Long defines "culinary tourism" as "the intentional, exploratory participation in foodways of an other—participation including consumption, preparation, and presentation of a food item, cuisine, meal system, or eating style considered to belong to a culinary system not one's own."[110] Essential to this definition are the concepts of choice and intentionality. Long contends that individuals who "participate in an exotic foodways [*sic*] out of consideration for one's host, in response to a challenge, as a statement of rebellion against the status quo, to conform to social obligations or norms, and so on" cannot be counted as culinary tourists.[111] James Bond has no intention of seeking new food experiences—the new dishes, as well as the drinks, are chosen by others—and when presented with a choice, he opts for the familiar. This conservatism contrasts with Fleming's own desire to eat the local fare. Meals at his winter home in Jamaica, cooked by his housekeeper, Violet, would include local vegetables, fish served with rice, and curried goat; a diary entry by Ann Fleming in 1948 recorded that Ian Fleming told Violet that he "did not come to the tropics to eat beef roll."[112] It could be argued even here, though, that like Bond, Fleming had relinquished food choices to the local expert.

Though Bond does not appear to be a food tourist, at least by Long's definition, food tourism is an unavoidable element of the novel, containing as it does detailed descriptions of food and restaurants. The real food tourists, though, are Ian Fleming's readers, rather than his creation. As each new Bond novel was published, readers came to expect not just the familiar ingredients of derring-do, adventure, violence, and sex, but also the exploration of different cultures, including their foodways. Readers *chose* to buy the next book in the expectation that they would read about new, exotic food, and *intended* to experience that food, even if, prevented by cost and availability, this was by proxy through Bond's actions.

For British readers of the 1950s and 1960s, if not beyond, much of the food presented in the novel was unusual and sophisticated and to some extent mysterious, and found no regular place in the readers' shopping basket or on the dining table, although it should be acknowledged that readers were not necessarily unfamiliar with the descriptions of the food. Some meals in the novel, however, are likely never to have ceased to mystify British readers. The expression "chicken dinner" conjures images of roast dinners, rather than fried chicken, while Brizzola must continue to leave many readers puzzled. Even in today's world of globalized mass consumerism, *Diamonds Are Forever* retains its role as a guide to the unfamiliar and exotic, and we, along with Bond, are grateful to Felix Leiter for the explanations.

The literary Bond's paucity of food knowledge, at least away from home (and France), would seem to contrast with the expertise that the cinematic Bond appears to demonstrate so effortlessly. Even here, though, there is some similarity. The cinematic Bond may know his sherry and wine, but his knowledge of diamonds is not so detailed. Similarly, the literary Bond's knowledge of (French) wines, including champagne is strong, but is weaker elsewhere. Both, however, are sophisticated men of the world and able to navigate their way through these information gaps. Rather than being a supercilious know-it-all, James Bond, both in print and on the big screen, is reassuringly human.

NOTES

1. *Diamonds Are Forever* (1971), written by Richard Maibaum, and Tom Mankiewicz, produced by Albert R. Broccoli and Harry Saltzman, directed by Guy Hamilton.

2. *Octopussy* (1983), written by George MacDonald Fraser, Richard Maibaum, and Michael G. Wilson, produced by Albert R. Broccoli, directed by John Glen.

3. *For Your Eyes Only* (1981), written by Richard Maibaum and Michael G. Wilson, produced by Albert R. Broccoli, directed by John Glen.

4. *On Her Majesty's Secret Service* (1969), written by Richard Maibaum, produced by Albert R. Broccoli and Harry Saltzman, directed by Peter Hunt.

5. *Live and Let Die* (1973), written by Tom Mankiewicz, produced by Albert R. Broccoli and Harry Saltzman, directed by Guy Hamilton.

6. *The Man with the Golden Gun* (1974), written by Richard Maibaum and Tom Mankiewicz, produced by Albert R. Broccoli and Harry Saltzman, directed by Guy Hamilton.

7. *The Living Daylights* (1987), written by Richard Maibaum and Michael G. Wilson, produced by Albert R. Broccoli, directed by John Glen.

8. *From Russia with Love* (1963), adapted for the screen by Johanna Harwood, written by Richard Maibaum, produced by Albert R. Broccoli and Harry Saltzman, directed by Terence Young.

9. *Thunderball* (1965), written by Richard Maibaum and John Hopkins, based on an original story by Kevin McClory, Jack Whittingham, and Ian Fleming, produced by Kevin McClory, directed by Terence Young.

10. *Casino Royale* (2006), written by Neal Purvis, Robert Wade, and Paul Haggis, produced by Barbara Broccoli and Michael G. Wilson, directed by Martin Campbell.

11. The paucity of food in the Bond films may be just as well. At a test screening of *Casino Royale* in London in 2006, one criticism offered to the producers and director was that Bond ate too much toast in the casino restaurant after winning the poker game. "Bond crunching is not Bond," was the verdict. The scene was subsequently trimmed; "Napoleon Solo Breaks into the Top Secret Screening of CASINO ROYALE!!!," *Ain't It Cool News*, last modified September 9, 2006, http://www.aintitcool.com/node/24436.

12. Ian Fleming, *Goldfinger* (London: Triad/Granada, 1978).

13. Ian Fleming, *On Her Majesty's Secret Service* (London: Triad/Panther Books, 1977).

14. cf. Matt Sherman, *James Bond's Cuisine: 007's Every Last Meal* (Gainesville: BCW Productions, 2014).

15. Ian Fleming, *Diamonds Are Forever* (Las Vegas: Thomas & Mercer, 2012).

16. Ian Fleming, "Ian Fleming on Writing Thrillers," in *Devil May Care*, by Sebastian Faulks (London: Penguin Books, 2009), 408.

17. Fleming, *Diamonds Are Forever*, 2.

18. Fleming, *Diamonds Are Forever*, 3.

19. Fleming, *Diamonds Are Forever*, 20.

20. Ian Fleming, *Moonraker* (London: Triad Grafton, 1982), 22.

21. Fleming, *Diamonds Are Forever*, 19.

22. Ian Fleming, *Thunderball* (London: Triad Grafton, 1978), 37.

23. Fleming, *Thunderball*, 46.

24. Fleming, *Diamonds Are Forever*, 50.

25. Fleming, *Moonraker*, 37.

26. Fergus Fleming, ed., *The Man with the Golden Typewriter: Ian Fleming's James Bond Letters* (London: Bloomsbury, 2015), 106.

27. Fleming, *Diamonds Are Forever*, 51.

28. Ian Fleming, *Live and Let Die* (London: Triad/Panther Books, 1978), 107.

29. Fleming, *Diamonds Are Forever*, 65.

30. Fleming, *Diamonds Are Forever*, 68.

31. Fleming, *Live and Let Die*, 41.

32. Virginia Nicholson, *Perfect Wives in Ideal Homes: The Story of Women in the 1950s* (London: Viking, 2015), 46, 206.

33. E. Phillips Oppenheim, *The Battle of Basinghall Street*, in *The Complete Works of E. Phillips Oppenheim: 109 Novels & 200+ Short Stories* (Prague: e-artnow, 2016), chapter 10, Kindle.

34. Fleming, *Diamonds Are Forever*, 64.

35. Fleming, *Live and Let Die*, 9.

36. Fleming, *Moonraker*, 39–40.

37. Earl Wilson, "Dining at 21: Fit for a President," *The Lowell Sun*, December 24, 1971, 22.

38. Ian Fleming, *Casino Royale* (London: Triad/Granada, 1978), 60.

39. Craig Claiborne, "Angels on Horseback, a Classic Savory," *Eugene Register-Guard*, August 21, 1979, 5E.

40. Fleming, *Moonraker*, 42.

41. Ian Fleming, *Dr. No* (London: Triad/Panther Books, 1977), 123.

42. Fleming, *Diamonds Are Forever*, 71.

43. Fleming, *Diamonds Are Forever*, 73–76.

44. Fleming, *Diamonds Are Forever*, 38.

45. Fleming, *Thunderball*, 113.

46. Fleming, *Moonraker*, 37.

47. Fleming, ed., *The Man with the Golden Typewriter*, 107.

48. Fleming, *Thunderball*, 145.

49. Fleming, *Diamonds Are Forever*, 80.

50. Ian Fleming, *The Man with the Golden Gun* (London: Triad/Granada, 1978), 82.

51. Fleming, *Casino Royale*, 60.

52. Fleming, *Moonraker*, 37.

53. Fleming, *Diamonds Are Forever*, 82.

54. Fleming, "Ian Fleming on Writing Thrillers," 408.

55. Elizabeth Hale, "James Bond and the Art of Eating Eggs," *Gastronomica* 12, no. 4 (Winter 2012): 84–90, doi:10.1525/gfc.2012.12.4.84.

56. Quoted in Henry Chancellor, *James Bond: The Man and His World* (London: John Murray, 2005), 89.

57. Fleming, *Thunderball*, 212.

58. Ian Fleming, "007 in New York," in *Quantum of Solace: The Complete James Bond Short Stories* (London: Penguin Books, 2008), 291.

59. Fleming, *Diamonds Are Forever*, 89.

60. Photograph of menu posted to flickr by Marical. Accessed November 16, 2017.

61. Fleming, *Live and Let Die*, 47.

62. Fleming, *Diamonds Are Forever*, 93.

63. Fleming, *Diamonds Are Forever*, 95.

64. Fleming, *Diamonds Are Forever*, 120.

65. Fleming, *Diamonds Are Forever*, 123.

66. Fleming, *Diamonds Are Forever*, 19.

67. Fleming, *Diamonds Are Forever*, 98.

68. Fleming, *Diamonds Are Forever*, 128.

69. Fleming, *Diamonds Are Forever*, 141–42.

70. Fleming, *Diamonds Are Forever*, 142.

71. Fleming, *Diamonds Are Forever*, 187.

72. Fleming, *Diamonds Are Forever*, 202.

73. Fleming, *Diamonds Are Forever*, 199.

74. Fleming, "Ian Fleming on Writing Thrillers," 408.

75. Chancellor, *James Bond: The Man and His World*, 9.

76. Mark Amory, ed., *The Letters of Ann Fleming* (London: Collins Harvill, 1985), 128.

77. Amory, ed., *The Letters of Ann Fleming*, 60.

78. Mary Wickham Bond, *How 007 Got His Name* (London: Collins, 1966), 35–36.

79. Andrew Lycett, *Ian Fleming: The Man behind James Bond* (Atlanta: Turner Publishing Inc., 1995), 200; Fleming, ed., *The Man with the Golden Typewriter*, 81.

80. Ian Fleming, *Thrilling Cities* (London: Jonathan Cape, 1963), 120–21.

81. Fleming, ed., *The Man with the Golden Typewriter*, 89.

82. Fleming, ed., *The Man with the Golden Typewriter*, 106.

83. Jeremy Strong, "James Bond: International Man of Gastronomy?," *Journal of European Popular Culture* 4, no. 2 (October 2013): 155–72, doi: 10.1386/jepc.4.2.155_1.

84. *Diamonds Are Forever* (1971).

85. *Diamonds Are Forever* (1971).

86. *The Spy Who Loved Me* (1977), written by Christopher Wood and Richard Maibaum, produced by Albert R. Broccoli, directed by Lewis Gilbert.

87. *Diamonds Are Forever* (1971).

88. *From Russia with Love* (1963).

89. *Diamonds Are Forever* (1971).

90. Fleming, *Casino Royale*, 61.

91. Fleming, *On Her Majesty's Secret Service*, 18.

92. *Casino Royale* (2006).

93. Anonymous, "MP wins prize at Young Tories' fete," *The Biggleswade Chronicle and Bedfordshire Gazette*, July 13, 1951, 7.

94. Anonymous, "Chicken dinner for skittles winner," *West Sussex County Times*, September 16, 1955, 10.

95. "KFC," Wikipedia, last modified November 7, 2017, https://en.wikipedia.org/wiki/KFC.

96. Anonymous, "Express from London," *Aberdeen Evening Express*, July 5, 1956, 4.

97. Helen Burke, "I advocate avocados," *The Tatler and Bystander*, July 23, 1958, 44.

98. Oliver Moody, "Marks & Spencer serves up an exotic dip into history of taste," *The Times*, April 20, 2013, https://www.thetimes.co.uk/tto/life/food/article3744548.ece.

99. "1953: Sweet Rationing Ends in Britain," BBC News, accessed November 19, 2017, http://news.bbc.co.uk/onthisday/hi/dates/stories/february/5/newsid_2737000/2737731.stm; "1954: Housewives Celebrate End of Rationing," BBC News, accessed November 19, 2017, http://news.bbc.co.uk/onthisday/hi/dates/stories/july/4/newsid_3818000/3818563.stm.

100. "Go to Work on an Egg," Egg Recipes: From Basic to Adventurous, accessed November 19, 2017, https://www.eggrecipes.co.uk/go-to-work-on-an-egg.

101. "Consumer Price Inflation Basket of Goods and Services: 2017," Office for National Statistics, last modified March 14, 2017, https://www.ons.gov.uk/economy/inflationandpriceindices/articles/ukconsumerpriceinflationbasketofgoodsandservices/2017.

102. "Consumer Prices Index (CPI) and Retail Prices Index (RPI) Basket of Goods and Services," The National Archives, last modified January 8, 2016, http://webarchive.nationalarchives.gov.uk/20160108054353/http://www.ons.gov.uk/ons/guide-method/user-guidance/prices/cpi-and-rpi/cpi-and-rpi-basket-of-goods-and-services/index.html.

103. The National Archives, "Consumer Prices Index (CPI) and Retail Prices Index (RPI) Basket of Goods and Services."

104. Office for National Statistics, "Consumer Price Inflation Basket of Goods and Services: 2017."

105. Marguerite Patten, *The Family Cookbook* (London: Paul Hamlyn, 1964), 5.

106. Patten, *The Family Cookbook*, 6, 12, 24, 36, 39, 60.

107. Marguerite Patten, *Marguerite Patten's Family Cookbook* (London: Bounty Books, 2007), 48.

108. Patten, *Marguerite Patten's Family Cookbook*, 54–55, 81, 83, 102, 128–30, 136, 155–56.

109. Strong, "James Bond: International Man of Gastronomy?," 160.

110. Lucy M. Long, "Culinary Tourism: A Folkloristic Perspective on Eating and Otherness," in *Culinary Tourism*, ed. Lucy M. Long (Lexington: The University Press of Kentucky, 2004), 21.

111. Long, "Culinary Tourism," 21.

112. Amory, ed., *The Letters of Ann Fleming*, 61.

BIBLIOGRAPHY

Ain't It Cool News. "Napoleon Solo Breaks into the Top Secret Screening of CASINO ROYALE!!!." Last modified September 9, 2006, http://www.aintitcool.com/node/24436.

Amory, Mark, ed. *The Letters of Ann Fleming*. London: Collins Harvill, 1985.

Anonymous. "MP wins prize at Young Tories' fete." *The Biggleswade Chronicle and Bedfordshire Gazette*, July 13, 1951.

Anonymous. "Chicken dinner for skittles winner." *West Sussex County Times*, September, 16, 1955.

Anonymous. "Express from London." *Aberdeen Evening Express*, July 5, 1956.

BBC News. "1953: Sweet Rationing Ends in Britain." Accessed November 19, 2017, http://news.bbc.co.uk/onthisday/hi/dates/stories/february/5/newsid_2737000/2737731.st.

BBC News. "1954: Housewives Celebrate End of Rationing." Accessed November 19, 2017, http://news.bbc.co.uk/onthisday/hi/dates/stories/july/4/newsid_3818000/3818563.stm.

Bond, Mary Wickham. *How 007 Got His Name*. London: Collins, 1966.

Burke, Helen. "I advocate avocados." *The Tatler and Bystander*, July 23, 1958.

Chancellor, Henry. *James Bond: The Man and His World*. London: John Murray, 2005.

Claiborne, Craig. "Angels on Horseback, a Classic Savory." *Eugene Register-Guard*, August 21, 1979.

Egg Recipes: From Basic to Adventurous. "Go to Work on an Egg." Accessed November 19, 2017, https://www.eggrecipes.co.uk/go-to-work-on-an-egg.

Fleming, Fergus, ed. *The Man with the Golden Typewriter: Ian Fleming's James Bond Letters*. London: Bloomsbury, 2015.

Fleming, Ian. *Casino Royale*. London: Triad/Granada, 1978.

———. *Diamonds Are Forever*. Las Vegas: Thomas & Mercer, 2012.

———. *Dr. No*. London: Triad/Panther Books, 1977.

———. *Goldfinger*. London: Triad/Granada, 1978.

———. *Live and Let Die*. London: Triad/Panther Books, 1978.

———. *The Man with the Golden Gun*. London: Triad/Granada, 1978.

———. *Moonraker*. London: Triad Grafton, 1982.

————. *On Her Majesty's Secret Service*. London: Triad/Panther Books, 1977.

————. *Thrilling Cities*. London: Jonathan Cape, 1963.

————. *Thunderball*. London: Triad Grafton, 1978.

————. "007 in New York." In *Quantum of Solace: The Complete James Bond Short Stories*. London: Penguin Books, 2008, 284–93.

————. "Ian Fleming on Writing Thrillers." In *Devil May Care*, by Sebastian Faulks, 405–12. London: Penguin Books, 2009.

Hale, Elizabeth. "James Bond and the Art of Eating Eggs." *Gastronomica* 12, no. 4 (Winter 2012): 84–90, doi:10.1525/gfc.2012.12.4.84.

Long, Lucy M. "Culinary Tourism: A Folkloristic Perspective on Eating and Otherness." In *Culinary Tourism*, edited by Lucy M. Long, 20–50. Lexington: The University Press of Kentucky, 2004.

Lycett, Andrew. *Ian Fleming: The Man behind James Bond*. Atlanta: Turner Publishing Inc., 1995.

Moody, Oliver. "Marks & Spencer serves up an exotic dip into history of taste." *The Times*, April 20, 2013, https://www.thetimes.co.uk/tto/life/food/article3744548.ece.

National Archives, The. "Consumer Prices Index (CPI) and Retail Prices Index (RPI) Basket of Goods and Services." Last modified January 8, 2016, http://webarchive.nationalarchives.gov.uk/20160108054353/http://www.ons.gov.uk/ons/guide-method/user-guidance/prices/cpi-and-rpi/cpi-and-rpi-basket-of-goods-and-services/index.html.

Nicholson, Virginia. *Perfect Wives in Ideal Homes: The Story of Women in the 1950s*, London: Viking, 2015.

Office for National Statistics. "Consumer Price Inflation Basket of Goods and Services: 2017." Last Modified March 14, 2017, https://www.ons.gov.uk/economy/inflationandpriceindices/articles/ukconsumerpriceinflationbasketofgoodsandservices/2017.

Oppenheim, E. Phillips. *The Battle of Basinghall Street*. In *The Complete Works of E. Phillips Oppenheim: 109 Novels & 200+ Short Stories*. Prague: e-artnow, 2016. Kindle.

Patten, Marguerite. *The Family Cookbook*. London: Paul Hamlyn, 1964.

————. *Marguerite Patten's Family Cookbook*. London: Bounty Books, 2007.

Sherman, Matt. *James Bond's Cuisine: 007's Every Last Meal*. Gainesville: BCW Productions, 2014.

Strong, Jeremy. "James Bond: International Man of Gastronomy?" *Journal of European Popular Culture* 4, no. 2 (October 2013): 155–72, doi: 10.1386/jepc.4.2.155_1.

Wikipedia. "KFC." Last modified November 7, 2017, https://en.wikipedia.org/wiki/KFC.

Wilson, Earl. "Dining at 21: Fit for a President." *The Lowell Sun*, December 24, 1971.

Index

"007 in New York" (short story), 143, 145, 149

Achtymichuk-Hardy, Elyn, 5
acousmatic voice, 5, 43, 44, 48, 49, 50, 51, 52, 53
Adam, Ken, 61, 68, 69, 70
Adele, 40
affect theory, 5, 26, 28, 34, 35
Agent for H.A.R.M. (film), 58
Ahmed, Sarah, 5, 16, 25, 26, 28, 35n6
Amalric, Mathieu, 67
Amanatullah, Ihsan, 8, 9
Ambler, Eric, 66, 83
Amis, Kingsley, 18, 28, 81, 106, 107, 121, 128, 146, 157; *The James Bond Dossier*, 81, 118n5, 118n12, 118n13
Anderson, Benedict, 21
Andress, Ursula, 47
Aristotle, 5, 26; catharsis, 5, 26, 27, 34

Bardem, Javier, 42, 100
Bassey, Shirley, 5, 41
Baudrillard, Jean, 158, 160–161, 166, 167–168, 169, 172
Belger, Thomas, 64
Bennett, Tony, 57, 58, 109, 117n3, 118n6, 118n12–118n13, 119n39, 122–123, 127, 131, 133
Benson, Raymond, 56, 149
Bergonzi, Bernard, 119n39, 148
Biddulph, Edward, x, 10–11
bin Laden, Osama, 172
Black, Jeremy, 22, 23, 117n3
Black, Joel, 25
Blackman, Honor, 45
Blaize, John, 2, 6–7, 75, 81, 82–85, 86n11. *See also* Collard, John
"Blofeld trilogy," 59
The Blue Dahlia (film), 162

Bold, Christine, 117n3, 118n5, 118n26, 126, 127
Bond, James (US ornithologist), 75, 186
"Bondmania," 58, 70n2
Boucher, Anthony, xi
Bourne, Stephen, 56
British Empire, x, 22, 23, 57, 67, 152; "Pax Britannica," 67
British film industry, 5, 40, 56
British Security Coordination (BSC), 80, 165
Broccoli, Albert R. "Cubby," 4, 55, 57, 63–64, 69–70, 153
Brosnan, John, 56
Brosnan, Pierce, 65
Bryce, Ivar, ix, x, 4, 75, 86n45
BSC. *See* British Security Coordination
Buchan, John, 66–67
Buckton, Oliver, ix, 6–7, 135
Bunyard, Jesc, 5
Butler, Judith, 7, 92

Cain, Syd, 61
Cannadine, David, 67
capitalism, 6, 50–52, 157, 161, 168
Caplan, Robert A., 114, 117n3, 118n5
Carmichael, Hoagy, 164
Carpenter, John, 50
Casino Royale (novel), ix, 1, 2, 3, 9, 18, 32, 57, 67, 75, 79, 108, 117n2, 121, 142, 143, 147, 164, 183, 184, 189
Casino Royale (1954 TV adaptation), 57, 166
Casino Royale (1967 film), 143, 154
Casino Royale (2006 film), 45, 47, 61, 97, 143, 178, 182, 189, 194n11
Central Intelligence Agency (CIA), x, 2, 3, 23–24, 62, 78, 102n31, 113, 124, 143, 145, 152, 180

Chandler, Raymond, ix, 1, 2, 3, 11n3, 73, 78, 124, 135, 141, 158, 162–163, 166, 170; *The Big Sleep*, 124; *Farewell, My Lovely*, 124; *The Little Sister*, 124, 158, 162–163

Chapman, James, 6, 42, 70n2, 106, 116, 117n3, 118n5–118n6, 118n26, 119n39

Chion, Michel, 43–44, 49–50

Churchill, Sir Winston, 68

CIA. *See* Central Intelligence Agency

Cold War, 22, 23, 57, 75, 78, 84

Collard, John., 7, 74–75, 81, 82. *See also* Blaize, John

Connery, Sir Sean, 1, 4, 5, 6, 39, 40–41, 42, 43–45, 46, 47, 51, 52, 55, 59–60, 63–64, 65, 68, 77, 87n51, 105, 116, 152, 164, 172

Cork, John, 144

Coward, Noël, 67, 146

Craig, Daniel, 41, 45, 46–47, 64, 100

Crichton, Michael, 157

Cuneo, Ernest, x, 4, 165, 166, 170, 186

Daily Express, 2, 57

Daily Mail, 100

Dalton, Timothy, 65

Davis Jr, Sammy, 65

Davies, Tony, 133

Deadlier Than the Male (film), 58

Dean, Jimmy, 49, 67

Deighton, Len, 66

Dench, Dame Judi, 45, 97, 102n34

Denning, Michael, 18, 66, 117n3, 119n39, 127, 128

Diamonds Are Forever (novel): Africa and Africans in, 5, 7, 15–16, 17, 29–32, 61, 76, 80; food and drink in, x, 9, 10–11, 20, 35, 132, 148, 151, 153, 178–186, 189–190, 190–194; gangsters in, 18; homosexuality in, x, 3, 7, 66, 78, 92, 95, 99, 126, 169; racial attitudes in, 5, 30–32, 34, 152; United States of America portrayed in, 21, 51, 62, 164

Diamonds Are Forever (film): box office performance, 68; camp style in, 4, 6, 42, 56, 65–66, 66–67, 69, 92, 171; food and drink in, 10, 177, 187–189, 194; homosexuality in, 66, 92, 93, 94, 99–100; United States of America portrayed in, 4, 9, 40, 51, 69, 116, 143, 152–154

The Diamond Smugglers, 2, 5, 6–7, 74, 81, 82–85, 86n11, 87n67

The Diamond Syndicate, 80–81

Die Another Day (film), 61

Dirty Harry (film), 66

Disneyland (theme park), 161, 168, 170

Disney, Walt, 161, 168, 171

Dolar, Mladen, 5, 43, 44

Donnelly, K.J., 40

double-0 status, 97, 100

Double Indemnity (film), 162

Dr. No (novel), 74, 107, 143, 148, 182

Dr. No (film), 3, 39, 41, 43, 45, 47, 52–53, 55, 57–58, 61, 69, 79, 143

Eastwood, Clint, 61, 63

Echo, myth of, 47, 48. *See also* Narcissus, myth of

Eco, Umberto, 1, 17–18, 34, 35n11, 79, 86n45, 118n12–118n13, 122, 135, 141, 142, 167, 170

Eon Productions, 79, 85

FBI. *See* Federal Bureau of Investigation

Federal Bureau of Investigation (FBI), 23, 143

feminism, 8, 57, 109. *See also* gender politics

Films and Filming (magazine), 58

Fisher, Mark, 50–51

Fleming, Ann (née Charteris), 74, 85n9, 193

Fleming, Fergus, 79, 85

Fleming, Ian: America, views of, 141, 145, 164, 166; book sales, 57, 58; culinary tastes, 148, 178, 183, 186, 193; literary career, 1, 57, 79, 91; misogyny of, 152; naming of James Bond, 75; racial attitudes of, 152; travels, 80. *See also* individual titles

"For Your Eyes Only" (short story), 143, 147

For Your Eyes Only (film), 61, 64, 178

Freud, Sigmund, 92, 95, 96–97, 159

The French Connection (film), 66

French Guinea, 15, 35n4, 179
Frobe, Gert, 62
From Russia with Love (novel), ix, xi, 2,
6, 9, 57, 61, 73–74, 76, 81, 84, 107,
109, 134, 135, 136, 146, 171–172, 192
From Russia with Love (film), 11, 39, 40,
41, 55, 57, 59, 61, 70, 77, 79, 178, 188
Furst, Joseph, 67

Gavin, John, 63
gender politics, 1, 3, 7, 45, 92, 101n3,
105, 110, 112, 117, 117n3, 127, 182.
See also feminism
Gibson, Mel, 63
Gilbert, Jon, 3
Gilbert, Lewis, 70
Glover, Bruce, 66
Goldeneye (Fleming home), 74, 75, 186
GoldenEye (film), 65, 102n34
Goldfinger (novel), 2, 32, 61, 81, 84, 92,
124, 143, 150, 172, 178
Goldfinger (film), 4, 5, 39, 40, 41, 45, 47,
55, 57, 58, 59, 61, 62, 68, 69, 70, 143,
172
The Graduate (film), 6, 60
Gray, Charles, 4, 49, 62, 67, 116
Green, Eva, 45
Greene, Graham, 66, 83

Hale, Elizabeth, 10, 184
Halliwell, Leslie, 56
Hamilton, Guy, vii, 1, 4, 5–6, 7, 8, 10,
40, 61, 69, 77, 105, 109, 110, 116, 117
Hammett, Dashiell, 124; *The Maltese
Falcon*, 124
Harris, Naomi, 45
Hartford, Jo, 4
Haskell, Molly, 60
Hester, Grant, 7–8
"The Hildebrand Rarity" (short story),
143
Hinds, Claire, 32
Hitchcock, Alfred, 46
Hitchens, Christopher, 141, 164, 165
Hollywood (US film industry), 6, 9, 60,
63, 152, 157, 158, 159, 161–163,
165–166, 167, 168–170, 171, 172
Hovey, James, 117, 118n6
Hughes, Howard, 67, 68, 153, 164

Hunt, Peter, 59, 61
Hyde, H. Montgomery, 80

identity theft, 43, 75–78, 80, 81

Jamaica, 74, 75, 186, 193
James, Clifton, 69
Johnson, Paul, 119n39
Jonathan Cape (publisher), 57, 164
Jones, Tom, 40

Kaufman, Mark David, 9–10
Keaton, Buster, 131, 169
Kennedy, John F., xi
Kine Weekly (magazine), 58
King, Hobart M., 28
Klosterman, Chuck, 93–94
Korda, Alexander, 85, 165

Ladenson, Elizabeth, 124
Larson, Lola, 48
Las Vegas, x, 2, 3, 9, 25, 40, 47, 49, 50,
51, 62, 69, 125, 130, 146, 147, 148,
150, 151, 153, 158, 164, 165, 166–167,
168, 170, 185, 189
Lawrence, Amy, 47
Lazenby, George, 4, 6, 43, 55, 59–60, 63,
87n51
Le Carré, John, 66
Lee, Christopher, 69
Liberia, 15, 84
Licensed to Kill (film), 58
The Liquidator (film), 58
Live and Let Die (novel), x, 1, 2, 4, 21, 75,
78, 85, 121, 143, 144, 148, 163, 164,
165, 166, 167, 178, 180, 181, 183, 184,
186, 193
Live and Let Die (film), 6, 69, 143; box
office performance, 69
Llewelyn, Desmond, 51
Long, Lucy, 193
Lorre, Peter, 166
Lycett, Andrew, 86n40, 86n45, 166

Macintyre, Ben, 117n3, 118n6, 118n31,
119n39
Maibaum, Richard, 4, 56, 59, 62, 63, 69,
70
Manchester Guardian, 82

Mankiewicz, Tom, 4, 56, 63, 65, 69, 70, 152
The Man With the Golden Gun (novel), 57, 62, 68, 93, 143, 183
The Man With the Golden Gun (film), 69, 178; box office performance, 69
Martinsen, Jennifer L., 8
Maugham, William Somerset, 83, 165
McClory, Kevin, 79, 86n45
McNeile, H.C. *See* "Sapper"
MI5, 6, 74, 80
MI6. *See* Secret Intelligence Service (SIS)
misogyny, 8, 102n34, 105–106, 152
Modesty Blaise (film), 58
Monro, Matt, 40
Monroe, Marilyn, 171–172
Monthly Film Bulletin , 68
Moonraker (novel), ix, 1, 2, 3, 75, 79, 85, 121, 163, 164–165, 166, 172, 179, 180, 182, 183
Moonraker (film), 61, 143
Moore, Sir Roger, 4, 6, 40, 64, 67, 69, 100
Moran, Christopher, 3
Mulvey, Laura, 7–8, 45, 46, 92, 95, 99, 111, 112, 127
Murderer's Row (film), 58

Naismith, Laurence, 65
Narcissus, myth of, 47. *See also* Echo, myth of
NATO, 143
Nelson, Barry, 57, 166
Never Say Never Again, 39, 143
Newman, Paul, 63
New Statesman , 73, 74
New York Times, xi, 60, 68, 70
Nichols, Mike, 6
Nixon, Richard, 68, 182

Octopussy and The Living Daylights (story collection), 57
Octopussy (film), 67, 143, 178
On Her Majesty's Secret Service (novel), 59, 61, 96, 178, 184, 189
On Her Majesty's Secret Service (film), 4, 6, 43, 55, 56, 58–62, 64, 65, 67, 68, 70, 143, 178; disappointing box office

of, 58–59, 60, 68
Oppenheim, E. Phillips, 181; *The Battle of Basinghall Street*, 181
Our Man Flint (film), 58
Ovid, 47; *Metamorphoses*, 47

Paluzzi, Luciana, 46
Parks, Trina, 48
Patten, Marguerite, 191
Pearson, John, xi, 165, 166, 172
Peary, Danny, 60
Picker, David, 63
Pleasence, Donald, 62
Plomer, William, 82–83, 85, 164
Polanski, Roman, 64
Pratt, Benjamin, 150, 151

Quantum of Solace (film), 67, 143
Queen Elizabeth II (monarch), 67, 94

racism, 29–31, 69, 152
Raven, Simon, 148
Rhodes, Chip, 10, 158, 159, 160, 163, 165
Rich, Frank, 70
Robinson, Joe, 42, 77
Russo, Vito, 93

Saltzman, Harry, 56, 57, 63, 69
"Sapper," 66
Saratoga, ix, x, 3, 4, 62, 77, 125, 146, 158, 183, 184–185, 189, 192
Sarris, Andrew, 68, 116–117
Savalas, Telly, 62
Scheurer, Timothy E., 41–42
scopophilia, 45, 46–47, 48, 52, 95. *See also* voyeurism
Secret Intelligence Service (SIS), 3, 23, 78, 79, 83, 126, 143
Secret Service. *See* Secret Intelligence Service (SIS)
Sherman, Matt, 9, 194n14
Sierra Leone, 15, 62
The Silencers (film), 58
Sillitoe, Sir Percy, 7, 74, 80–81, 82–83
Silverman, Kaja, 48
simulacra, 9, 10, 158, 161, 162, 166, 167, 172
Sinatra, Nancy, 40

SIS. *See* Secret Intelligence Service
Skyfall (film), 42, 97, 100
Smith, Putter, 66
Smith, Sam, 41
Sontag, Susan, 7, 92, 98–99
Soviet Union, x, 1, 7, 22, 23, 33, 62, 68, 73, 78, 79, 143, 146
Spectre (film), 91, 143
Spender, Stephen, 163
The Spy Who Loved Me (novel), 2, 61, 143, 168
The Spy Who Loved Me (film), 64, 70, 117, 143, 188; box office performance, 70
The Spy With a Cold Nose (film), 58
Star Wars (film), 41, 51–52
Stephenson, Sir William, 80
St. John, Jill, 47, 77, 99, 110, 111, 112, 114, 115–116, 119n38, 152
Strakovksy, Yevgenya, 151
Strong, Jeremy, 186, 192
Sullivan, Nikki, 96
The Sunday Times, 81, 135
Swanson, "Swanee," 166

Tangier, 74
The Tatler (magazine), 190
Thrilling Cities, 145, 147, 161, 168, 173n27
Thunderball (novel), 1, 61, 79, 86n45, 108, 143, 180, 183, 184
Thunderball (film), 40, 41, 46, 55, 57–59, 61, 70, 143, 178; box office success, 58
Time (magazine), 55, 58
Tomorrow Never Dies (film), 67

Ulfsdotter, Boel, 106, 110, 118n6, 127

United Artists, 57, 63

Vermont, ix, 4, 11n8, 143, 147
Vietnam war, 60
Village Voice (magazine), 60, 68–69, 116–117
voyeurism, 45, 95, 106, 119n39, 127, 128, 171. *See also* scopophilia

Wagner, Richard, 41
Walker, Alexander, 59, 64
Washington Post, 69
Waugh, Evelyn, 10, 158, 161, 166, 168, 173n27; *Brideshead Revisited*, 161; *The Loved One*, 10, 158, 161–162, 168, 173n27
Welles, Orson, 63, 165
West, Nathanael, 10, 158, 159–161; *The Day of the Locust* (novel), 10, 159–161
West, Nigel, 81
When the Bullets Fly (film), 58
Where the Spies Are (film), 58
Whittingham, Jack, 79
Wilder, Billy, 162
Wood, Christopher, 70
Wood, Lana, 47, 63
Woodward Jr., William, x
Woollacott, Janet, 57, 58, 109, 117n3, 118n6, 118n12–118n13, 119n39, 122–123, 127, 131, 133

You Only Live Twice (novel), 61, 108, 169, 192
You Only Live Twice (film), 4, 6, 40, 55, 58, 59, 61, 62, 64, 65, 68, 70, 77, 143; box office of, 58, 68

Žižek, Slavoj, 172

About the Editor

Oliver Buckton is professor of English at Florida Atlantic University in Boca Raton, where he specializes in modern British literature and culture, spy fiction and film, and critical theory. He is the author of *Secret Selves: Confession and Same-Sex Desire in Victorian Autobiography* (1998), *Cruising With Robert Louis Stevenson: Travel, Narrative, and the Colonial Body* (2007) and *Espionage in British Fiction and Film since 1900: The Changing Enemy* published by Lexington Books in 2015, and issued in paperback in 2017. Buckton has published essays on some of the leading British spy novelists including Len Deighton, Frederick Forsyth, and Charles Cumming. He is currently working on a critical and biographical study of Ian Fleming and James Bond, and is the recipient of a Helm Visiting Fellowship from the Lilly Library, Indiana University, to research the Ian Fleming papers.

About the Contributors

Elyn Achtymichuk-Hardy is a PhD candidate at the University of Saskatchewan in Saskatoon, Saskatchewan, Canada. Her areas of focus within English literature include gender studies, popular culture, and cultural studies, and the ways that these areas conflict and intersect. Her current work—her dissertation—will focus on the changes that the James Bond franchise has undergone as it responds to changing cultural needs and desires, based on performance(s) of gender; the audience's fears and anxieties; and the sociohistorical facts that bind the novels and films to the times in which they are produced.

Ihsan Amanatullah studied at the University of California, Davis and San Francisco State University. Since 2007 he has worked for the National Film Preservation Foundation. He has written various film notes for the NFPF and entries for the encyclopedias *Movies in American History* and *Race in American Film: Voices and Visions That Shaped a Nation*.

Edward Biddulph is an independent researcher and the author of *Licence to Cook: Recipes Inspired by Ian Fleming's James Bond* (2010, Lulu Enterprises). His study on the "archaeology" of James Bond's diet was published in the journal, *Food, Society and Culture*, in 2009, and his essay on the cultural perception of Bond on the eve of the launch of the Bond film series was published in the 2014 edited volume, *James Bond and Popular Culture*. Edward contributes to Bond-related magazines and websites, including *MI6 Confidential*, *Artistic Licence Renewed*, and the *James Bond Dossier*, and he writes the blog, *James Bond memes*, which explores the ideas and influences in the Bond books and films and the impact of Ian Fleming's creation on wider culture. Beyond Bond studies, Edward is an archaeologist based in Oxford, UK, and is the author of many archaeological monographs, journal articles, and reports.

Jesc Bunyard is an independent artist and writer. Her work has led her to examine sound within a moving image in both the gallery and cinema. Bunyard has written for numerous publications including *Little White Lies* and *Hunger Magazine*. In her artistic work, Bunyard seeks to continue her exploration into moving image and sound, this has led her to exhibit at various galleries including at the National Theatre in London. She is currently researching the fetishization of the mouth and the mask within superhero films.

James Chapman is professor of film studies at the University of Leicester and editor of the *Historical Journal of Film, Radio and Television*. He has a particular interest in the histories of British popular cinema and television: his books include *Licence to Thrill: A Cultural History of the James Bond Films* (2007), *Saints and Avengers: British Adventure Series of the 1960s* (2002), *Inside the Tardis: The Worlds of 'Doctor Who'—A Cultural History* (2013), *Swashbucklers: The Costume Adventure Series* (2015), and *Hitchcock and the Spy Film: Authorship, Genre and National Cinema* (2018). He is currently writing *Comics at the Movies*—a history of comic book film adaptations—and in a different vein is researching a history of the fiscal politics of the British film industry since 1945.

Grant C. Hester is currently a PhD candidate in the cultures, languages, and literatures track of the comparative studies program at Florida Atlantic University. He holds a master's degree with a double concentration of English and art history from the University of St. Thomas and a bachelor's degree in accounting from the University of Arkansas. His creative non-fiction article appeared in *Laurels*. He has presented papers on James Bond at the conferences for the Southwest Pop/American Culture Association and the South Atlantic Modern Language Association.

Mark David Kaufman is assistant professor of English at Alvernia University in Reading, Pennsylvania. His scholarship has appeared in *Hypermedia Joyce Studies, Biography, Public Domain Review, Virginia Woolf Miscellany, European Journal of American Studies, Twentieth-Century Literature*, and *The Space Between*. Currently, he is completing his first book, a study of the relationship between modernism and security legislation, the weaponization of the humanities during wartime, and the cultivation of writers as spies by the Anglo-American intelligence community.

Jennifer L. Martinsen, PhD, is an associate professor of English at Newberry College in South Carolina. She specializes in nineteenth, twentieth, and twenty-first-century British literature. Her research interests include the intersection of humor and shame in Jane Austen as well as the examination of how writers and artists used humor to help formulate British national identity throughout the nineteenth century. Her article on humor, humility, and national identity in *Pride and Prejudice* was published in the Fall 2013 special issue on humor and culture in *Proteus: A Journal of Ideas*.

Matthew B. Sherman is an independent scholar and a leading expert on James Bond, in particular *Diamonds Are Forever*. Sherman has led tour groups to visit *DAF* film and book locations, meet *DAF* actors, screenwriters, and musicians, and to even climb aboard *DAF* vehicles. His newest book, *James Bond's Cuisine: 007's Every Last Meal*, is in print worldwide. Sherman's spy collectibles and spy meets have featured on C-SPAN, DISCOVERY, HGTV, VH-1, TLC, TNN and in *Ripley's Believe It or Not!* His contributions have appeared in the *Daily Mail, The Chicago Tribune, The Los Angeles Times, The New York Times, The Washington Post, Parade Magazine, Time,* and *Time Europe*.

CPSIA information can be obtained
at www.ICGtesting.com
Printed in the USA
LVHW091931160721
692904LV00003B/51